HTML
QuickSteps

GUY HART-DAVIS

McGraw-Hill/Osborne

New York Chicago San Francisco
Lisbon London Madrid Mexico City
Milan New Delhi San Juan
Seoul Singapore Sydney Toronto

McGraw-Hill/Osborne
2100 Powell Street, 10th Floor
Emeryville, California 94608
U.S.A.

To arrange bulk purchase discounts for sales promotions, premiums, or fund-raisers, please contact **McGraw-Hill/** Osborne at the above address. For information on translations or book distributors outside the U.S.A., please see the International Contact Information page following the index of this book.

HTML QUICKSTEPS

1234567890 WCK WCK 0198765
ISBN 0-07-225895-0

VICE PRESIDENT, GROUP PUBLISHER / Phillip Ruppel

VICE PRESIDENT, PUBLISHER / Jeffrey Krames

ACQUISITIONS EDITOR / Roger Stewart

ACQUISITIONS COORDINATOR / Agatha Kim

SERIES CREATORS & EDITORS / Marty and Carole Matthews

TECHNICAL EDITOR / Marty Matthews

COPY EDITOR / Lisa McCoy

PROOFREADER / Karyle Kramer

INDEXER / Valerie Perry

LAYOUT ARTIST / Bailey Cunningham

ILLUSTRATORS / Kathleen Edwards, Pattie Lee, Bruce Hopkins

SERIES DESIGN / Bailey Cunningham

COVER DESIGN / Pattie Lee

Contents at a Glance

Chapter 1 **Creating Your First Web Pages with HTML** 1
Begin and organize your web site, choose HTML tools, create web pages, and describe and check your web pages

Chapter 2 **Choosing an ISP and Getting Your Own Web Site** 19
Understand the basics of the Web; choose a web host or ISP; plan, design, and create your site; and transfer it to the Web

Chapter 3 **Applying Manual Formatting to Web Pages** 39
Apply manual formatting, create lists, apply indents and alignment, use inline styles, and work with the style attribute

Chapter 4 **Adding Graphics** 63
Create graphics with Paint and Paint Shop Pro, use a camera or scanner, add inline graphics, and place background graphics

Chapter 5 **Adding Links** 85
Link to another web page or the same page, create links that download files or send e-mail, and create imagemaps

Chapter 6 **Creating Tables** 105
Create a table, add rows and columns, format table borders, format and group cells, and create nested tables

Chapter 7 **Creating Frames** 127
Create frameset documents and component documents, lay out the frames, add alternative text, and create inline frames

Chapter 8 **Applying Formatting Using Style Sheets** 141
Create style rules; create embedded and external style sheets; and set alignment, indents, margins, and line height.

Chapter 9 **Creating Web Pages Using Microsoft Office** 159
Configure web options; insert hyperlinks; create web pages using Word or from spreadsheets, presentations, and data-access pages

Chapter 10 **Using Forms, Scripts, and Special Tags** 181
Create forms to collect information, use scripts in your web pages, and use special tags for eBay and Blogger.com

Index 207

Dedication

To Rhonda and Teddy

Acknowledgments

My thanks go to the following people, who put in a huge amount of work on this book:

Marty Matthews, series editor and technical editor, developed the book, checked it for technical accuracy, and made countless suggestions for improvements throughout.

Lisa McCoy, editor, edited the book skillfully and with good humor.

Bailey Cunningham, series designer and layout artist, laid out the book with great skill, turning the raw manuscript and graphics into a highly polished book.

Karyle Kramer, proofreader, caught widely varied inconsistencies throughout the text.

Valerie Perry, indexer, created the index for the book with speed and precision.

Roger Stewart, Editorial Director at Osborne, helped create the series and pulled strings in the background throughout the process.

Contents

Acknowledgments..iv

Introduction...ix

Chapter 1 **Creating Your First Web Page with HTML**.............. 1
    Create a Folder for Your Web Site..2
    Organizing Your Site..3
    Open Notepad 3
    Create the Page's Structure...3
    Understanding the Header and the Body 4
    Add Content to the Page...4
    Apply Formatting 9
    Add a Picture 10
    Understanding Tools for Creating HTML 11
    Add a Hyperlink 11
    Create Linked Files 13
    Describe Your Pages with Meta Tags 15
    Reload a Page Automatically 15
    Understanding How Search Engines Work..16
    Redirect the Browser to Another Page 16
    Check Your Pages with Other Browsers 17

Chapter 2 **Choosing an ISP and Getting Your Own Web Site**.. 19
    Understand Web Basics 19
    Understand Web Clients and Servers 19
    Access a Web Page 20
    Understanding URLs...22
    Assess Your Requirements..22
    Choose an ISP or Web-Hosting Service...22
    Understanding Intranets and Extranets...23
    Decide on Web-Hosting Features 23
    Running Your Own Web Server..25
    Evaluate an ISP 25
    Understanding Domains...26
    Evaluate a Web-Hosting Service 26
    Register a Domain Name 26
    Plan, Design, and Create Your Site... 28
    Plan Your Site's Contents 28
    Make Your Site Effective 29
    Check Your Web Site...31
    Update and Maintain Your Web Site..31
    Transfer Your Site to the Web 32
    Transfer Your Site Using Internet Explorer 33
    Transfer a Site Using an FTP Client...37

1

2

3

Chapter 3 **Applying Manual Formatting to Web Pages** 39
- Using Proportional and Monospaced Fonts 40
  - Understand Considerations for Web Formatting 40
  - Use Paragraphs, Divisions, Breaks, and Hyphens 40
- Inserting Special Characters 43
  - Create Headings 43
  - Create Numbered, Bulleted, and Definition Lists 44
  - Apply an Indent 49
  - Align Elements 50
  - Use Preformatted Text 50
  - Apply Inline Styles 51
- Understanding Other Inline Styles 53
  - Control Font Formatting 53
- Working with Fonts 54
  - Change Style Using the Style Attribute 55
  - Catch the Eye with Moving Text 60

4

Chapter 4 **Adding Graphics** 63
- **Create Graphics for Your Web Pages** 64
  - Create Graphics with Paint..64
- Choosing Graphics Applications 66
  - Create Graphics with Paint Shop Pro...67
- Understanding GIF, JPEG, and PNG...68
  - Download Pictures from Your Digital Camera...71
  - Scan Graphics from Documents or Pictures...72
- Keeping Down Graphic Size to Make Pages Load Faster................................73
- **Use Graphics in Your Web Pages**..73
  - Add an Inline Graphic..73
- Using Graphics to Control How Text Appears..78
  - Add a Background Graphic...80
  - Add a Horizontal Rule..80
- Laying Out Your Web Pages..82
  - Create an E-Mail Signature Containing a Graphic...82

5

Chapter 5 **Adding Links** 85
  - Link to Another Web Page..85
- Understanding Absolute and Relative Links...86
  - Link within a Web Page..88
- Making Your Site Navigable 90
  - Link to a Particular Point on a Web Page 90
  - Open a Link in a New Window 90
  - Create a Link to Download a File 91
  - Display a ScreenTip for a Link 92
  - Create Links to Send E-Mail 92
- Making Useful Imagemaps..95
  - Create Two or More Links in a Graphic...95
- Creating an Imagemap with Paint Shop Pro 98
  - Add Audio and Video to Your Web Pages 98

Chapter 6 **Creating Tables** 105

Understand How Tables Work and When to Use Them 105
Plan a Table 106
Create the Table's Structure 107
Add Rows and Columns to a Table...110
Add Table Borders 111
Group Cells by Rows and Columns...112
Set Table and Cell Width 115
Add Padding and Spacing..116
Setting Table and Cell Height 117
Align a Table, Row, or Cell..118
Make a Table Span Two Columns or Rows 121
Apply a Background Color or Picture...121
Create a Nested Table 123
Create a Vertical Line...125

Chapter 7 **Creating Frames** 127

Understand How Frames Work 128
Plan a Web Page That Uses Frames...128
Deciding Whether to Use Frames in Your Web Pages 129
Define Frame Height and Width...129
Create the Component Documents 130
Create the Frameset Document..130
Lay Out the Frames..131
Add the Component Documents to the Frameset...............................133
Add Alternative Text 134
Change a Frame's Borders and Margins..135
Control Whether a Frame Scrolls..137
Prevent Visitors from Resizing the Frame 137
Nest One Frameset Inside Another 138
Create Inline Frames...138
Create a Link That Changes the Contents of a Frame 140

Chapter 8 **Applying Formatting Using Style Sheets** 141

Understand CSS Essentials...142
Understanding the Style Cascade..143
Create a Style Rule 144
Understanding Other Ways of Creating Style Rules..............................145
Create an Embedded Style Sheet 145
Understanding CSS Versions...146
Create and Apply an External Style Sheet..146
Use Special Selectors...148
Apply a Style to Part of an Element 152
Override Style Sheets...153
Control Font Formatting 153
Set Alignment, Indents, Margins, and Line Height 154
Overriding Style Sheets in Your Browser...157
Prevent a Background Graphic from Being Tiled or Scrolled....................157

10

Chapter 9 **Creating Web Pages Using Microsoft Office** 159

🍭 Understanding How the Office Applications Use HTML............................160
Configure Web Options in the Office Applications...160
Start a New Web Page in Word 167
Create a Hyperlink..168
Check How a Page Will Look 171
Remove Personal Information from the File Properties 172
Save Word Documents as Web Pages...173
🍭 Choosing Suitable Web File Formats..174
Remove Office-Specific Tags from a Word Document....................................174
Create Web Pages from Excel Workbooks 175
🌑 Using Word to Create HTML Elements 176
Create Web Pages from PowerPoint Presentations...178
Create Web Pages from Data-Access Pages in Access 180

9

Chapter 10 **Using Forms, Scripts, and Special Tags** 181

Create Forms 182
Understand the Basics of Forms 182
Define the Form Structure...183
🍭 Understanding the method Attribute 184
Add Fields to the Form 184
Complete a Form...189
🌑 Letting Visitors Upload Files 191
Create a Form that E-Mails Its Contents to You...191
Use Scripts in Your Web Pages... 192
Understand the Different Categories of User Events 193
🍭 Dealing with Script Threats 195
Show When a Page Was Last Updated 195
Redirect the Browser to Another Page 195
Display a Pop-Up Window...195
Verify that a Form Is Filled In...198
Use Special Tags.. 201
Develop Your "About Me" Page on eBay...201
🍭 Understanding Item-Level Tags and Page-Level Tags 205
Use Blogger.com Tags...205

Index 207

Introduction

QuickSteps books are recipe books for computer users. They answer the question "How do I...?" by providing quick sets of steps to accomplish the most common tasks in a particular operating system or application.

The sets of steps are the central focus of the book. QuickSteps sidebars show how to quickly perform many small functions or tasks that support primary functions. QuickFacts sidebars supply information that you need to know about a subject. Notes, Tips, and Cautions augment the steps, presented in a separate column so as not to interrupt the flow of the steps. Introductions are minimal rather than narrative, and numerous illustrations and figures, with callouts, support the steps.

QuickSteps books are organized by function and the tasks needed to perform that function. Each function is a chapter. Each task, or "How To," contains the steps needed for accomplishing the function with the relevant Notes, Tips, Cautions, and screenshots. You can easily find the tasks you need through:

- The Table of Contents, which lists the functional areas (chapters) and tasks in the order they are presented

- A How To list of tasks on the opening page of each chapter

- The index, which provides an alphabetical list of the terms that are used to describe the functions and tasks

- Color-coded tabs for each chapter or functional area with an index to the tabs in the Contents at a Glance (just before the Table of Contents)

Conventions Used in this Book

HTML QuickSteps uses several conventions designed to make the book easier for you to follow. Among these are:

- A 🎨 in the table of contents and in the How To list in each chapter references a QuickSteps sidebar in a chapter, and a 🖊 references a QuickFacts sidebar.

- **Bold type** is used for words or objects on the screen that you are to do something with—for example, "click the **Start** menu, and then click **My Computer**."

- *Italic type* is used for a word or phrase that is being defined or otherwise deserves special emphasis.

- <u>Underlined type</u> is used for text that you are to type from the keyboard.

- SMALL CAPITAL LETTERS are used for keys on the keyboard such as **ENTER** and **SHIFT**.

- When you are expected to enter a command, you are told to press the key(s). If you are to enter text or numbers, you are told to type them.

- `Red font` (for example, "the opening `<title>` tag") distinguishes HTML code terms that appear within body text.

- Code lines show examples of HTML code—for example:

```
<html>
<head>
<title>Greener Seeds - Your One-Stop Solution for
    Professional and Home Gardening</title>
</head>
```

How to...

- Create a Folder for Your Web Site
- *Organizing Your Site*
- Open Notepad
- Create the Page's Structure
- *Understanding the Header and the Body*
- Add Content to the Page
- Apply Formatting
- Add a Picture
- *Understanding Tools for Creating HTML*
- Add a Hyperlink
- Create Linked Files
- Describe Your Pages with Meta Tags
- Reload a Page Automatically
- *Understanding How Search Engines Work*
- Redirect the Browser to Another Page
- Check Your Pages with Other Browsers

Chapter 1

Creating Your First Web Pages with HTML

Hypertext Markup Language, or HTML, is responsible for many of the wonders of the Web. HTML lets you specify the contents of a web page and control how it looks in a web browser. All modern computer operating systems have browsers, so HTML pages can be displayed on almost any computer.

An HTML file consists of plain text with *tags* (formatting codes), so you can create an HTML file quickly and easily using only a text editor and a browser. This chapter shows you how to start creating web pages using only the Notepad text editor and the Internet Explorer browser, both of which are included with Windows.

This book assumes that you are using Windows, because Windows has the bulk of the computer market. The examples use Windows XP with Service Pack 2.

TIP

If you plan to use Notepad frequently, pin it to the left section of the Start menu by right-clicking its entry on the Start menu and then clicking **Pin To Start Menu** on the shortcut menu.

TIP

If FrontPage is installed on your computer, your My Documents folder will contain a folder named My Webs. If you choose, you can use this folder to contain your web sites.

Create a Folder for Your Web Site

You will typically store your web site on your local computer while you create it and then transfer it to a web server when it is ready for public consumption. While many HTML tools enable you to create and edit web pages directly on a web server, creating the site locally has three advantages:

- You can create the site more quickly if it is stored locally. You can work on your site without an Internet connection if necessary.
- The pages on your final web site (on the Web) should be in a finished state for public consumption rather than in an intermediate state.
- Your local copy safeguards your site even if your ISP or web host has a server disaster; once the server is back up, you can simply upload your site again.

Start by creating a folder on your computer for your web site, if you do not already have one, and such subfolders within that folder as you need for the content. See the "Organizing Your Site" QuickFacts for suggestions on how to organize your web site.

1. Click the **Start** button and then click **My Documents**. The My Documents window opens.

2. Click the **File** menu, click **New**, and then click **Folder** on the submenu. Windows creates a new folder with the default name "New Folder" and displays an edit box around the name so that you can change it.

3. Type the name for the folder, for example Web_Site, (include the underscore), and press **ENTER** to apply the name.

4. Double-click the new folder to display its contents.

5. Repeat steps 2 and 3 to create as many new folders as needed within the main folder.

6. Click the **File** menu and click **Close** to close the Windows Explorer window.

ORGANIZING YOUR SITE

The first rule of web sites is that even the smallest site quickly grows far beyond the size and complexity originally intended—so even if you're planning a "small" site, you should organize it with care. Thoughtful organization is even more important if you know from the outset that you'll be creating a larger site.

The three key elements to organizing your site are:

- **Separate Content by Folder** Create a separate folder for each different type or category of content: graphics, different text topics, scripts, and so on. For example, for a family site, you might create folders such as html, pictures, music, and recipes. Keep the folder names short for ease of use. Create subfolders as necessary within the main folders.

- **Use Naming Conventions** Develop naming conventions for the files that make up your site's content so that you can figure out easily what a file would be called and where to locate it if you've forgotten its name or location. Short, descriptive names using lowercase letters are usually best. When you need to use multiple words in a name, separate the words with underscores rather than with spaces.

- **Document Your Site** Create a short document that explains how the site is structured, how files are named, and which content goes in which folder. You don't need to be excessively formal, but this document will help you and anyone else who assists you in creating and managing your site.

NOTE

This book shows HTML tags in red text where they appear in body paragraphs in order to help you pick them out easily.

Open Notepad

To open Notepad, click the **Start** button, click **All Programs**, click **Accessories**, and then click **Notepad**. A Notepad window opens, containing a new, blank text document.

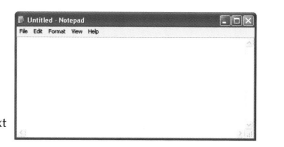

Create the Page's Structure

HTML is a set of tags that identify the elements of your web pages. A *tag* (or *markup tag*) is a name contained within angle brackets (< >) and usually comes in pairs (an opening tag and a closing tag). The tags may enclose a page element, such as text or a graphic, that you want to format. The closing tag has a slash preceding the tag name to identify it as the closing tag. Tags may also have *attributes* that further define the formatting or function of the tag.

The following sections show you how to create the structure of the web page.

ADD THE <HTML> TAGS

All web pages have a basic set of tags that identify the page as an HTML document, with all the major sections defined. These tags state the page is written in HTML so that the browser knows that it should use HTML rules for displaying the page. (Other markup languages have different rules from HTML.) The tags may also give the version of HTML used, the language (for example, "en" for English or "es" for Spanish), or other information.

1. On the first line of your text document in Notepad, type the opening tag, <html>, and press **ENTER**. This tag indicates the beginning of the HTML document.

2. On the second line, type the closing tag, </html>. This tag indicates the end of the HTML document. The remainder of the HTML document goes between the <html> tag and the </html> tag.

QUICK**FACTS**

UNDERSTANDING THE HEADER AND THE BODY

Each HTML web page consists of a header and a body:

- The *header* (also called the *document head*) typically contains the title for the web page and information about the document, including terms for search engines, information on links, and information about the style and scripts used.

- The *body* is the rest of the HTML web page. The body contains the text that appears when you display the web page as well as instructions for other objects (for example, pictures) to be included in the web page.

NOTE

HTML tags aren't case-sensitive, so you can write them in uppercase, lowercase, or even mixed case. You'll often see uppercase tags because they make the tags easier to locate by eye on a busy page; mixed case is seldom used because it has no advantage beyond idiosyncrasy; but modern practice is to use lowercase for tags because more advanced markup languages (for example, XHTML) *are* case-sensitive. This book uses lowercase for all tags and recommends that you follow this practice.

ADD HEADER AND BODY TAGS

The header of an HTML web page is delimited by an opening `<head>` tag and a closing `</head>` tag, and the body is similarly delimited by `<body>` and `</body>` tags. Type these into your web page between the existing `<html>` and `</html>` tags:

```
<head>
</head>
<body>
</body>
```

The elements that make up the header go between the `<head>` and `</head>` tags, and the elements that make up the body go between the `<body>` and `</body>` tags.

Add Content to the Page

After creating the structure for the web page, add content to it as described in this section.

ADD THE TITLE FOR THE PAGE

Most web pages begin with a title—the text that appears in the browser's title bar when the web page is loaded and that is used as the default text for a Favorite or for a Bookmark created for the page. Create your title by placing an opening `<title>` tag, the title text, and the closing `</title>` tag between the `<head>` tag and the `</head>` tag, as shown:

```
<head>
<title>Greener Seeds, Inc. — Home Page</title>
</head>
```

SAVE THE PAGE

Save the page so that you can view it in your web browser.

1. Click the **File** menu and then click **Save**. The Save As dialog box appears.
2. Navigate to the folder for your web site. (Note which folder it is, because you'll need to access it again in a minute.)
3. Select the contents of the File Name text box, and type "index.html" (including the double quotation marks) over the selection, replacing it.
4. Click **Save**.

VIEW THE PAGE

Start your web browser and view the page you're creating so that you can see the effects of the HTML tags you enter.

1. Click the **Start** button and then click **Internet**. Internet Explorer starts.
2. Click the **File** menu, click **Open**, and then click **Browse**. The Microsoft Internet Explorer dialog box appears.
3. Navigate to your site's folder, click the **index.html** file, click **Open**, and then click **OK**.

Figure 1-1 shows the page open in Internet Explorer. All you see is the title in the title bar because the body of the web page is blank.

Figure 1-1:
Use your browser to see the progress in the page you create. At first, only the title is visible.

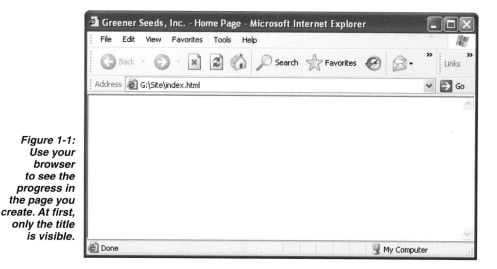

TIP

ADD A HEADING

Add a level-1 (top-level) heading to your web page by entering the heading text inside the `<h1>` and `</h1>` tags within the body section (between the `<body>` and `</body>` tags). For example:

```
<body>
<h1>Welcome to Greener Seeds, Inc.!</h1>
</body>
```

Save the web page (click the **File** menu and then click **Save**), switch to Internet Explorer, and click the **Refresh** button to force Internet Explorer to read the web page again. Figure 1-2 shows the page.

Figure 1-2: To see the effect of the changes you make, click the Refresh button to update the display after each change you save to the page.

TIP

For speed, you may want to use keyboard shortcuts to save the web page, switch to your browser, and then refresh or reload the page. Press **CTRL+S** to save, **ALT+TAB** to switch (you may need to press **TAB** multiple times while holding down **ALT** if the application to which you're switching is not the last application you used), and **F5** to refresh Internet Explorer.

NOTE

Browsers ignore line breaks in HTML documents, so you must explicitly tag each paragraph mark that you want the browser to display in a page. Using the `<p>` and `</p>` tags in matching pairs is usually best, because doing so makes your web pages easier for people to read; however, you can omit the closing `</p>` tags if you prefer.

ADD TEXT PARAGRAPHS

To add a text paragraph, enter the paragraph's text between an opening `<p>` tag and a closing `</p>` tag.

1. Immediately below the heading, add two or more text paragraphs to the page, putting each paragraph within `<p>` and `</p>` tags. For example:

```
<p>Greener Seeds, Inc., is the leading supplier of premium organic
seeds in the United States and Canada.</p>
<p>We also offer customized advice on what to plant in different
types of garden, depending on your climate, soil, and needs. </p>
```

2. Save the page, switch to your browser, and then refresh the display so that you can see the change. Figure 1-3 shows the example page with the text added.

Figure 1-3: Paragraphs without specific attributes appear in the browser's default font.

ADD A LINE BREAK

Most browsers accept only one paragraph tag at a time, figuring that multiple `<p>` tags in sequence are an error. To put space between paragraphs, you must use a line-break tag, `<br>`, instead of using multiple `<p>` tags.

1. Add a `<br>` tag before "premium" in the first paragraph:

```
<p>Greener Seeds, Inc., is the leading supplier of <br>premium
organic seeds in the United States and Canada.</p>
```

2. Add a `<br>` tag between the two text paragraphs:

```
<br>
```

3. Save the page, switch to your browser, and then refresh the display so that you can see the change. Figure 1-4 shows the example page with the breaks added, making the words "premium organic seeds" appear at the start of the second line of the first paragraph and adding extra space between the first and second paragraphs.

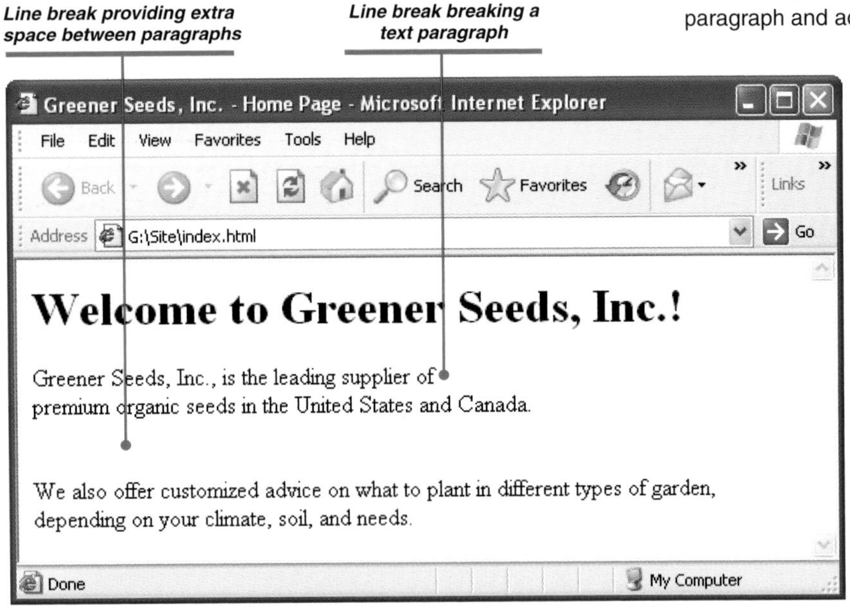

Line break providing extra space between paragraphs

Line break breaking a text paragraph

Figure 1-4: Use a `<br>` (line-break) tag to break a line at a specific point or add extra space between paragraphs.

ADD A COMMENT

Comments are text that the browser is instructed not to display. You can add comments to a web page to note a change you need to make, explain an effect you're trying to achieve, or add other information for yourself or others helping you to create and manage your site.

To add a comment, use the `<!-- -->` tag, placing the comment between the two pairs of dashes. Put a space between each pair of dashes and the comment.

1. Add a comment to the line after the line break you just inserted, together with a new text paragraph below it:

```
<br>
<!-- Insert the picture here -->
<p>Greener Seeds can help make your garden
flourish.</p>
```

2. Save the page, switch to your browser, and then refresh the display so that you can see that the comment is not displayed, while the new paragraph is displayed.

VIEW THE SOURCE CODE

Although browsers don't display comments when they display the web page, anyone who can view your pages can view the comments by examining the source code for the pages. Most browsers include a View Source or View Source Code command (often on the View menu) for displaying the source code.

To view the source code for the page currently displayed in Internet Explorer:

1. Click the **View** menu and then click **Source**. XP opens the page in Notepad (or your default text editor).

2. When you've finished examining the source code, click the **File** menu and then click **Exit** to close Notepad.

Apply Formatting

To apply direct formatting using HTML, use tags. Chapter 3 shows you how to perform the most widely used manual formatting. For now, you'll quickly apply centering to a paragraph by adding the `align` attribute to the paragraph tags that contain it.

1. Click before the closing angle bracket of the `<p>` tag at the beginning of the paragraph you want to center. In the example, the paragraph is "Greener Seeds can help make your garden flourish."

2. Press **SPACEBAR** and then type align="center" before the closing angle bracket, as in this example:

   ```
   <p align="center">Greener
   Seeds can help make your
   garden flourish.</p>
   ```

3. Save the page, switch to your browser, and then refresh the display so that you can see the change.

NOTE

Instead of changing a picture's size, you can change the size at which the browser displays the picture. Chapter 4 shows you how to do this.

NOTE

Adobe Photoshop Elements is a powerful entry-level graphics program that can be used for sizing and many other graphics-editing tasks. See *Photoshop Elements 3.0 QuickSteps*, published by McGraw-Hill/Osborne.

Add a Picture

Add a picture to the page by using an `<img src=>` tag that specifies the source file used for the image.

1. Choose the picture you want to display.

2. Copy it to your site's folder.

3. Open the copy in your graphics application, and check its dimensions. Ideally, the picture should be around 200 to 400 pixels wide. Resize your copy of the picture to around this width if necessary.

4. Type the tag on the line below the line break (`<br>`) tag, substituting your picture's name for "red_rose_13.jpg".

   ```
   <img src="red_rose_
   13.jpg">
   ```

5. Save the page, switch to your browser, and then refresh the display so that you can see the change. Figure 1-5 shows an example of a page with an image added.

6. If the picture is too big for the page, use your graphics application to make it smaller, and then reload the page in your browser.

Figure 1-5: You will often need to reduce the size of digital photographs so that they fit on a web page and do not take too long to download.

QUICK**FACTS**

UNDERSTANDING TOOLS FOR CREATING HTML

You can create effective HTML using just a text editor, as described in this chapter, but you will probably be able to create pages faster using more capable tools much of the time. This sidebar explains some of your options.

MICROSOFT OFFICE APPLICATIONS OR EQUIVALENTS

If you want to create HTML files quickly from your existing documents, you can use the tools built into the Microsoft Office applications and into most of their major competitors, including Lotus SmartSuite, Corel WordPerfect Office, and the open-source StarOffice and OpenOffice.org suites. Because Microsoft Office is the leading office suite, this book uses it for examples of creating HTML using office applications.

The disadvantage to using office applications to create HTML is that these applications are almost never optimized for creating small web pages or tidy HTML. For example, when you save a Word document as a web page, Word includes all the information needed to allow you to continue to edit the web page as a Word document. Technically, this is extremely impressive, but it means that even a simple web page created in Word contains a large amount of data that's useless to most browsers. This extra data makes the web page significantly larger than it needs to be, so the page takes longer to transfer across an Internet connection.

Unless you have a compelling reason to create and save your web pages directly from office applications, you'll do best to use an HTML editor or a web-authoring application to ensure that the web pages contain only the information they need.

Continued...

Add a Hyperlink

A *hyperlink* is a link in a web page that leads to another page or to another point on the same page. You click the hyperlink to switch the browser to the hyperlink's target or destination. Hyperlinks are usually implemented as text or graphics.

Add hyperlinks from this page to another page by using a pair of anchor tags, `<a>` and `</a>`, with the `href` (hypertext reference) attribute and the path and name of the linked file.

1. Position the insertion point where you want the hyperlink—for example, after the last `</p>` tag in the file—and press **ENTER** to create a new line.

2. Create any heading or other text that you want to immediately precede the hyperlink. For example, type a new level-2 heading using the `<h2>` and `</h2>` tags, as shown:

   `<h2>Today's Specials</h2>`

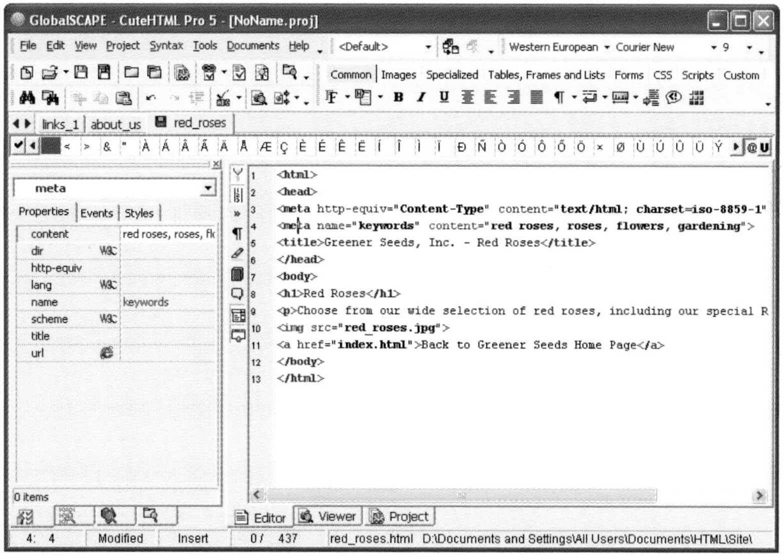

Figure 1-6: HTML editors, such as CuteHTML Pro, make the process of inserting and checking codes easier and may include an integrated browser for viewing pages as you work.

UNDERSTANDING TOOLS FOR CREATING HTML *(Continued)*

HTML EDITOR

An HTML editor is an editing application that's customized for creating HTML manually. An HTML editor typically includes options for creating and editing HTML tags quickly (for example, creating tags via drag and drop or by using property sheets), powerful search and replace functionality, and HTML templates that you can use to create particular types of documents quickly.

Figure 1-6 shows CuteHTML (www.globalscape.com; $49.99), a popular Windows HTML editor.

WEB-AUTHORING APPLICATION

A web-authoring application is an application designed for creating web pages (as opposed to creating another kind of document) using a graphical interface. Instead of typing the HTML codes your pages need, you can apply codes by using formatting commands, toolbars, and menu options as you would apply formatting or styles in a word processor or in a page layout program.

The advantage of a web-authoring application is that you can see the layout of the page you're creating. This is sometimes called What You See Is What You Get, or WYSIWYG (pronounced *whizzy-wig*).

Widely used web-authoring applications include:

- **Microsoft FrontPage** runs only on Windows. FrontPage works best with servers that run the FrontPage Extensions (FrontPage-specific features), so make sure that your web host offers this service. (For information about FrontPage, see *Microsoft Office FrontPage 2003 QuickSteps*, published by McGraw-Hill/Osborne.)

- **Adobe GoLive** (shown in Figure 1-7) is available for both Windows and Mac OS X.

- **Macromedia Dreamweaver** is available for both Windows and Mac OS X.

3. Type the actual hyperlink. For example, a link to a page named yellow_roses.html that uses the words *Yellow Roses* as the object that a user would click to use the hyperlink:

```
<a href="yellow_roses.html">Yellow Roses</a>
```

4. Type additional hyperlinks as needed—for example:

```
<a href="red_roses.html">Red Roses</a>
<a href="pink_roses.html">Pink Roses</a>
```

5. Save the page, switch to your browser, and then refresh the display so that you can see the change. Don't click any of the links, however, because there are no linked files yet.

Figure 1-8 shows the bottom of the page with the hyperlinks added. Notice that even though the hyperlinks appear on separate lines in the text editor, they appear on one line in the browser because there are no paragraph tags or break tags between them.

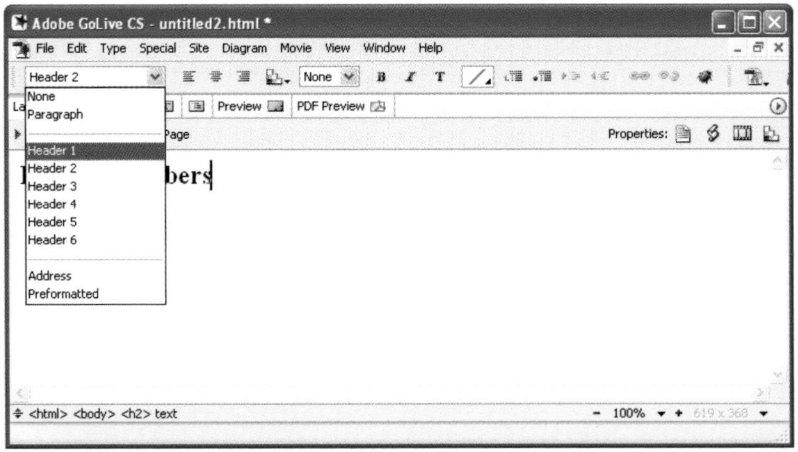

Figure 1-7: Web-authoring applications, such as Adobe GoLive (shown here running on Windows XP), let you apply formatting graphically rather than by entering the HTML codes manually.

Create Linked Files

Create the files that are referred to by the hyperlinks you just created.

1. Create a new text file by clicking the **File** menu and then clicking **New**. Notepad automatically closes the index.html file because it can work with only one file at a time.

2. Type the structure of the new file and any contents that can be common to each of the hyperlinked pages, such as a hyperlink back to the index.html page. For example:

```
<html>
<head>
<title></title>
</head>
<body>
<h1></h1>
<a href="index.html">Back to Greener Seeds home page</a>
</body>
</html>
```

Figure 1-8: Text hyperlinks provide an easy way of letting visitors access other pages on your web site.

NOTE

HTML files use the file extensions .htm and .html more or less interchangeably. When you're browsing the Web, you'll often enter an address that ends with one or another of these extensions, but you'll often use other extensions as well, such as .php, .asp, and .mspx. These file extensions indicate technologies used by the servers to provide dynamic web pages (web pages that change as the user interacts with them).

3. Click the **Edit** menu and then click **Select All** to select all the contents of the file.

4. Click the **Edit** menu and then click **Copy** to copy the structure of the file to the Clipboard.

5. Enter the unique contents of the page using the techniques discussed earlier in this chapter to add a title, a heading, some text, and perhaps a picture. This example shows the HTML for a short page (shown in Figure 1-9) that contains those items:

```html
<html>
<head>
<title>Greener Seeds, Inc. - Yellow Roses</title>
</head>
<body>
<h1>Yellow Roses</h1>
<p>Choose from our wide selection of yellow roses, including our
special Yellow Devils, shown here.</p>
<img src="y_roses.jpg">
<br>
<a href="index.html">Back to Greener Seeds Home Page</a>
</body>
</html>
```

6. Save the file under the file name you assigned to the first hyperlink you created in your site's folder. Remember to use double quotation marks to force Notepad to use the .html extension rather than the .txt extension.

7. Switch to your browser and then click the first link at the bottom of the page. Your browser displays the page you just created. Click the link on the page to return to the home page.

8. If you have additional hyperlinks, create a new text document for each, paste in the document structure and common elements that you copied, and then add the unique elements desired. Save each file under the name used for the hyperlink, and test the links from the index.html page to each file and back to the index.html page.

Figure 1-9: Use the techniques discussed earlier in this chapter to create a short page that includes a hyperlink back to the index.html page.

NOTE

Unlike most of the tags discussed in this chapter, meta tags don't have a closing tag.

TIP

Often, you may want to use meta tags to describe your site (or an area of your site) rather than simply the content of the page to which you're adding the tag. This will help increase your site's presence in search engines, but you will need to ensure that users can easily navigate to the other areas of your site to find the contents that have drawn them to it.

NOTE

You can place the meta tags anywhere in the header, but you'll probably find it best to choose a standard location for all your pages. For example, you might decide always to put the meta tags after the page's title.

TIP

There's a special meta tag called robots that you can use to request search engines not to scan a page or follow links on it. You might do this if you want to avoid having a page appear in search engines—for example, if it's private or if you're still testing your site. It's not 100 percent effective, as search engines can disregard it, but it's still worth doing. Add this tag to the header area: `<meta name="robots" content="noindex,nofollow">`.

Describe Your Pages with Meta Tags

To enable search engines to determine the contents of your web pages and catalog them correctly, you can use meta tags with the appropriate information. You place these tags inside the head of a web page, where they're read by search engines but not displayed in the browser.

The main attributes for the meta tag are the name attribute and the content attribute:

- name specifies the name of the meta tag you want to create. HTML supports a wide variety of names for recording details, such as the author, editor, purpose and rating of the page, and more. For describing your pages, you'll typically want to use the description name and the keywords name because search engines typically concentrate on these tags.

- content specifies the content of the meta tag.

To add meta tags to a page:

1. Position the insertion point within the header of the web page you want to affect.
2. Type the first meta tag, making it a description tag and assigning it a brief description of the page—for example:

   ```
   <meta name="description" content="mail-order seeds and plants">
   ```
3. Type the next meta tag, making it a keywords tag and assigning it the keywords you want to use for the page, separated by commas—for example:

   ```
   <meta name="keywords" content="seeds, plants, gardening">
   ```
4. Type further meta tags as required—for example:

   ```
   <meta name="author" content="Greener Seeds">
   ```
5. Save the page.

Reload a Page Automatically

Sometimes you may need to create a web page that automatically reloads itself without the user's intervention so that it can display the latest information available. For example, you might need to update a page of sports events with the latest statistics.

QUICKFACTS

UNDERSTANDING HOW SEARCH ENGINES WORK

To find specific content on the Web, you're probably used to using a search engine, such as Google (http://www.google.com), Yahoo! (http://www.yahoo.com), MSN (http://www.msn.com), or another search engine. You type your search criteria, click the **Search** button or the **Go** button, and receive the results within seconds.

Most search engines create their catalogs by using the titles, headings, and meta tags in web pages. By making sure that your titles and headings contain terms that describe the contents of your pages, and by adding meta tags with suitable descriptions and keywords to reinforce the titles and headings, you increase the likelihood of search engines categorizing your site correctly.

CAUTION

Don't set too short a refresh interval on a page no matter how frequently the information is updated or how eagerly viewers will want to get the latest information; even when you use a meta tag to update the page automatically, users can reload it manually as frequently as they wish. In particular, don't set `content` to 0, as this will cause the page to reload constantly.

NOTE

You can also redirect the browser to another web page using JavaScript. Chapter 10 shows you how to do so.

To update a page automatically, use a meta tag with the `http-equiv` attribute set to `refresh`.

1. Position the insertion point within the header of the web page you want to affect.
2. Type the meta tag in the following format, assigning to `content` the number of seconds after which you want the page to be refreshed:

```
<meta http-equiv="refresh" content="60">
```

3. Save the page, switch to your browser, and then refresh the display.
4. Wait the specified number of seconds, and the page will automatically reload itself.

Redirect the Browser to Another Page

If you've used the Web much, you'll be familiar with being redirected from one page to another. You'll often need to use redirection in your pages as well. For example, you might need to redirect browsers from your old web site to your new web site or from an alternate domain (such as .org or .net) to your main domain.

To redirect the browser, use an `http-equiv` meta tag with the `url` attribute set to the destination URL.

1. Position the insertion point within the header of the web page you want to affect.
2. Type the `<meta>` tag and specify the `http-equiv` attribute with the `refresh` value:

```
<meta http-equiv="refresh">
```

3. Add the `url` attribute with the URL that you want to use—for example:

```
url="http://www.htmlq.com"
```

4. Add the `content` attribute with the number of seconds to wait before the redirection takes effect:

```
content="2">
```

The entire tag should look like this:

```
<meta http-equiv="refresh" url="http://www.htmlq.com" content="2">
```

Check Your Pages with Other Browsers

Internet Explorer has more than 90 percent of the browser market (as of September 2004), so you should use Internet Explorer as your primary browser for testing your web pages to make sure that the vast majority of people on the Web can see them.

The remainder of the browser market is split among the other browsers listed in Table 1-1. After ensuring that your pages work with Internet Explorer, it's a good idea to test your pages with several other browsers as well to make sure that you're not accidentally excluding part of your audience or market from your site.

TIP

If you already have both a PC and a Mac, you'll be in a good position to check how your web pages look on both platforms. If you have just a Mac, consider buying a copy of Microsoft's Virtual PC emulator so that you can run Windows XP (and perhaps other PC-based operating systems, such as Linux) on your Mac and check how your pages look. You can download a trial copy of Virtual PC from www.microsoft.com/windows/virtualpc/default.mspx. There are currently no PC-based emulators for Mac OS X, so if you use a PC and want to check how your pages look on Mac OS X, you'll need to use an actual Mac.

TABLE 1-1: WEB BROWSERS

BROWSER	OPERATING SYSTEMS	SOURCE
Internet Explorer	Windows, System 9, Mac OS X	Included with the operating systems
Safari	Mac OS X	Included with Mac OS X
Opera	Windows, System 9, Mac OS X, Linux	www.opera.com
Mozilla Firefox	Windows, Mac OS X, Linux	www.mozilla.org
Mozilla	Windows, Mac OS X, Linux	www.mozilla.org
Netscape	Windows, Mac OS X, Linux	www.netscape.com
Konqueror	Linux	www.konqueror.org
Lynx	Windows	Various sites, including www.download.com
MacLynx	System 9, Mac OS X	Various sites, including www.download.com

Figure 1-10 shows Mozilla Firefox, a browser that offers the convenience of opening multiple pages on different tabs in the same window.

All these browsers are free, except for Opera, which costs $35. All the browsers are graphical, except for Lynx and MacLynx, which are text-only browsers. (Text-only browsers display only text but are useful for checking that your web pages provide the necessary information even on the most limited computers, cell phones, or text-to-speech devices.)

To access a web page:

1. Start the browser, if it's not already running. For example, click the **Start** button, click **All Programs**, and then click the browser's entry on the Start menu.

2. Drag across the browser's address bar to select the address.

3. Type the URL (uniform resource locator) of a web page on the Internet or the path and file name of the web page on a local drive, and then press **ENTER**.

Figure 1-10: Most browsers, such as Mozilla Firefox, have similar interfaces and controls.

- *Understand Web Clients and Servers*

- *Access a Web Page*

- *Understanding URLs*

- *Assess Your Requirements*

- *Choose an ISP or Web-Hosting Service*

- *Understanding Intranets and Extranets*

- *Decide on Web-Hosting Features*

- *Running Your Own Web Server*

- *Evaluate an ISP*

- *Understanding Domains*

- *Evaluate a Web-Hosting Service*

- *Register a Domain Name*

- *Plan Your Site's Contents*

- *Make Your Site Effective*

- *Check Your Web Site*

- *Update and Maintain Your Web Site*

- *Transfer Your Site Using Internet Explorer*

- *Transfer a Site Using an FTP Client*

Chapter 2

Choosing an ISP and Getting Your Own Web Site

Understand Web Basics

The *Internet* is the umbrella term for the worldwide network of computers that are connected together and use the TCP/IP (Transmission Control Protocol/Internet Protocol) protocol suite of controlling standards. The Internet uses several different forms of communication, including e-mail, file transfer, and the Hypertext Transfer Protocol, or HTTP. The World Wide Web (hereafter, simply *the Web*) is that part of the Internet that uses HTTP to transfer information.

Understand Web Clients and Servers

If you have an Internet connection, you're probably already familiar with using a web browser, such as Microsoft's Internet Explorer, to view the contents of a web site and navigating from one web page to another by following hypertext links. The mesh of links among pages gives the Web its name.

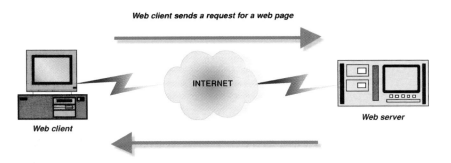

Web client sends a request for a web page

INTERNET

Web client

Web server

Web server sends the web page to the client

Figure 2-1: A web client (using a browser) typically connects to a web server across the Internet. You can also use a browser to open an HTML document on your local hard drive or network.

Web sites (a *site* is a collection of linked web pages) are stored on *servers*, computers that provide data to other computers (*clients*) on request. Web servers can run almost any TCP/IP-capable operating system, such as UNIX, Linux, Solaris, Windows, or Mac OS X. Likewise, Web clients can run almost any operating system, although most run client operating systems rather than server operating systems. Figure 2-1 shows a web client requesting a web page from a web server across the Internet.

Access a Web Page

Every computer on the Internet has a unique address called its *Internet Protocol address*, or *IP address*, that enables the computer to be identified. If you enter that address in a browser, you will access the public web page on that computer (provided that it has one).

Since an IP address is a complex series of up to 12 digits, most web servers have a domain name associated with that address that is simpler to remember and use. For example, the IP address 198.45.19.151 is registered to the computer associated with the domain host name "mcgraw-hill.com," home of McGraw-Hill, publishers of this book. To access their web site, you can also enter their domain name using their URL, or Uniform Resource Locator, http://www.mcgraw-hill.com, in your browser (see Figure 2-2). Your browser consults a domain name service (DNS) server (usually at your ISP) to resolve the URL to the appropriate IP address. See the QuickSteps "Understanding URLs," later in this chapter.

CAUTION

Most browsers also let you omit the www designation and the domain type suffix (such as .com or .org), so you can often type just the keyword in the domain and let your browser fill in the rest. For example, you might type ibm and let your browser expand the address to http://www.ibm.com. The danger is that sometimes the site you want may not use the .com domain suffix—but another site will. This can lead to some unpleasant surprises.

Long URLs tend to be hard to remember, so most companies try to keep them as short as possible. For example, on the back of this book, you'll see the URL www.mcgraw-hill.com for the McGraw-Hill web site. To access the McGraw-Hill web site:

1. Click the **Start** button and then click **Internet**.

2. Type www.mcgraw-hill.com into the address bar of your browser, and then press ENTER.

When you enter a URL like this, your browser automatically adds *http://* to the beginning of the address, because most web sites use HTTP rather than another protocol. The request doesn't include a file name, so the web server supplies the default file for the web site. The default file is usually named index.html, but may also be named index.htm (without an L) or default.html, depending on the server technology used.

Figure 2-2: When you enter a host name, your browser resolves the IP address and displays the appropriate web site.

QUICK**FACTS**

UNDERSTANDING URLS

A typical full URL has the format http://
www.quicksteps.com/products/plants/greens.html.

The first part of a URL, http://, tells the client and
the server that the site uses HTTP as opposed to
another protocol. If the URL begins with https://, it uses
encryption to secure the data transmitted between the
client and the server. For example, if you connect to your
bank via the Web, the connection will almost certainly
use HTTPS rather than unsecured HTTP so that your
sensitive data is secured in transit.

The next part of the URL, www, indicates that the server
being contacted is a web server. This part appears in
most URLs, but is not always required. For example,
URLs such as http://store.apple.com do not use www.

The next part of the URL identifies the domain name
or IP address of the server to which to connect.
Typically, the URL uses the domain name—in the format
quicksteps.com—because domain names are easier
for people to remember and to type. Sometimes, the
URL uses the server's IP address instead of the domain
name—for example, http://216.239.37.99.

The last part of the URL is the address of the file
that's being opened—for example, /products/plants/
greens.html. The address consists of the file name
(greens.html) preceded by the folder path (/products/
plants/). The folders are divided using forward slashes (/)
rather than backward slashes (\) because much of the
Internet is based on Unix (which uses forward slashes to
denote directory divisions).

Choose a Web Host or ISP

Before you can put up a web site, you'll probably need to choose a web host or
ISP. This section discusses how to assess your requirements, decide whether
to run your own web server, establish which features you need, and choose a
web host.

Assess Your Requirements

First, assess your requirements for an ISP and a web site:

- If you're planning to build your own web site, you'll need to find an Internet location
  to host your site (unless you have a location already). Follow the instructions in this
  chapter to choose an ISP or a web-hosting service and create your own web site.

- If you're creating pages for your school, organization, or company, however, that body
  will probably have set up a hosting arrangement for the site, so you'll put the pages
  either on an existing web site or on an intranet site (an *intranet* is a web network
  similar to the Internet but contained within and limited to a single organization; see the
  "Understanding Intranets and Extranets" QuickFacts, later in this chapter). In this case,
  you can skip most of this chapter, provided that you learn the details of the server that
  will contain your web site.

- If you're creating HTML content for pages on a special site (for example, eBay or
  Blogger.com), you won't need to get a web site, but the site may have specific con-
  straints on the tags you can use and where you can place them.

Choose an ISP or Web-Hosting Service

If you're looking for web space, your choices are usually between your ISP, a
web hosting service, and online communities. You can research your options on
the web by visiting ISPs' web sites, web hosts' sites, and host-finding sites, such as
TopHosts.com (www.tophosts.com) and HostSearch (www.hostsearch.com), but
you should also ask your friends and co-workers. In particular, if you're part of a
company or a school, ask its system administrator or webmaster for suggestions,
because they should be able to steer you toward suitable ISPs or hosts.

UNDERSTANDING INTRANETS AND EXTRANETS

A web site is a site on the World Wide Web that anyone with an Internet connection and a web browser can access. Most large companies and many small companies have web sites that provide information and support to their customers. Companies also tend to have internal web sites for their staff that people outside the company cannot access. These web sites are called *intranets* and are separated from the Web by firewalls.

Beyond intranets and web sites, some companies have web sites that allow people outside the company to access certain types of information that are kept on the company's internal network rather than on its web server. For example, at web sites such as FedEx (www.fedex.com) and UPS (www.ups.com), you can enter the tracking number for a package and learn its current location, status, and routing information. This information comes from the company's internal network but is accessible to customers.

Having a valid tracking number establishes you as a bona fide customer; without the tracking number, you can't (for example) learn the delivery information about hundreds of packages on the off-chance of finding one that interests you. At other extranet sites, users must log in using a password.

From the customer's point of view, an extranet works in the same way as a web site except that it provides more useful information and may require logging in. The difference lies in how the extranet provides information to the customer from inside the firewall instead of simply providing the set of information available on the web server.

Continued…

Decide on Web-Hosting Features

When choosing an ISP or web host for your web site, decide which features you will need for your site.

AMOUNT OF SPACE

The web host rents you a certain amount of space on its web servers for your site. 10 MB is enough for a small site; as soon as you add more than a handful of pages with graphics or post one or more of your musical compositions (even in a compressed format, such as MP3), you'll need to get more space.

AMOUNT OF TRAFFIC

The web host allows you a certain amount of *traffic*, or data transferred, measured in megabytes or (more often) gigabytes per month. If your site exceeds your allowance, the web host charges you extra for each megabyte or gigabyte.

How much traffic you need depends on how many people visit your site and what they do when they're there—for example, viewing pages consisting of compact files generates far less traffic than downloading your audio or video files. Even if your site fits comfortably within, say, 10 MB, you may need gigabytes of traffic if your site is busy.

Some hosts have creative accounting policies for traffic, such as excluding the heaviest-traffic day of the month from the total calculation, which allows your site to ride out brief surges of visitor interest without incurring extra cost. Other hosts are less generous and deduct all data transfer from your allowance.

NUMBER OF E-MAIL ACCOUNTS

Most web hosts include some e-mail accounts with the web space. Make sure that your host offers enough e-mail accounts and that you can add further accounts at reasonable rates should you need them.

UNDERSTANDING INTRANETS AND EXTRANETS (Continued)

In addition to being used to make information available to customers on the web, as in the examples given here, extranets can also be used to provide information securely to the employees of another company without the information being available to users of the Web as a whole.

DOMAIN NAME SUPPORT

For impact and ease of access, you'll probably want your web site to have its own domain name (for example, www.quicksteps.com) rather than a name that includes your ISP's name or web host's name (for example, www.earthlink.net/~quicksteps).

All web hosts support domain names, but some ISPs do not. Check whether your intended host or ISP will handle the domain registration process for you if necessary.

INTERNET CONNECTION SPEED AND UPTIME

Check that the web host has a fast connection to the Internet's *backbone*, the main lines of connection of the Internet, so that would-be visitors will be able to access your web site quickly. Most serious web hosts will have at least a T3 communications channel (44.7 megabits per second, or Mbps). Better is a web host with one or more OC (optical carrier) channels. OC-1 provides 51.8 Mbps, OC-3 provides 155.5 Mbps, OC-12 provides 622.1 Mbps, and so on, up to OC-48, which provides 2.5 Gbps (gigabits per second). It is also valuable for a web host to have multiple, independent connections to the Internet backbone through separate carriers, such as AT&T, Sprint, or UU-Net.

A good web host will publish statistics for its *uptime*—the percentage of time that its servers and network are typically available. Look for an uptime above 99.9 percent.

SUPPORT FOR ANY WEB TOOLS

Some ISPs and web-hosting services limit you to using their custom tools for building and maintaining your web site. Some of these custom tools consist of online templates and wizards that walk you through the process of creating a site; others are executable programs that you download and install on your computer. Many of these custom tools enable you to put together a good-looking web site with minimal time and effort, but they do not provide the flexibility that you will need to create a full-featured web site that meets your needs. Make sure that you can use your preferred tools as well as any tools that the host provides.

QUICK**FACTS**

RUNNING YOUR OWN WEB SERVER

Instead of renting space from an ISP or from a web-hosting service, you may be tempted to run your own web server, especially if you have all the tools needed:

- Windows XP Professional includes a stripped-down version of Internet Information Services (IIS) web server that permits up to 10 connections at a time. (Windows XP Home Edition doesn't include IIS.)
- Mac OS X includes Apache, a full-bore web server.
- Most Linux distributions also include Apache.
- A broadband, high-speed connection to the Internet.

In most cases, however, running your own web server makes sense only for a medium- to large-size company, because you need to keep your web server running all the time (so that the site is always accessible) and provide enough bandwidth for however many users choose to visit the site. Even minor outages, such as those caused by having to restart your computer after installing software, can cost you part of your audience.

Worse, most broadband Internet connections are *asymmetrical*, delivering fast download speeds but slower upload speeds, so your site will not respond speedily to multiple visitors. In addition, most ISPs specifically exclude running a server from residential and SOHO (small office/home office) service agreements and will notice—and object—if you try to run a popular web site on such a connection.

AUDIO AND VIDEO STREAMING

If you plan to place audio or video files on your web site for streaming rather than for download, make sure your host offers streaming, and check what they will charge you for it (it can be expensive). *Streaming* is a way of splitting up an audio or video file so that it can be played as it is being transferred. Streamed files are usually not permanently saved on the computer that plays them. By contrast, downloaded files are permanently saved (unless the user chooses to delete them).

Audio and video streaming can quickly use up even a generous traffic allowance, so you may need to limit the number of files you offer for streaming.

SHOPPING CARTS AND SECURE SERVERS

If you plan to sell items from your web site, look for a web host that offers shopping carts and secure servers.

Evaluate an ISP

If you already have an Internet connection via an ISP (rather than through a school, company, or organization), investigate the web-hosting services that the ISP provides. Having your ISP host your web site is a convenient solution as long as the ISP provides all the web features you need (see the section "Decide on Web-Hosting Features" for a discussion of the features you should evaluate).

Many ISPs provide enough web space for a small web site with their basic accounts and provide more space with more expensive accounts; most ISPs also let you pay for as much additional space as you need. For example, at this writing, Earthlink's basic dial-up account offers up to eight e-mail accounts, with 10 MB of web space for each of those accounts. This is enough to establish a modest site and decide whether you want to pay for additional space.

QUICKFACTS

UNDERSTANDING DOMAINS

The *Domain Naming System* or *Domain Name Service* (abbreviated to DNS in either case) is a system (or service) that maps domain names to IP addresses. A domain name is essentially a human-friendly shortcut to a particular IP address. For example, at this writing, the domain name yahoo.com maps to the IP address 66.94.231.99.

Domains are divided into different organizational types and geographical areas. The key organizational types are .com (commercial organization), .edu (educational institution), .gov (government agency), .mil (U.S. military), and .net (networking organization); there are other types, such as .biz (business) and .name (personal name). All types are widely available except for .gov and .mil.

The most widely used geographical areas are .us (United States), .de (Germany or Deutschland), .cn (China), .jp (Japan), .uk (United Kingdom), .es (Spain or España), .in (India), .br (Brazil), and .it (Italy); there are others for most major, and many minor, countries.

The .com designation is king of the domain world, which is why almost all web browsers default to the .com address when the domain type isn't specified. So if you're planning to register a domain name, .com should be your first choice.

NOTE

Most registration services provide suggestions of available domain names that are similar to unavailable domain names you request, but you will do better to start with your own list and work through it in order of preference.

Evaluate a Web-Hosting Service

Unless your ISP specializes in hosting web sites, you will find more options and greater flexibility in a web-hosting service—a service that hosts web sites but does not provide Internet access. Most web-hosting services offer various hosting packages aimed at different levels of users, from basic packages (for example, 200 MB disk space, 10 mailboxes, 200 MB a day traffic, and basic scripting capabilities) to developer packages (for example, 1 GB disk space, 100 mailboxes, 1 GB a day traffic, extra FTP logins for extra users with different privileges, secure server facilities, and advanced scripting capabilities). By choosing a suitable web-hosting service and an appropriate package, you can get almost exactly the space, traffic, and capabilities you need.

Evaluate the cost of paying separately for your Internet access and for your web hosting. If your web site requires only the features and amount of space that your ISP includes with an Internet access account, paying for separate web hosting will be more expensive. If your site needs a significant amount of space and bandwidth, however, using a web-hosting service is likely to be less expensive than getting that same amount of space and bandwidth from your ISP.

Register a Domain Name

To make your web presence not only felt but also easy to find, you'll probably want to register your own domain name. (See the "Understanding Domains" QuickFacts for an overview of domain names and how they work.) Having a domain name (for example, www.quicksteps.com) gives your web site much more impact than—and makes it easier to access than—a name contained within another domain (for example, www.yourisp.com/~yourname).

Draw up a short list of domain names that would be suitable for your site. Huge numbers of domain names have already been registered, so you'll need to be creative to find a suitable name that's still available.

TIP

Most people consider it more satisfactory to spend the time and effort coming up with a unique domain name for which you can get the .com extension rather than settle for one of the less usual extensions (such as .ws or .cc). Even if you prefer an extension other than .com for your site, you may choose to register the .com domain as well so that you can redirect it to your site. For example, if your site is for a non-profit organization, the .org domain type would more accurately reflect its nature. By securing the .com domain name and redirecting it to the .org site, however, you can avoid losing traffic to someone who subsequently registers it. Also, because most browsers default to the .com domain type, visitors who type only the basic name of your site rather than the full address will be directed to the correct site.

Domain name registration used to be centrally controlled, but nowadays there are many registration sites. Three of the most popular sites are:

- Network Solutions (www.networksolutions.com; shown in Figure 2-3) was the first domain registration site and remains the largest.

- Register.com (www.register.com) is another large registration site with a good reputation.

- Joker.com (www.joker.com) is a low-cost registration site that's popular with many users.

Figure 2-3: You can register a domain name— or just find out whether a name is available—at a registration site such as Network Solutions.

CAUTION

Make sure any domain name you register doesn't infringe on any trademark. If it does, the trademark holder may be able to claim the domain name from you.

NOTE

If you have a web-authoring application (such as FrontPage, Dreamweaver, or GoLive), you may be able to use its automated features to set up your web site.

Many web hosts can also register domain names for you, thus simplifying the process of registering the domain name and finding somewhere to host it.

Start your web browser and go to a domain name registration site. The procedure for registering a domain name starts by searching to see if it is available. If it is and you decide to proceed, you will need to provide payment (via credit card), billing information, and the name and address of an administrative contact (usually you) and a technical contact (usually the web host) for the domain name. Ideally, you will also provide the IP addresses of the web server that will host the domain name. If you don't know them yet, you can leave the domain name with the registration service until you find a web host, but you may then have to pay extra to transfer the domain name to the web host.

Plan, Design, and Create Your Site

You can start a web site by creating individual web pages using a text editor (as discussed in Chapter 1), an HTML editor, or a web-authoring application and linking the pages to each other using hyperlinks. Before you start creating your site, however, you should plan the site's contents and decide its basic design.

Plan Your Site's Contents

A snappy URL may stick in a web surfer's mind, and a good design will please the eye (assuming that the browser renders it correctly), but content is what makes or breaks your web site. To make people come to your site and to persuade them to come back, you need strong—and preferably unique—content.

Focus on what your site's purpose is—why you're creating it in the first place. This should be obvious: you'd think few people would create a web site for no reason, but a surprising number of people do start off with at best a nebulous idea of what they're trying to achieve. While you *can* start creating pages without a firm goal and then let it grow in whichever direction your enthusiasm takes you, you're unlikely to end up with a focused, unified site that will draw interest. (If you do begin creating your web site this way, be prepared to start again from scratch if you realize you should have chosen a different direction.)

Establish what value you will provide to the people who visit your site. Will you provide tips, resources, or evaluations of products? Will you link to other sites? Will you sell, promote, or support products?

Once you have decided the purpose of your web site, focus on how you will deliver that purpose. In particular, decide who is going to generate content, who is going to edit it, who will create the web pages, and who will post them to the site and maintain it. On a small site, such as a personal site, you may end up doing all the tasks yourself.

Make Your Site Effective

You must design your web site so that it can be viewed successfully by everyone who accesses it. That's not as easy as it might seem, for several reasons:

- How a given page looks will depend on the browser, the screen resolution the computer is using, and the window size of the browser.
- Visitors to your site may use one of several browsers that interpret HTML a little differently. Over 90 percent of all Internet users, however, are on computers running Windows and using Internet Explorer as their browser, so that should be the focus of your development unless you are deliberately targeting a niche that you know uses a different operating system or browser.
- Even if the users are using the same browser, the operating system on their computers may cause the pages to be displayed in slightly different ways. For example, font sizes appear smaller on a Mac than on Windows, so your pages will typically look different on a Mac.
- Most browsers have highly configurable display settings that will affect how the pages look. You can change the text size, text color, background color, and even the display resolution of most browsers.

TIP

If possible, have several other people look at your web site while it is in development to make sure that they find it navigable and workable. Ask these people to make notes of difficulties that they have with the layout, navigation, text, or graphics. Resolve any persistent difficulties that surface. For example, you might need to add explanatory text to your home page to help visitors find parts of the site or add redundant links to simplify navigation.

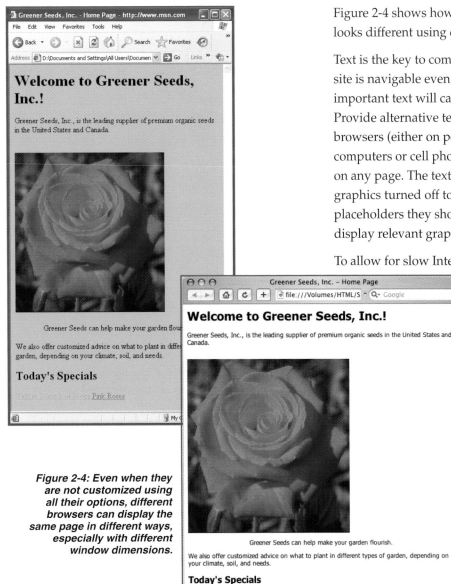

Figure 2-4 shows how even the simple page used as the example in Chapter 1 looks different using different browsers and browser settings.

Text is the key to communicating via web pages, so you must ensure that your site is navigable even if only the text is displayed. Organize it so that the most important text will catch the reader's eye and draw him or her into the page. Provide alternative text for all graphics used so that visitors using text-only browsers (either on personal computers or on other devices, such as handheld computers or cell phones) will be able to see all the important information on any page. The text will also benefit visitors using a browser with the graphics turned off to speed up browsing, because they'll be able to tell which placeholders they should click to navigate your site, which they should click to display relevant graphics, and which they can ignore.

To allow for slow Internet connections, keep the file sizes of your pages as small as possible. HTML files themselves contain only text, so their file sizes remain quite compact unless you add unnecessary tags and comments, but graphics quickly increase the time it takes to download a web page.

Figure 2-4: Even when they are not customized using all their options, different browsers can display the same page in different ways, especially with different window dimensions.

If your site is primarily providing information, use graphics with discretion rather than as a rule and keep their sizes small. (Chapter 4 discusses how to use graphics and how to prepare them for the web.) On the other hand, if your site is demonstrating examples of design, you may need to use more graphics to produce the effects you need.

Where possible, reuse the same small graphics, such as those for your logo and navigation buttons. Most browsers cache graphics so that they can quickly supply them the next time the user requests the same page or another page that uses the same graphics.

Check Your Web Site

Once you've gotten your web site to a stage at which you want to make it available to your audience, check it using Internet Explorer before transferring it to your web host. If possible, it's also a good idea to check your web site using browsers other than Internet Explorer, such as Mozilla Firebird and Netscape Navigator. (See Table 1-1 in Chapter 1 for a list of other browsers for Windows, Mac OS X, and Linux.) Verify that the site functions correctly and that all pages are readable. As discussed earlier in this chapter, it's quite normal for the pages to look different on different browsers and operating systems even if the browsers are configured with default settings.

Be sure to use different sizes of browser window as you test and, if it's practical to do so, assorted screen resolutions as well, concentrating on 800 × 600 and 1024 × 768 resolutions. (These are the resolutions that most users will probably use.) If you want your web pages to be accessible to the widest possible audience, check it at 640 × 480 resolution as well; this resolution is still widely used on near-obsolete computers and is also used by some recent handheld computers.

Try turning down the display to 256 colors, and make sure that the pages are viewable. Graphics that use more colors will be noticeably dithered, using a mixture of colors to deliver roughly the colors you specified.

Update and Maintain Your Web Site

Few web sites are static; almost all sites contain information that needs updating, either every day (for example, a restaurant's menu pages) or from time to time. New content will help to bring visitors back to your site, provided that they know it is there and can easily find it, so make sure your new content is easy to access and that it is flagged from the home page.

Develop a schedule for creating and posting new content and for moving previously new content to the longer-established areas of your site or to an archive. Decide how frequently the different areas of your web site will need to be updated and, if you have a team, establish whose responsibility the updates are.

Add this information to your site-description document (the document explaining your site, its structure, and its contents, as discussed in Chapter 1) so that it is recorded and available to those who need to know it.

Transfer Your Site to the Web

To transfer your site to the web server, you typically need to use the File Transfer Protocol, or FTP, an old and reliable protocol that's responsible for the majority of file transfer on the Internet. Windows XP includes built-in support for transferring files via FTP, but its capabilities are limited, so if you need to transfer many files via FTP, you may choose to buy a third-party FTP application, such as CuteFTP. If you have FrontPage, Dreamweaver, or GoLive, you won't need to buy a third-party FTP application because these applications all include built-in FTP functionality that is superior to the FTP functionality built into Windows.

To transfer files via FTP, you must get the following information from the server's administrator (at your ISP, at the hosting service, or on your company's or organization's network):

- The web server's address (for example, ftp.quicksteps.com) and the folder in which you should put the files.

- Your user name and password for the web server.

NOTE

A *protocol* is a specification or set of rules for doing something—in this case, for communicating between computers.

NOTE

Many web server administrators configure their servers to direct you automatically to your folder when you log in using your user name and password, but you may also need to navigate to a particular subfolder within your folder.

1
2
3
4
5
6
7
8
9
10

Transfer Your Site Using Internet Explorer

The best way to transfer your web site to the FTP server via Internet Explorer is to create a network place for the web server. The network place enables you to access the web server quickly in the future. Another option is to use Internet Explorer to access the FTP server directly. Both of these methods are discussed here.

ACCESS AN FTP SITE USING INTERNET EXPLORER

If you need to access an FTP server only once from a particular computer, it's probably not worth creating a network place. Instead, you can simply use Internet Explorer.

1. Click the **Start** button and then click **Run**. The Run dialog box appears.

2. Type the address of the FTP server in the format ftp:// *username*:*password*@ *ftpserver*, and then press **ENTER**. For example, to access the FTP server named amut-ka.pair.com using the username "jpublic" and the password "sixpack", you would type ftp://jpublic:sixpack@amutka.pair. com and then press **ENTER**.

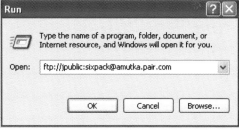

3. Internet Explorer starts and displays the contents of the FTP site in a window.

See "Transfer Files to the Network Place," later in this chapter, for instructions on how to transfer files once you've connected.

CREATE A NETWORK PLACE FOR A WEB SERVER

To create a network place for a web server:

1. Click the **Start** button and then click **My Network Places**. A My Network Places window opens.

2. Click the **Add A Network Place** link in the Network Tasks list. The Add Network Place Wizard starts. Click **Next**. The Where Do You Want To Create This Network Place? screen appears.

Windows XP also includes a command-line FTP client named ftp that you can run from a Command Prompt window (click the **Start** button, click **All Programs**, click **Accessories**, and then click **Command Prompt**). Unless you're comfortable with Unix-style FTP commands, however, chances are that Internet Explorer or a third-party FTP client with a graphical interface will be faster and easier to use.

Add Network Place Wizard

What is the address of this network place?

Type the address of the Web site, FTP site, or network location that this shortcut will open.

Internet or network address:

ftp://amutka.pair.com

Browse...

View some examples

Examples:
\\server\share   (shared folder)
http://webserver/share   (Web Share)
ftp://ftp.microsoft.com   (FTP site)

< Back   Next >   Cancel

3. Click **Choose Another Network Location**, and then click **Next**. The What Is The Address Of This Network Place? screen appears (see Figure 2-5).

4. Type the address of the FTP server in the Internet Or Network Address text box, and then click **Next**. The User Name And Password screen appears (see Figure 2-6).

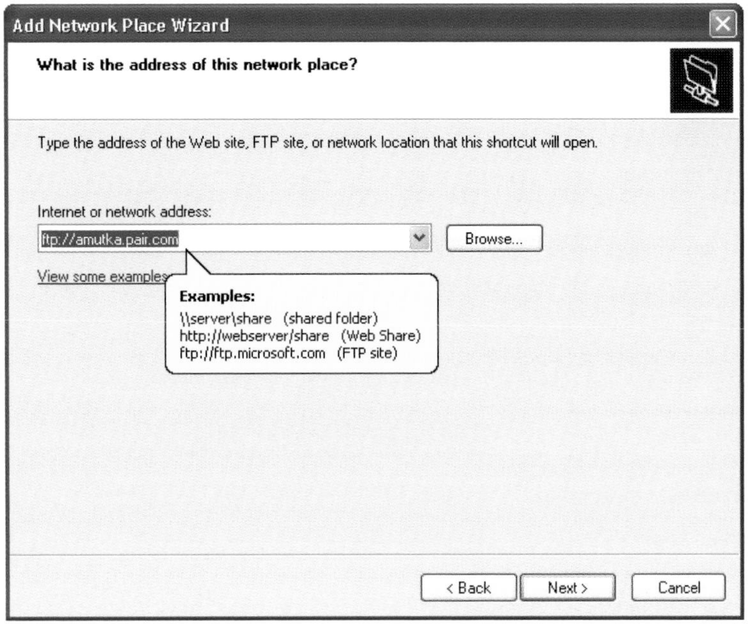

Figure 2-5: Type the details of the FTP server on the What Is The Address Of This Network Place? You can click the View Some Examples link if you want a quick reminder of the address format.

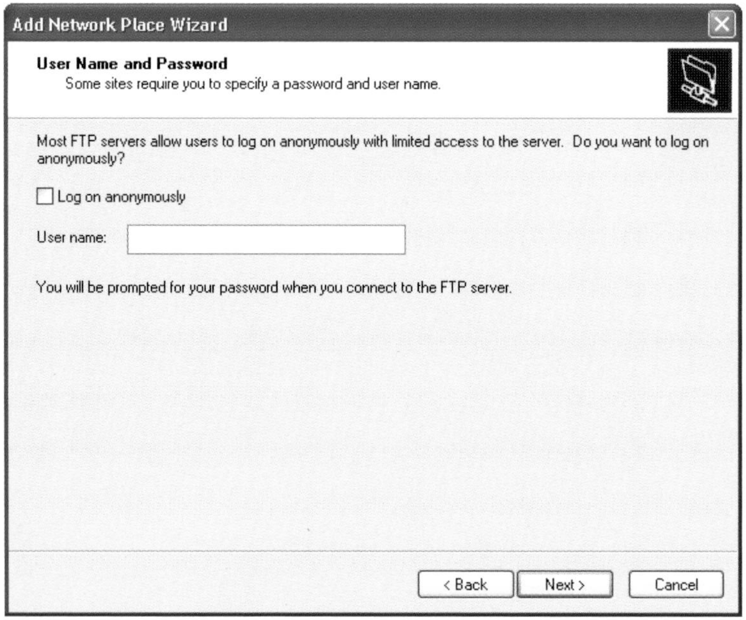

Add Network Place Wizard

User Name and Password
   Some sites require you to specify a password and user name.

Most FTP servers allow users to log on anonymously with limited access to the server. Do you want to log on anonymously?

☐ Log on anonymously

User name: [   ]

You will be prompted for your password when you connect to the FTP server.

< Back   Next >   Cancel

Figure 2-6: You will need to provide your user name (and password, in due course) for the FTP site rather than logging on anonymously.

5. Clear the **Log On Anonymously** check box, type your user name, and click **Next**. The What Do You Want To Name This Place? screen appears.

6. Type a descriptive name for the site, click **Next**, and then click **Finish** on the final screen of the wizard. The wizard creates the network place and tries to connect to it. As you have not yet entered your password, the wizard displays the Log On As dialog box (shown in Figure 2-7), prompting you for your password.

7. Type your password, select the **Save Password** check box if you want to store your password so that you will not have to type it each time you access the FTP site, and then click **Log On**.

8. Internet Explorer displays the contents of the FTP site in a window.

See "Transfer Files to the Network Place," later in this chapter, for instructions on how to transfer files once you've connected.

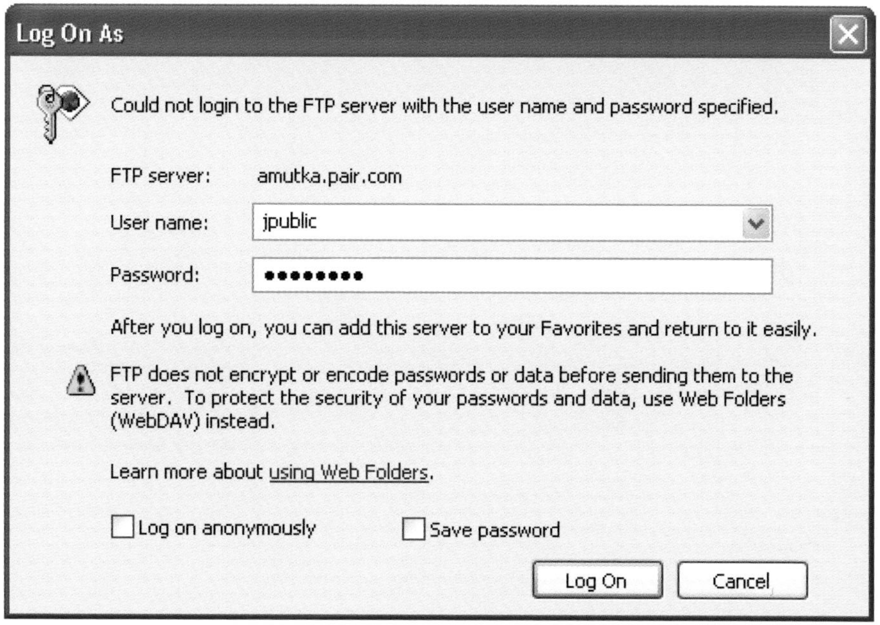

Log On As

Could not login to the FTP server with the user name and password specified.

FTP server: amutka.pair.com

User name: jpublic

Password: ●●●●●●●●

After you log on, you can add this server to your Favorites and return to it easily.

⚠ FTP does not encrypt or encode passwords or data before sending them to the server. To protect the security of your passwords and data, use Web Folders (WebDAV) instead.

Learn more about using Web Folders.

☐ Log on anonymously   ☐ Save password

[Log On]   [Cancel]

Figure 2-7: The Log On As dialog box lets you save your password for the FTP site if you choose.

TIP

For instant access to your FTP site, right-click the site's icon in the My Network Places window, and then choose **Desktop (Create Shortcut)** from the shortcut menu to create a shortcut on the desktop. Alternatively, drag the icon to the Start menu to place an icon on the Start menu.

OPEN THE NETWORK PLACE

After creating the network place, as described in the previous section, you can access it quickly.

1. Click the **Start** button and then click **My Network Places**. A My Network Places window opens.

2. In the section named The Internet, double-click the icon for your site.

3. If the Log On As dialog box prompts you for your password, type it and then click **Log On**.

4. Internet Explorer displays the contents of the FTP site in a window.

TRANSFER FILES TO THE NETWORK PLACE

Once you've connected to the FTP site, you'll see an Internet Explorer window (see Figure 2-8) that works like a Windows Explorer window. You can select an object (a folder or a file) by clicking it, open an object by double-clicking it, drag an object to or from the Windows Explorer window to copy it, and so on.

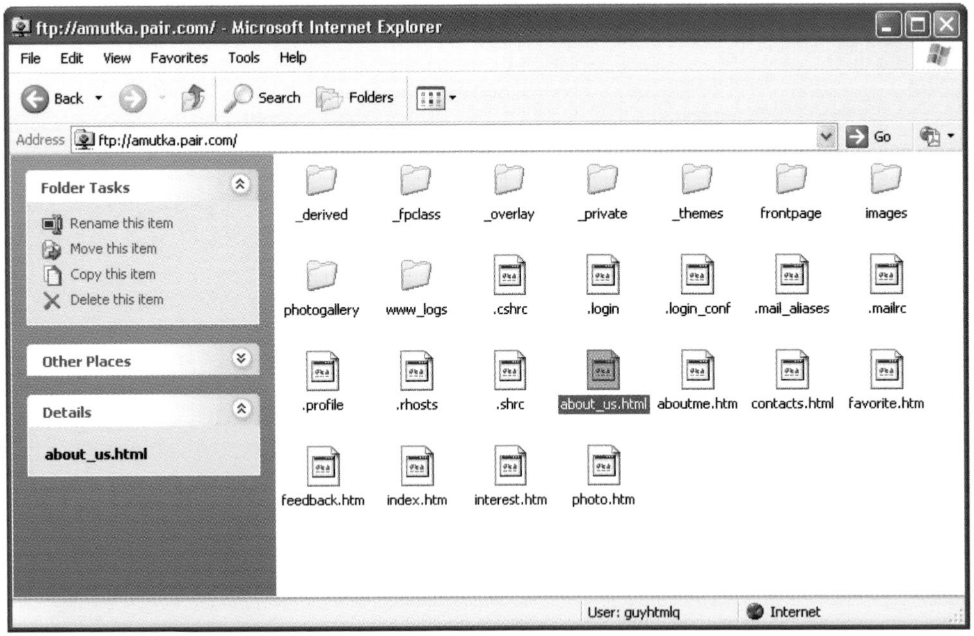

Figure 2-8: Internet Explorer opens the FTP site in a Windows Explorer–like view that enables you to copy files and folders easily to and from the FTP site.

Figure 2-9: CuteFTP is a third-party FTP client that simplifies the process of transferring files to and from your FTP site.

You can copy objects in several ways:

- The easiest way to copy objects is usually to open a Windows Explorer window to your site's folder on your local computer, arrange the Internet Explorer window and the Windows Explorer window so that you can see both, and then drag objects from one window to the other.

- You can also click the **Copy This File** link (for a local file), the **Copy This Item** link (for a file on the FTP server), or the **Copy This Folder** link to copy the selected object. In the Copy Items dialog box, select the destination folder and then click the **Copy** button. The My Network Places list appears at the bottom of the list box.

To end your session with the FTP site, click the **File** menu and then click **Close**.

Transfer a Site Using an FTP Client

If you find Internet Explorer too clumsy for regular FTP use, buy and install a third-party FTP client, such as CuteFTP (www.globalscape.com) or WS_FTP (www.ipswitch.com). You can download and try a time-limited evaluation version of both these FTP clients from the URLs given.

With most FTP clients, you create a new site, and then connect to it:

- With CuteFTP, click the **File** menu, click **Connect**, and then click **Connection Wizard**. The CuteFTP Connection Wizard starts. Follow the steps of the wizard to specify the details of the FTP site to which you want to connect. The wizard then opens the site (see Figure 2-9).

● With WS_FTP, click the **File** menu, click **Connect**, and then click **Connection Wizard**. The Connection Wizard starts. Follow the steps of the wizard to specify the details of the FTP site to which you want to connect. The wizard then opens the site by default unless you prevent it from doing so. Figure 2-10 shows an example.

Once you've connected to the site, transfer files by dragging them from the pane showing your local folders to the pane showing the folders on the FTP site, or vice versa.

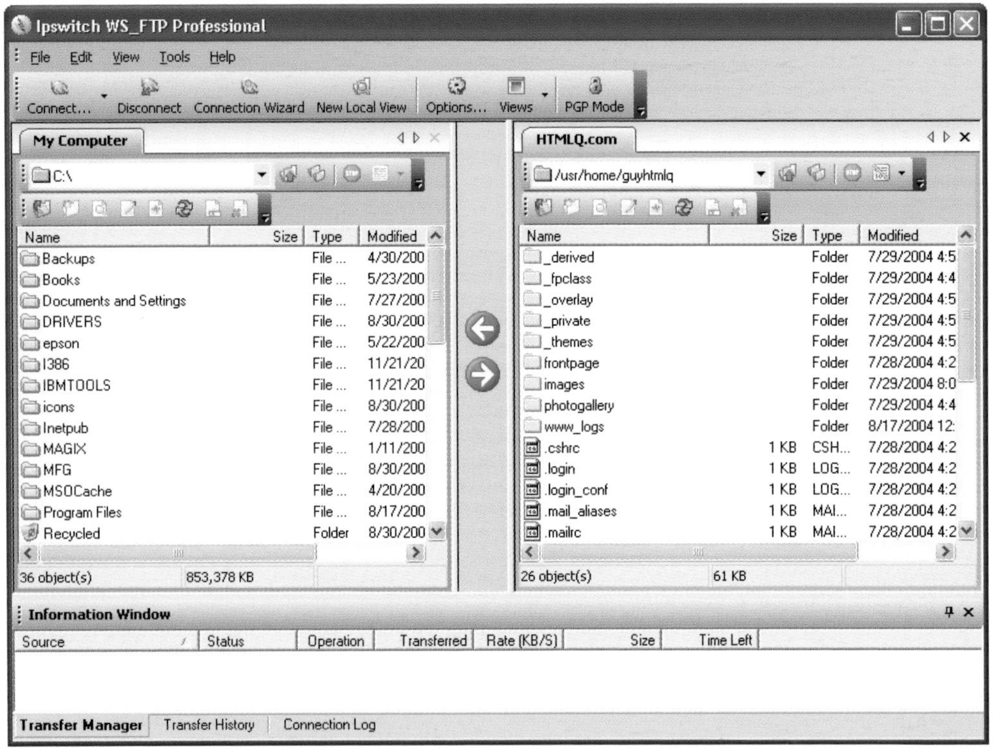

Figure 2-10: WS_FTP is a widely used third-party FTP client.

How to...

- *Using Proportional and Monospaced Fonts*
- *Understand Considerations for Web Formatting*
- *Use Paragraphs, Divisions, Breaks, and Hyphens*
- *Inserting Special Characters*
- *Create Headings*
- *Create Bulleted, Numbered, and Definition Lists*
- *Apply an Indent*
- *Align Elements*
- *Use Preformatted Text*
- *Apply Inline Styles*
- *Understanding Other Inline Styles*
- *Control Font Formatting*
- *Working with Fonts*
- *Change Style Using the Style Attribute*
- *Catch the Eye with Moving Text*

Chapter 3

Applying Manual Formatting to Web Pages

HTML offers two ways of formatting the web pages you create: by applying manual formatting to individual elements in a web page, or by using Cascading Style Sheets (CSS) to define styles for the elements that make up your web pages. This chapter shows you how to apply formatting manually, while Chapter 8 shows you how to create and apply CSS.

Which type of formatting you use for your web pages will depend on what you're trying to achieve with them. Manual formatting is a good way to get started, and you will probably want to use it for individual pages that you create for special purposes (for example, for eBay or Blogger.com). CSS enable you to standardize your formatting and implement changes centrally across an entire site without editing each page separately, so it's a powerful tool for creating consistent sites.

USING PROPORTIONAL AND MONOSPACED FONTS

Each browser has a default proportional font and a default monospaced font:

- A *proportional* font is one in which the letters are different widths, like the body fonts used in this book. For example, an uppercase M is wider than a lowercase i or l.

- A *monospaced, constant-width,* or *fixed-width* font is one in which all the letters are all the same width (in the same font size). Courier, the font used on most typewriters, is the most widely used monospaced font.

Proportional fonts are easier on the eye than monospaced fonts, and normal practice is to use proportional fonts for most of the text that appears on web pages, keeping monospaced fonts for when you need to differentiate some text or display it in a very clear format. The `<pre>` tag and some other tags automatically use the monospaced font. While you *can* use monospaced fonts more widely, there's usually little to be gained from doing so.

When checking your web pages, try changing the default proportional and monospaced fonts used by your browsers. In most Windows browsers, you'll find the settings in the Options dialog box (click the **Tools** menu and then click **Internet Options** or **Options**). For example, to change the fonts on Internet Explorer:

1. If Internet Explorer isn't running, click the **Start** button and then click **Internet**.

2. Click the **Tools** menu and then click **Internet Options**. The Internet Options dialog box appears.

Continued...

Understand Considerations for Web Formatting

When you create a document with a word processor, such as Microsoft Word or Corel WordPerfect, you can specify the exact formatting you want for each character, paragraph, and page. For example, you can make a character bold, underlined, 18-point Times New Roman font; apply one-inch indents and 1.5-line spacing for a paragraph; and set one-inch margins for the top, bottom, and sides of a page. When you print out the page, you'll get the formatting you applied.

Similarly, you can apply formatting to elements in the web pages you create: font formatting, line breaks, alignment, indentation, and more. But you can't be sure that this formatting will appear as you intended it to when your pages are displayed in a browser, for several reasons:

- Different browsers interpret even standard HTML tags differently.

- If the fonts you use in the page are installed on the browser's computer, they will be displayed; if not, the browser will substitute its default proportional font for any proportional font you use and its default monospaced (fixed-width) font for any monospaced font you use.

- The viewer can change the way his or her browser displays particular items. For example, the viewer can increase or decrease the text size to make a page readable, or change the text color or the background color.

- Unless you use CSS (discussed in Chapter 8), you can't apply precise indents to paragraphs.

Use Paragraphs, Divisions, Breaks, and Hyphens

As discussed in Chapter 1, each web page you create must include an HTML statement, a header section, and a body section. Each page should have a title that appears in the browser's title bar (or on a tab, if it is a tabbed browser) when the page is displayed.

USING PROPORTIONAL AND MONOSPACED FONTS *(Continued)*

3. On the General tab, click the **Fonts** button. The Fonts dialog box appears.

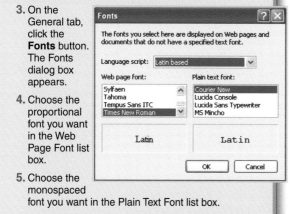

4. Choose the proportional font you want in the Web Page Font list box.

5. Choose the monospaced font you want in the Plain Text Font list box.

6. Click **OK** to close the Fonts dialog box, click **OK** again to close the Internet Options dialog box, and, if desired, close Internet Explorer.

TIP

If you use a text editor to create all your web pages, save the basic structure of one of your pages in a file as a template so that you can reuse it quickly to save yourself typing the common elements.

TIP

You can indent text in your web pages to make their structure easier to read. Browsers automatically remove extra spaces, so such indentation will not appear in the pages when they are displayed in a browser.

The basic structure of a web page typically looks like this:

```
<html>
<head>
<title></title>
</head>
<body>
</body>
</html>
```

Within the body of the web page, you use *block elements*, such as headings, paragraphs, and images, to form the major parts of the page.

CREATE PARAGRAPHS

Use the `<p>` and `</p>` tags to create a body text paragraph in the default proportional font. A body text paragraph includes extra space afterward to separate it from the next paragraph. It's best to use both the opening tag (`<p>`) and the closing tag (`</p>`), although many browsers will display pages correctly that use only the opening tag to indicate a paragraph.

You can apply formatting directly to paragraphs or to text within paragraphs.

GROUP PARAGRAPHS INTO DIVISIONS

If you need to apply formatting to two or more paragraphs, you can create a *division*, or group of paragraphs, and apply the formatting to the division. By doing so, you can cut down on the number of formatting codes. You can also achieve different effects, such as applying a border around the division as a whole instead of applying a separate border around each of the paragraphs.

To create a division:

1. Type the opening `<div>` tag before the first paragraph you want to include in the division.

2. Include in the opening `<div>` tag any formatting instructions for the division as a whole—for example:

```
<div align="center">
```

Rosemary

Rosmarinis

Perfect for lamb and for rosemary bread!

3. Type the closing `</div>` tag after the last paragraph you want to include in the division.

For example, a division that includes a heading, an image, and two paragraphs looks like:

```
<div align="center">
<h3>Rosemary</h3>
<p><i>Rosmarinis</i></p>
<img src="rosemary.jpg" height="150" width="110">
<p>Perfect for lamb and for rosemary bread!</p>
</div>
```

CONTROL BREAKS

Web browsers automatically rebreak the lines within paragraphs as necessary to display all the text within the current window size, so viewers will see your web page differently depending on their screen resolution, browser window size, and the default text size they've chosen.

To force browsers to break a line at a particular point or to insert extra space between paragraphs, insert a `<br>` tag.

KEEP TEXT TOGETHER WITH NONBREAKING SPACES

To prevent two words from being broken at the end of a line, use the ` ` code to create a nonbreaking space. For example, you might want to prevent your name or your company's name from being broken:

```
<p>To contact us at Greener Seeds, write to:</p>
```

CONTROL HYPHENATION WITH OPTIONAL HYPHENS

If a compound word always uses a hyphen, type a hyphen in it, just as you would in any document. You can also instruct the browser to break a long word when it is at the end of a line but not break it at other times. To do so, you place one or more *soft hyphens*, or *optional hyphens*, by typing the `&shy;` code at the appropriate places in the word—for example:

```
<p>These products are for both horti&shy;cultural and non&shy;h
orti&shy;cultural use.</p>
```

TIP

You can prevent a line of text from being broken by putting it within no-break tags, `<nobr>` and `</nobr>`. Usually, this isn't a good idea, because if the browser can't break a line that's too long, the line will continue to the right of the visible area, and the user will have to scroll the window to see the rest of the line.

CAUTION

Avoid using nonbreaking spaces on more than three consecutive words because doing so can create awkward breaks in lines.

TIP

You can also use nonbreaking spaces at the beginning of a paragraph to force indentation. Such usage is discouraged, but is nonetheless effective.

INSERTING SPECIAL CHARACTERS

If you can type a character on the keyboard, you can enter it in a web page with minimal effort. To use a character that you can't type directly on a keyboard, such as a registered trademark symbol, ®, or smart quotes (" "), you must enter the code that HTML uses to represent that character. HTML refers to these codes as "character entities." You can enter these characters by using either their name or their code. Table 3-1 shows the names and codes for the character entities you're most likely to need in your web pages.

TIP

When structuring your documents, use as few heading levels as is practical. Start by breaking each document into major sections: these become your Heading 1s. Within each Heading 1 section, create Heading 2s as necessary; if those sections need subsections, use Heading 3s. You'll seldom need to use the lower heading levels. For example, most of the chapters in this book use three levels of headings—and your web pages should normally be much shorter than even the shortest chapter in this book. If not, consider breaking up your material into separate pages.

Create Headings

HTML offers six levels of headings, using paired tags, from Heading 1 (opening tag `<h1>`, closing tag `</h1>`) to Heading 6 (opening tag `<h6>`, closing tag `</h6>`). Each browser displays the headings in boldface, using its default proportional font and descending font sizes from Heading 1 (the biggest) to Heading 6 (the smallest). The actual font size used depends on the browser and on the user's display settings: if the user increases the text size to make a page more readable, the font size of the headings increases as well.

TABLE 3-1: SPECIAL CHARACTER CODES

CHARACTER	NAME	CODE
®	&reg;	&#174;
©	&copy;	&#169;
TM	&trade;	&#153;
"		&#147;
"		&#148;
<	&lt;	&#60;
>	&gt;	&#62;
¡	&iexcl;	&#161;
¿	&iquest;	&#191;
¢	&cent;	&#162;
±	&plusmn;	&#177;
¼	&frac14;	&#188;
½	&frac12;	&#189;
¾	&frac34;	&#190;
×	&times;	&#215;
√	&divide;	&#247;
ñ	&ntilde;	&#241;
←	&larr;	&#8592;
↑	&uarr;	&#8593;
→	&rarr;	&#8594;
↓	&darr;	&#8594

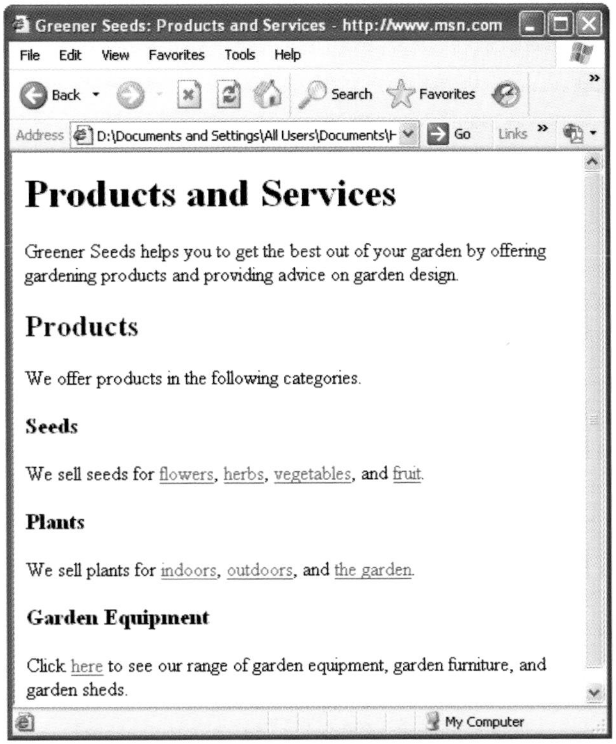

Figure 3-1: Use two or three levels of headings to break your documents into major sections.

For example, to create a short section of headings and text on an existing web page:

1. Position the insertion point within the body of the web page.

2. Type the opening tag for a Heading 1, the text for the heading, and then the closing tag—for example:

   `<h1>Products and Services</h1>`

3. Type a text paragraph between `<p>` and `</p>` tags—for example:

   `<p>Greener Seeds helps you to get the best out of your garden by offering gardening products and providing advice on garden design.</p>`

4. Type the opening `<h2>` tag for a Heading 2, the text for the heading, and then the closing `</h2>` tag—for example:

   `<h2>Products</h2>`

5. Type a text paragraph after the Heading 2—for example:

   `<p>We offer products in the following categories.</p>`

6. Type the opening `<h3>` tag for a Heading 3, the text for the heading, and then the closing `</h3>` tag—for example:

   `<h3>Seeds</h3>`

7. Enter further headings and paragraphs (or other items, such as links) as necessary.

8. Save the file, switch to your browser, and update the display. Figure 3-1 shows an example of three levels of headings.

Create Bulleted, Numbered, and Definition Lists

HTML lets you create three different types of lists:

- **Unordered list** A bulleted list (like this one). The browser automatically displays the bullets and indents the list items.

- **Ordered list** A numbered list, like those used for the steps in this book. The browser automatically displays the numbers in the correct sequence.

- **Definition list** A list that alternates paragraphs aligned with the left margin and indented paragraphs. The first of each pair of paragraphs is the term being defined, and the second is the definition of the term. (You'll see an example of this a little later in this chapter.)

CREATE A BULLETED LIST

A bulleted list is a block element that starts with a `<ul>` (unordered list) tag and ends with a `</ul>` tag. Within the list, each item starts with an `<li>` (list item) tag and ends with a `</li>` tag.

To create a bulleted list:

1. Type the opening and closing tags for the unordered list:

```
<ul>
</ul>
```

2. Within the tags, type the list items, one to a line, marking each with `<li>` and `</li>` tags—for example:

```
<ul>
<li>French beans</li>
<li>Climbing beans</li>
<li>Black beans</li>
</ul>
```

We sell three main categories of beans:

- French beans
- Climbing beans
- Black beans

3. Save the file, switch to your browser, and update the display. Your list will be displayed with default black bullets, as in the example shown.

4. Try changing the bullets to squares by adding the `type` attribute to the `<ul>` tag and specifying the square parameter:

```
<ul type="square">
```

We sell three main categories of beans:

- French beans
- Climbing beans
- Black beans

5. Save the file, switch to your browser, and update the display. The bullets will have turned to squares. Depending on your browser, the squares may be filled in (as in the example shown) or empty.

6. Change the bullets to empty circles by changing the `type` attribute to `circle`:

```
<ul type="circle">
```

7. Save the file, switch to your browser, and update the display. The bullets will have turned to circles.

We sell three main categories of beans:

- French beans
- Climbing beans
- Black beans

8. Change the bullets back to regular bullets by either changing the `type` attribute to `disc` or by removing the attribute altogether. `disc` is the default bullet type, so you don't need to specify it if you want a default bulleted list.

9. Save the file.

CREATE A NUMBERED LIST

A numbered list is a block element that begins with an `<ol>` (ordered list) tag and ends with a `</ol>` tag. Within the list, each item starts with an `<li>` (list item) tag and ends with a `</li>` tag.

To create a numbered list:

1. Type the opening and closing tags for the ordered list:

```
<ol>
</ol>
```

2. Within the tags, type the list items, one to a line—for example:

```
<ol>
<li>Burdock</li>
<li>Mugwort</li>
<li>Caraway</li>
<li>Myrrh</li>
<li>Goldenseal</li>
</ol>
```

Herbs of the Week

These are our Top 5 herbs for this week:

1. Burdock
2. Mugwort
3. Caraway
4. Myrrh
5. Goldenseal

3. Save the file, switch to your browser, and update the display. Your list will be numbered from 1 to 5, as in the example shown.

CHANGE THE NUMBERING TYPE

The default type of numbered list uses standard numbers, as in the previous example. You can specify different types of numbering by adding the type attribute to the `<ol>` tag, as described in Table 3-2.

1. Change the numbering on the numbered list to uppercase roman numerals by changing the `type` attribute to `I`:

```
<ol type="I">
```

2. Save the file, switch to your browser, and update the display (see the example).

3. Change the numbering back to standard numbering by either changing the `type` attribute to `1` (`<ol type="1">`) or removing the `type` attribute altogether. Standard numbering is the default for numbered lists, so you don't need to specify the `type` attribute if you want a list with standard numbering.

4. Save your file again.

TABLE 3-2: TYPES OF NUMBERED LISTS

	EFFECT	EXAMPLE
1	Standard numbering	1, 2, 3
I	Uppercase roman numerals	I, II, III
i	Lowercase roman numerals	i, ii, iii
A	Uppercase letters	A, B, C
a	Lowercase letters	a, b, c

Herbs of the Week

These are our Top 5 herbs for this week:

I. Burdock
II. Mugwort
III. Caraway
IV. Myrrh
V. Goldenseal

CHANGE THE STARTING NUMBER

By default, HTML starts each numbered list with 1 or the equivalent in the numbering scheme used: I, i, A, or a. Sometimes, you may need to use a different starting number for a list. For example, if you break a numbered list with a graphic or a paragraph, you will need to start the second part of the list with the appropriate number rather than with 1.

To change the starting number, add the `start` attribute to the `<ol>` tag, and specify the appropriate number—for example:

```
<ol type="1" start="5">
```

CREATE A DEFINITION LIST

A definition list is a block element that begins with a `<dl>` (definition list) tag and ends with a `</dl>` tag. Each of the terms defined begins with a `<dt>` tag and ends with a `</dt>` tag. Each of the definitions for those terms begins with a `<dd>` tag and ends with a `</dd>` tag.

To create a definition list:

1. Type the opening and closing tags for the definition list:

```
<dl>
</dl>
```

2. Within the tags, type each of the definition terms within `<dt>` and `</dt>` tags, and type the definitions for those terms within `<dd>` and `</dd>` tags:

```
<dl>
<dt>Burdock</dt>
<dd>Burdock helps soothe eczema and other skin diseases and
is reputed to purify the blood. Burdock grows wild in many
locations around the world.</dd>
<dt>Mugwort</dt>
<dd>Mugwort is a perennial herb with a bitter taste. It can
help the digestion of rich foods, such as heavy meat and fish
dishes.</dd>
</dl>
```

3. Save the file, switch to your browser, and update the display. The example list is shown to the left.

Burdock
  Burdock helps soothe eczema and other skin diseases and is reputed to purify the blood. Burdock grows wild in many locations around the world.
Mugwort
  Mugwort is a perennial herb with a bitter taste. It can help the digestion of rich foods, such as heavy meat and fish dishes.

CREATE A NESTED LIST

You can *nest*, or position, any list within another list—for example, a bulleted list within a numbered list, a numbered list within a bulleted list, a definition list within a bulleted list, or a list within the same type of list as itself.

To nest a list, place the tags for the nested list within the tags for the list that will contain it. The browser then displays the nested list with more indent than the list that contains it. You can nest another list within the nested list if necessary; the second nested list receives even more indent than the first nested list.

To create a nested list:

1. Position the insertion point at the appropriate point within the existing list.

2. Type the opening and closing tags for the sublist—for example, as shown in bold font here:

```
<ol type="I">
<li>Burdock</li>
<li>Mugwort</li>
<li>Caraway</li>
<li>Myrrh</li>
<li>Goldenseal</li>
<ul>
</ul>
</ol>
```

3. Within the bulleted list tags (`<ul>` and `</ul>`), type the items for the sublist:

```
<li>Goldenseal, dried roots</li>
<li>Goldenseal, powder</li>
<li>Goldenseal, fresh</li>
```

4. Save the file, switch to your browser, and update the display. The example list looks like this:

Herbs of the Week

These are our Top 5 herbs for this week:

1. Burdock
2. Mugwort
3. Caraway
4. Myrrh
5. Goldenseal
   - Goldenseal, dried roots
   - Goldenseal, powder
   - Goldenseal, fresh

TIP

Nest lists when you need to, but try to avoid listing more than one level of lists. Excessive nesting is not only confusing to the eye, but can also push too much of the text to the right edge of a small window, making for short lines of text in the display.

Apply an Indent

Indentation is a standard feature of word-processing applications, but HTML doesn't offer a direct means of creating an indent. CSS (discussed in Chapter 8) make it easy to indent paragraphs; without them, you need a workaround.

INDENT ONLY THE LEFT MARGIN

To indent only the left margin, create an unordered list but don't specify any list items. This indents all lines in the paragraph around half an inch. For example:

```
<h3>Caraway Seeds</h3><ul>Latin name: <i>Carum carvi</i></ul>
<p>Caraway seeds have a pungent taste that works well with
cabbage dishes, rye and other breads, and stews and soups.
Caraway not only improves the flavor of cabbage dishes, but also
works as an anticarminative, making digestion easier.</p>
```

To increase the amount of indent, create a nested list without any list items in the first list:

```
<ul><ul>Latin name: <i>Carum carvi</i></ul></ul>
```

INDENT BOTH THE LEFT AND RIGHT MARGINS

To indent both margins, use the block quote tags, `<blockquote>` and `</blockquote>`. A block quote is indented at both the left and right margins. The tag works both for longer quotations and for other types of text that need indentation. The following is an example of a block quote:

```
<h3>Burdock</h3>
<p>Here's what John Gerard, the famous herbalist of Shakespeare's
era, had to say about burdock in his <i>Herball or General
Historie of Plantes</i> (1633):</p>
<blockquote>The stalke of Clot-burre before the burres come
forth, the rinde pilled off, being eaten raw with salt and
pepper, or boyled in the broth of fat meate, is pleasant to be
eaten.... Also it is a good nourishement, especially boyled:
if the kernell of the Pine Apple be likewise added it is the
better.</blockquote>
```

Caraway Seeds

Latin name: *Carum carvi*

Caraway seeds have a pungent taste that works well with cabbage dishes, rye and other breads, and stews and soups. Caraway not only improves the flavor of cabbage dishes, but also works as an anticarminative, making digestion easier.

Burdock

Here's what John Gerard, the famous herbalist of Shakespeare's era, had to say about burdock in his *Herball or General Historie of Plantes* (1633):

The stalke of Clot-burre before the burres come forth, the rinde pilled off, being eaten raw with salt and pepper, or boyled in the broth of fat meate, is pleasant to be eaten.... Also it is a good nourishement, especially boyled: if the kernell of the Pine Apple be likewise added it is the better.

Burdock and Nettle Brew

This traditional Welsh brew, sometimes referred to as an "ale" or even a "wine," claims to have healing properties. It also tastes great, especially considering the ingredients used.

To make the brew, pick two quarts of fresh nettle leaves, using rubber gloves to avoid being stung. Simmer the nettle leaves with 3 oz hops and 3 oz chopped burdock in five quarts of water for 45 minutes. Strain the mixture, and then stir into the strained liquid 2 lb sugar and the juice of a lemon. Allow to cool, sprinkle the yeast on top, cover, and leave overnight before bottling in airtight containers. Allow to mature for two days before using.

Figure 3-2: You can align elements (such as paragraphs) left, right, or center.

NOTE

Preformatted text is ideal for displaying programming code, where precise layout is vital, but you can use it for any element that needs the text to be displayed in exactly the way you enter it. The disadvantage of preformatted text is that it always appears in the browser's default monospaced font, which doesn't suit all purposes.

CAUTION

Browsers don't rebreak lines tagged as preformatted text, so long lines will go beyond the right edge of small windows using average-size text. For best results, keep your preformatted-text lines relatively short.

Align Elements

As in a word-processing document, you can apply left, center, and right alignment to an element such as a paragraph, heading, or image. To do so, you use the `align` attribute in the element's tag and specify the appropriate value: `left`, `center`, or `right`. Left is the default alignment, so you don't need to specify it.

For example, the following code centers the heading, aligns the first paragraph right, and aligns the second paragraph left (see Figure 3-2):

```
<h3 align="center">Burdock and Nettle Brew</h3>
<p align="right">This traditional Welsh brew, sometimes referred
to as an "ale" or even a "wine," claims to have healing
properties. It also tastes great, especially considering the
ingredients used.</p>
<p align="left">To make the brew, pick two quarts of fresh nettle
leaves, using rubber gloves to avoid being stung. Simmer the
nettle leaves with 3 oz hops and 3 oz chopped burdock in five
quarts of water for 45 minutes. Strain the mixture, and then
stir into the strained liquid 2 lb sugar and the juice of a
lemon. Allow to cool, sprinkle the yeast on top, cover, and leave
overnight before bottling in airtight containers. Allow to mature
for two days before using.</p>
```

Use Preformatted Text

If you need to lay out text precisely using spaces and carriage returns, use preformatted text. To create preformatted text, which is monospaced or (fixed-width) text, enter the text between the opening `<pre>` tag and the closing `</pre>` tag.

```
Prices

Stock #    Description            Quantity (g)   Price (US$)
------------------------------------------------------------
A3892      Wormwood, dried                  25          4.99
A3893      St. John's Wort                   5          3.99
A3894      Stevia                           50          8.99
------------------------------------------------------------
```

NOTE

The bold-text tags are considered "physical" style tags, meaning that they change the font itself, and the strong-text tags are considered "logical" style tags, meaning that they change the meaning of the text. Most people find physical style tags easier when formatting text manually, because you know exactly what effect they will produce. Depending on the browser's configuration, logical-style tags can produce a different effect.

CAUTION

Whereas most applications use a separate font for italic text (for example, Times New Roman Italic instead of Times New Roman), browsers simulate italic by slanting the default font. The result is that the italic often doesn't look like real italics and is best used only for emphasis on small amounts of text. Don't apply italic-text or emphasis-text formatting to whole sentences or paragraphs at a time.

The following is an example of preformatted text:

```
<h3>Prices</h3>
<pre>
Stock # Description Quantity (g) Price (US$)
------------------------------------------------------
A3892 Wormwood, dried 25 4.99
A3893 St. John's Wort 5 3.99
A3894 Stevia 50 8.99
------------------------------------------------------
</pre>
```

Apply Inline Styles

After setting the basic formatting for the blocks of text in a page, you can apply specific formatting to individual words, phrases, or elements using inline styles. Inline styles are the HTML equivalent of direct formatting or character styles in a word processor.

APPLY BOLDFACE

To apply boldface, enclose the text in either the bold-text tags (`<b>` and `</b>`) or the strong-text tags (`<strong>` and `</strong>`). Both pairs of tags typically have the same effect:

```
<p>This is an example of <b>boldface</b> using &lt;b&gt; and
&lt;/b&gt; tags.</p>
<p>This is an example of <strong>boldface</strong> using
&lt;strong&gt; and &lt;/strong&gt; tags.</p>
```

> This is an example of **boldface** using <b> and </b> tags.
>
> This is an example of **boldface** using <strong> and </strong> tags.

APPLY ITALICS

To apply italics, enclose the text in either the physical italic-text tags (<i> and </i>) or the logical emphasis-text tags (<em> and </em>):

```
<p><i>Today Only</i>: 15% discount on cash sales!</p>
<p><em>Special offers</em> on <b>pots</b> and <b>planters</b>.</p>
```

APPLY UNDERLINE

Figure 3-3: You can apply underline manually, but because most browsers use colored underline to indicate hyperlinks on text, underline can be confusing. In most cases, italics are a better means of adding emphasis to text than underline.

This traditional <u>Welsh</u> brew, sometimes referred to as an <u>ale</u> or even a <u>wine</u>, claims to have healing properties. It also tastes great, especially considering the <u>ingredients</u> used.

To apply a single underline, enclose the text in `<u>` and `</u>` tags, as in the example shown (see Figure 3-3):

```
<p>This traditional <a href="wales_general.html">Welsh
</a> brew, sometimes referred to as an <u>ale</u> or
even a <u>wine</u>, claims to have healing properties.
It also tastes great, especially considering the <a
href="burdock_nettle.html">ingredients</a> used.</p>
```

APPLY STRIKETHROUGH

To apply strikethrough, enclose the text in either `<strike>` and `</strike>` tags or `<s>` and `</s>` tags:

```
<p>40-gallon planter <s>$19.99</s> NOW ONLY $14.99</p>
```

APPLY MONOSPACED FONT

TIP

You can apply multiple inline styles to the same text by nesting one pair of tags inside another. For example, `<b><i>Special Offers</i></b>` produces bold italic text.

As well as displaying whole paragraphs in monospaced font using the `<pre>` and `</pre>` tags, you can format characters as monospaced font by using the teletype inline style. To apply this style, enclose the text in the `<tt>` and `</tt>` tags, as in the example shown, which also uses the `<big>` and `</big>` tags to increase the size of the monospaced font displayed:

```
<h3>Contact Us</h3>
<p>You can contact us via e-mail at
<big><tt>questions@quicksteps.com</tt></big>.</p>
```

Contact Us

You can contact us via e-mail at `questions@quicksteps.com`.

APPLY SUBSCRIPT AND SUPERSCRIPT

To apply subscript, enclose the text in `<sub>` and `</sub>` tags. To apply superscript, enclose the text in `<sup>` and `</sup>` tags. For example, to use both subscript and superscript text:

```
<ul>
<li>Remember to add plenty of H<sub>2</sub>0 to your plants in
the summer!</li>
<li>To calculate the volume of your compost heap in cubic meters
(m<sup>3</sup>), multiply its dimensions in meters.</li>
</ul>
```

- Remember to add plenty of $H_2 0$ to your plants in the summer!
- To calculate the volume of your compost heap in cubic meters (m^3), multiply its dimensions in meters.

Control Font Formatting

The `<font>` tag lets you control the typeface, type size, and type color displayed in the browser.

CONTROL THE TYPEFACE

To specify the typeface the browser should use for some text, enter the opening `<font>` tag with the face attribute and the name of the font or fonts you want to use, then the text on which to use the font, and then the closing `</font>` tag. The font name can be either a specific font name (for example, Times New Roman) or one of the five generic font families (serif, sans-serif, monospace, fantasy, and cursive) that all browsers recognize. For example, you can specify the Times New Roman typeface as follows:

```
<font face="Times New Roman">Shipping and Handling</font>
```

Unless you know that visitors to your web site will have specific fonts installed (as you might know if you are designing an internal web site for a company), you can provide a list of alternative fonts or families to ensure that the browser doesn't substitute its default proportional font or monospaced font if it doesn't have the exact font you specify; for example:

```
<font face="Times New Roman, Times, serif">Shipping and Handling</font>
```

CONTROL THE TYPE SIZE

To control the type size via HTML, you do not use the point size (as in most word-processing applications), but rather the type size relative to the default size set in the browser.

Browsers use the values 1 through 7 to measure type sizes, with 1 being the smallest and 7 the largest. Each size is about 20 percent bigger than the size preceding it: size 2 is 20 percent bigger than size 1, size 3 is 20 percent bigger than size 2, and so on. Each browser assigns the value 3 to its default type size, no matter how big or small that size is. You can then control the type size by using

WORKING WITH FONTS

While you *can* control font formatting using the <font> tag, you should usually avoid doing so. Any font you specify in a web page will be displayed correctly only if it is installed on the computer that's viewing the page. If the font isn't installed, the computer substitutes its default proportional font (for a proportional font) or its default monospaced font (for a monospaced font). This substitution can wreck the effects you carefully create.

Cascading Style Sheets (CSS) are now the preferred method for applying formatting such as font formatting; because CSS let you instantly apply a font change to a whole document, they can save you a great deal of time and effort.

To avoid font substitutions changing the look of your pages, stick with widely used fonts as much as possible, and design your pages so that fonts can be substituted without the pages suffering. The most widely used serif fonts are Times New Roman, Times, and Georgia. The most widely used sans-serif fonts are Arial, Helvetica, Trebuchet, and Verdana. The most widely used monospaced font is Courier.

If you simply *must* ensure that a particular font is used, create a graphic containing the text, and insert the graphic at the appropriate place in the web page. Remember that anyone who has turned off the display of pictures or who is using a text-only browser will not see such graphics. See Chapter 4 for more information.

the size attribute with either an absolute value (1 through 7) or a relative value, the amount to be added to or subtracted from the current type size. For example:

- `size="4"` is an absolute value that makes the type size 4, about 20 percent bigger than the default size.
- `size="+2"` is a relative value that makes the type size 5, about 40 percent (two 20-percent increments) bigger than the default size.
- `size="-1"` is a relative value that makes the type size 2, about 20 percent smaller than the default size.

CONTROL THE TYPE COLOR

To change the font color, use the `<font>` tag with the `color` attribute. You can display many different colors by using either their names (for example, `color="blue"` or `color="red"`) or the hexadecimal (base 12) code for the color (for example, `color="#99FF00"` for a lime-green shade). Most web-authoring tools and HTML editors make it easy to find the exact color you want. If you're working in a text editor, consult a color-codes reference, such as that found at webmonkey.wired.com/webmonkey/reference/color_codes/, to learn the hexadecimal codes you need.

The following example changes the formatting of the text to sans-serif (preferring Arial or Trebuchet), blue, and two sizes larger than the default:

```
<p><font face="Arial, Trebuchet, sans-serif" size="+2"
color="blue">Trees</font></p>
```

The next example changes the formatting of the text to sans-serif (preferring Comic Sans MS or Trebuchet) and one size smaller than the default:

```
<p><font face="Comic Sans MS, Trebuchet, sans-serif" color="red"
size="-1">Evergreens</font> remain verdant all year through.</p>
```

Trees

Evergreens **remain verdant all year through.**

Change Style Using the Style Attribute

You can change the style of an element (such as a paragraph or a heading) by applying the `style` attribute to the element's tag. The `style` attribute takes the format `style="property1:value1; property2:value2"`, where *property1* and *property2* are properties of the `style` attribute, and *value1* and *value2* are the values assigned to those properties.

To change the style of an element, follow these general steps. See the rest of this section for specific examples using the `style` attribute.

1. Type the opening tag (except for its closing angle bracket), and enter the `style` attribute, an equal sign, and double quotation marks:

   ```
   <p style="
   ```

2. Type the name of the first property that you want to set for the element, a colon, and the value for that property:

   ```
   <p style="line-height:3
   ```

3. If you want to set a second property for the element, type a semicolon, the name of the property, a colon, and the value for that property:

   ```
   <p style="line-height:3;text-align:center
   ```

4. If you want to set a third property for the element, repeat step 3.

5. When you've set all the properties for the element, type the closing angle bracket, the text for the element, and then the closing tag:

   ```
   <p style="line-height:3;text-align:center/>Yard-long beans are
   tolerant of hot and wet conditions.</p>
   ```

6. Save the page, switch to your browser, and view the effect.

CHANGE LETTER AND WORD SPACING

To increase the spacing between letters in a paragraph, use the `letter-spacing` property with the number of pixels you want to put between each pair of letters. For example, to add 10 pixels between each pair of letters:

```
<h1 style="letter-spacing:10">Bitter Gourds</h1>
```

To increase the spacing between words in a paragraph, use the word-spacing property with the number of pixels you want to put between each pair of words. For example, to add 15 pixels between each pair of words:

```
<p style="word-spacing:15">Bitter gourds, such as Naja, are
widely used in Cambodian cooking.</p>
```

Figure 3-4 shows the effect of letter spacing and word spacing.

Bitter Gourds

Bitter gourds, such as Naja, are widely used in Cambodian cooking.

Figure 3-4: Letter spacing can be useful for drawing attention to headings. Word spacing is best reserved for special effects.

CREATE A FIRST-LINE INDENT

To apply a first-line indent to a paragraph, use the text-indent property and specify the indent as a number of pixels or as a percentage. For example, to apply a first-line indent of 10 percent to the paragraph:

```
<p style="text-indent:10%">This paragraph is indented 10 percent.</p>
```

CHANGE LINE SPACING

To change the line spacing of a paragraph, use the line-height property and specify the spacing as 1 (single spacing), 1.5 (one-and-a-half line spacing), 2 (double spacing), or a higher number. For example, to apply double spacing to the paragraph:

```
<p style="line-height:2">Zenith is an attractive sweet pepper that
varies in color from dark green to dark red when it is fully
mature. Suitable for cultivation in hot climates, Zenith matures
in 10 weeks from transplanting and offers high yields.</p>
```

CHANGE THE CAPITALIZATION OF TEXT

To change the capitalization of the text in an element, use the text-transform property and specify the case you want:

- uppercase capitalizes every letter in the text.
- lowercase lowercases every letter in the text.
- capitalize applies initial capitals to the text. HTML changes the first letter in every word to a capital but doesn't change the case of other letters in the words.

For example, to apply initial capitals to the text:

```
<h1 style="text-transform:capitalize">sweet peppers</h1>
```

TIP

The text-transform property is most useful when you need to control the appearance of text that is automatically entered in your web pages. If you're typing the text yourself, it's easier to type the letters with the correct capitalization.

APPLY UNDERLINING, OVERLINING, OR STRIKETHROUGH

As discussed earlier in this chapter, you can apply underlining to individual words using the `<u>` and `</u>` tags, and you can apply strikethrough using either the `<s>` and `</s>` or `<strike>` and `</strike>` tags. To affect an entire paragraph, you can use the `text-decoration` property of the `style` attribute with the `underline` value (for an underline) or the `line-through` value (for strikethrough). You can also use the `text-decoration` property to apply *overlining*—a line above the text—by using the `overline` value.

For example, to apply underline to the first paragraph, strikethrough to the second paragraph, and overline to the third paragraph:

```
<p style="text-decoration:underline">Flower
Seed Specials</p>
<p style="text-decoration:line-
through">Alyssum Snow Crystals</p>
<p style="text-decoration:overline">Aster
Assortment</p>
```

Flower Seed Specials

~~Alyssum Snow Crystals~~

Aster Assortment

MAKE TEXT BLINK ON BROWSERS OTHER THAN INTERNET EXPLORER

To make a text element blink on and off, use the `text-decoration` property of the `style` attribute with the `blink` value—for example:

```
<h2 style="text-decoration:blink">Don't Miss This Offer!</h2>
```

TABLE 3-3: FONT PROPERTIES FOR THE `style` ATTRIBUTE

PROPERTY	CONTROLS	VALUES
font-family	The font displayed	A specific font name—for example, Arial
font-size	The font size	Either an absolute size (xx-small, x-small, small, medium, large, x-large, or xx-large) or a relative size (smaller or larger)
font-style	The font style—normal, italic, or oblique	normal, italic, or oblique. oblique works only if the font includes oblique characters; otherwise, oblique produces slanted text that gives an italic effect
font-variant	Whether the font is normal or small caps	normal or small-caps
font-weight	How bold the font is	normal, lighter, bold, bolder, 100, 200, 300, 400, 500, 600, 700, 800, or 900
color	The color of the font	A specific color name or hex code

CHANGE FONT FORMATTING

To set font formatting on an element, you can use the `style` properties shown in Table 3-3.

For example, to apply bold, blue, extra-large Comic Sans MS font to the text:

```
<p style="font-family:Comic
Sans MS;font-size:x-large;font-
weight:bold;color:blue">Emerald
Kohlrabi</p>
```

White Heat, Red Face

¡Red Savina Habañero Now Available!

Figure 3-5: *To make text stand out, you can apply a background color that contrasts with the text color.*

TIP

If you need to make sure that a box doesn't have other material floating on its left or right, add the `clear` property set to `left` or `right`.

APPLY A BACKGROUND COLOR TO AN ELEMENT

To apply a background color to an element, use the `background-color` property of the `style` attribute, and specify the color either by name or by its hex code. For example, to apply a red background to a division so that the white heading and yellow paragraph text stand out (see Figure 3-5):

```
<div style="background-color:red">
<br>
<h1 style="color:white">White Heat, Red Face</h1>
<p style="color:yellow;font-family:serif;font-weight:bold;font-size:
x-large">&iexcl;Red Savina Haba&ntilde;ero Now Available!</p>
</br>
</div>
```

CREATE BOXES

To create a box that occupies a certain area of the page, use the `width` and `height` properties of the `style` attribute to specify the area. For example, to create a box that is 400 pixels wide and 200 pixels high:

```
<div style="width:400;height:200">
</div>
```

By default, a box appears flush with the left margin. To make a box float so that another element can appear alongside it, add the `float` property set to `left` (to make the box float left) or `right` (to make the box float right). For example, to create a box with a purple background and white text that floats to the left of the text that follows it:

```
<p style="width:140;height:80;float:left;background-color:
purple;color:white;font-weight:bold">If you've never tried bitter
gourds, try them today!</p>
<h1>Bitter Gourds</h1>
<p>Bitter gourds, such as Naja, are widely used in Cambodian
cooking.</p>
```

If you've never tried bitter gourds, try them today!

Bitter Gourds

Bitter gourds, such as Naja, are widely used in Cambodian cooking.

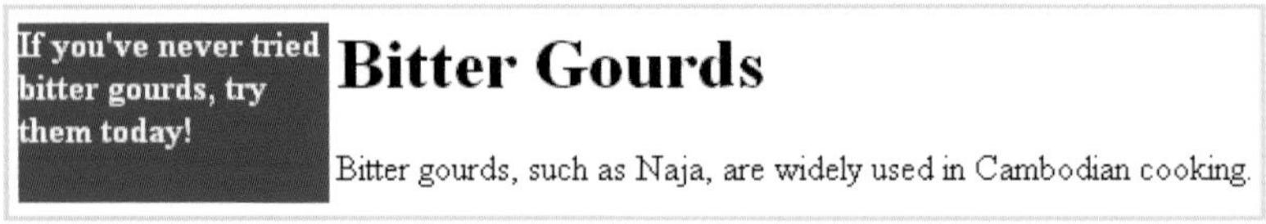

APPLY BORDERS

To apply borders to an element, you can use the `style` properties shown in Table 3-4.

For example, to use most of the border settings and many of the other properties of the `style` attribute discussed in this section to create the two boxes with borders:

```
<p style="border-style:solid;border-color:red;border-width:thick;w
idth:100;height:85;float:left;margin-left:10;margin-right:10;margin-
bottom:10;padding-top:10;padding-left:10;padding-right:10;background-
color:yellow;color:red"><b>Red Bird Chilli Sauce</b></p>
<p style="border-style:solid;border-color:blue;border-width:
thick;width:300;height:85;margin-top:10;padding-left:10;font-
weight"><br>You've heard of
fuel injection for cars?
<br>This is fuel injection
for <em>you</em>!</p>
```

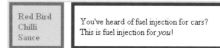

TIP

The margin for borders is the space between the previous element, or the edge of the page, and the start of the border. The padding is the space between the border and the element inside the border.

CAUTION

Borders may be displayed somewhat differently in some browsers (for example, Netscape), so it's a good idea to check your pages with any browser for which you want to be sure that your web pages work correctly.

TABLE 3-4: BORDER PROPERTIES FOR THE `style` ATTRIBUTE

PROPERTY	CONTROLS	VALUES
border-style	Whether the border is hidden or appears as a single line or a double line	none (for no border), solid, or double
border-color	The border color	A specific color name or hex code
border-width	The border width	undefined, a number of pixels, thin, or thick
border-top-width	The width of the top border	medium, a number of pixels, thin, or thick
border-bottom-width	The width of the bottom border	medium, a number of pixels, thin, or thick
border-left-width	The width of the left border	medium, a number of pixels, thin, or thick
border-right-width	The width of the right border	medium, a number of pixels, thin, or thick
margin-top	The width of the top margin	A number of pixels
margin-bottom	The width of the bottom margin	A number of pixels
margin-left	The width of the left margin	A number of pixels
margin-right	The width of the right margin	A number of pixels
padding-top	The amount of padding from the top edge	A number of pixels
padding-bottom	The amount of padding from the bottom edge	A number of pixels
padding-left	The amount of padding from the left edge	A number of pixels
padding-right	The amount of padding from the right edge	A number of pixels

HIDE AN ELEMENT

To hide an element, set the `visibility` property of the `style` attribute to `hidden`; to display the element, set the `visibility` property to `visible` (or remove the `visibility` property).

Catch the Eye with Moving Text

You can add moving text to a web page using the `<marquee>` tag. Moving text can help draw the viewer's eye to important information, such as an advertisement or the latest headline. Moving text is best used in moderation, however, as it can be distracting.

The `<marquee>` tag uses the following attributes:

- `behavior` can be `scroll`, `alternate`, or `slide`. `scroll` is the default and makes the text scroll in the direction specified by `direction`. `alternate` makes the text scroll in alternating directions. `slide` makes the text appear from the direction specified by `direction` and stop when it reaches the opposite margin.

- `direction` can be `left` (the default), `right`, `up`, or `down`. Scrolling left is the most common usage. Scrolling up or down can be effective but takes up more space.

- `bgcolor` specifies the background color for the marquee. `bgcolor` can be any valid color—either a color name (such as `red`) or a hexadecimal code (such as `#FFFF00`).

- `loop` specifies how many times the marquee repeats the scrolling. The default setting is to loop endlessly, which you can also specify explicitly using the value `infinite`.

For example, to create a marquee with a cyan (light blue) background, such as that shown in Figure 3-6:

1. Type the opening `<marquee>` tag:

   ```
   <marquee>
   ```

2. Before the closing angle bracket, type the `behavior` attribute and specify `scroll`, `alternate`, or `slide`, as appropriate—for example:

   ```
   <marquee behavior="scroll">
   ```

3. Type the `direction` attribute and specify `left`, `right`, `up`, or `down`, as appropriate—for example:

```
<marquee behavior="scroll" direction="left">
```

4. Type the `bgcolor` attribute and specify the color you want to use—for example:

```
<marquee behavior="scroll" direction="left" bgcolor="cyan">
```

5. Type the `loop` attribute and specify either the number of loops or the value `infinite`—for example:

```
<marquee behavior="scroll" direction="left" bgcolor="cyan"
loop="2">
```

6. On the next line, type the text you want the marquee to display—for example:

```
Special low prices TODAY ONLY! Stout Planter Pots $5 each, Tall
Planter Pots $8 each…
```

7. Type the closing `</marquee>` tag:

```
</marquee>
```

8. Save the file, switch to your web browser, and refresh the page to see the effect.

Figure 3-6: Use moving text to draw the viewer's eye to key information you want to convey.

How to...

- *Create Graphics with Paint*
- *Choosing Graphics Applications*
- *Create Graphics with Paint Shop Pro*
- *Understanding GIF, JPEG, and PNG*
- *Download Pictures from Your Digital Camera*
- *Scan Graphics from Documents or Pictures*
- *Keeping Down Graphic Size to Make Pages Load Faster*
- *Add an Inline Graphic*
- *Using Graphics to Control How Text Appears*
- *Add a Background Graphic*
- *Add a Horizontal Rule*
- *Laying Out Your Web Pages*
- *Create an E-Mail Signature Containing a Graphic*

Chapter 4

Adding Graphics

Much of the Web's popularity is due to its ability to present graphical content rather than only text, and even a few graphics can make a huge difference in the look of a web page. Graphics of any size increase the time it takes to download a page, however, so you should use them with discretion to avoid making your pages awkward to access.

This chapter starts by showing you how to create graphics for your web site using tools such as a digital camera, scanner, and a graphics application. The chapter then explains how to insert graphics in your web pages as inline graphics and background graphics and control how they appear. You'll also learn how to add horizontal rules to your pages.

Create Graphics for Your Web Pages

Many web pages benefit from graphics. Depending on the types of web pages you're creating, you may want to create or acquire graphics in any of the following ways:

- Create graphics in a graphics application, such as Paint or Paint Shop Pro.
- Take photos with a digital camera and download them to your computer.
- Scan hard-copy documents or photos to create graphics files.
- Find clip-art graphics that are free to use, or get permission to reuse other people's copyrighted graphics on your web site.
- Buy the rights to use professional stock photos.

Create Graphics with Paint

All desktop or laptop versions of Windows (as opposed to versions of Windows that run on Pocket PCs) include Paint, a simple graphics application. You can use Paint to create your own pictures and to perform basic operations with graphics. For greater control over your graphics, use a more advanced graphics application, such as Paint Shop Pro, which is discussed in the next section.

CREATE A NEW GRAPHIC WITH PAINT

To create a new graphic with Paint:

1. Click the **Start** button, click **All Programs**, click **Accessories**, and then click **Paint**. Paint opens with a blank image.

2. Click the **Image** menu and then click **Attributes**. The Attributes dialog box appears.

CAUTION

Never use someone else's copyrighted graphic without specific permission. You may be tempted to scan a picture you like and use it on your web site, or simply save a graphic that you find on a web site other than your own. Both these actions are violations of copyright law. The only exception is if a graphic is in the public domain, either because its copyright term has expired or because the copyright holder has specifically put the graphic in the public domain. Always verify that a graphic is in the public domain, get permission, or pay for it before you use it.

3. In the Units area, select the option button for the measurement units you want to use: Inches, Cm, or Pixels. For web graphics, pixels work best, because dimensions on web pages are usually specified in pixels.

4. Type the dimensions for the graphic in the Width and Height text boxes.

5. Click **OK**. The Attributes dialog box closes, and Paint changes the blank image to the dimensions you specified.

6. Use Paint's tools (see Figure 4-1) to create the graphic you want.

7. Click the **File** menu and then click **Save**. The Save As dialog box appears. Specify the name and location for the file, choose the format in the Save As Type drop-down list, and then click **Save**.

8. If you've finished working with Paint, click the **File** menu and then click **Exit**.

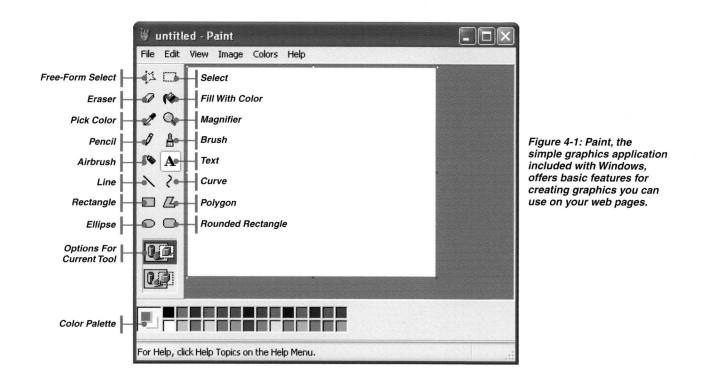

Figure 4-1: Paint, the simple graphics application included with Windows, offers basic features for creating graphics you can use on your web pages.

QUICKFACTS

CHOOSING GRAPHICS APPLICATIONS

The Paint application included with Windows lets you perform basic operations on graphics, including converting them from one major format to another, changing their size, and changing their resolution.

If you need to use pictures extensively, however, you will probably need to get a more capable graphics application that can perform graphical transformations on a graphic— for example, sharpening it or blurring it. You should also make sure that the application can create interlaced and transparent GIFs and progressive JPEGs. (See the "Understanding GIF, JPEG, and PNG" QuickFacts in this chapter for a discussion of these formats.)

One of the most affordable commercial software applications for Windows is Paint Shop Pro from JASC Software (www.jasc.com, around $99), which also includes Animation Shop, a tool that enables you to create animated GIFs. This chapter uses Paint Shop Pro for examples of how to create graphics.

Beyond Paint Shop Pro, the main Windows tools for manipulating graphics are:

- **Photoshop Elements** from Adobe Systems, Inc. (www.adobe.com, $120) is an introductory version of Photoshop but has enough features to take care of all but the most advanced operations. (See *PhotoShop Elements 3.0 QuickSteps*, published by McGraw-Hill/Osborne, for more information.) The full version of Photoshop, a standard professional tool, costs around $600. Photoshop is part of the Adobe Creative Suite ($1,100), which includes Illustrator (a drawing program), ImageReady (for creating web graphics, including animations), GoLive (a leading web-authoring application), Acrobat Professional (an application for creating and editing PDFs), and InDesign (a layout application).

Continued...

CHANGE THE SIZE OF A GRAPHIC WITH PAINT

To change the size of a graphic with Paint:

1. Click the **Start** button, click **All Programs**, click **Accessories**, and then click **Paint**. Paint opens with a blank image.

2. Click the **File** menu and then click **Open**. The Open dialog box appears. Select the graphic you want to change, and then click **Open**. Paint opens the graphic.

3. Click the **Image** menu and then click **Stretch/Skew**. The Stretch And Skew dialog box appears.

4. In the Stretch area, type the percentage (of the current size) to which you want to reduce or increase the graphic. For example, type 25 in both the Horizontal and Vertical text boxes to reduce the height and width of the graphic to a quarter of the original dimensions.

5. Click **OK**. Paint changes the dimensions of the graphic.

6. To save the graphic under its current name, click the **File** menu and then click **Save**. To save the graphic under another name, click the **File** menu, click **Save As**, enter the name in the Save As dialog box, and then click **Save**.

7. If you've finished working with Paint, click the **File** menu and then click **Exit**.

CONVERT A GRAPHIC TO A DIFFERENT FORMAT WITH PAINT

To convert an existing graphic to a different format with Paint:

1. Click the **Start** button, click **All Programs**, click **Accessories**, and then click **Paint**. Paint opens with a blank image.

2. Click the **File** menu and then click **Open**. The Open dialog box appears. Select the graphic you want to change, and then click **Open**. Paint opens the graphic.

3. Click the **File** menu and then click **Save As**. The Save As dialog box appears. Choose the file format you want in the Save As Type drop-down list, and then click **Save**.

4. If you've finished working with Paint, click the **File** menu and then click **Exit**.

Create Graphics with Paint Shop Pro

Paint Shop Pro is an affordable Windows application for creating and manipulating graphics. This section shows you how to use Paint Shop Pro to create progressive JPEGs and interlaced GIFs, which are explained more in the "Understanding GIF, JPEG, and PNG" QuickFact on the next page. If you don't already own Paint Shop Pro, download the free trial version from http://www.jasc.com and try it out here.

CREATING PROGRESSIVE JPEGS WITH PAINT SHOP PRO

To create a progressive JPEG from an existing graphic with Paint Shop Pro:

1. Click the **Start** button, click **All Programs**, click **Jasc Software**, and then click **Paint Shop Pro**. Paint Shop Pro opens.

2. Click the **File** menu and then click **Open**. The Open dialog box appears. Select the graphic file you want to open, and then click **Open**. Paint Shop Pro opens the graphic.

3. Click the **File** menu and then click **Save As**. The Save As dialog box appears.

4. In the Save As Type drop-down list, select **JPEG – JFIF Compliant**. Depending on the version of Paint Shop Pro you are using, the name may be different—for example, JPEG (*.jpg, *.jif, *.jpe, .jpeg)—and some interface elements may be different.

5. Click **Options**. The Save Options dialog box for JPEG files appears.

UNDERSTANDING GIF, JPEG, AND PNG

Most images used in web pages are in one of the three main graphics formats that the majority of browsers support: PNG, JPEG, or GIF.

LOSSY AND LOSSLESS COMPRESSION

All three formats use compression to reduce the size of the image file so that it will download faster. There are two main types of compression:

- *Lossless compression* doesn't discard any of the information required to display the graphic, so graphics compressed with lossless compression are as high in quality as the original, uncompressed file.

- *Lossy compression* discards some of the information required to display the graphic, so graphics compressed with lossy compression are lower in quality than the original file.

PNG

PNG (Portable Network Graphics) is a relatively new graphics format developed for Internet usage. PNG uses lossless compression to create a high-quality picture with as small a file size as possible. PNG doesn't offer different compression levels, but it lets you make parts of the graphic transparent so that the background shows through.

PNG is a good choice for web graphics and is supported by all current browsers. Some older versions of browsers don't support PNG.

JPEG

JPEG (Joint Photographic Experts Group) is a graphics format widely used on the web. JPEG uses lossy compression and is supported by all browsers. JPEG offers different levels of compression, allowing you to choose a suitable quality of picture. JPEG does not let you make parts of the graphic transparent.

Continued...

6. In the Encoding area, select the **Progressive Encoding** option button.

7. In the Compression area, drag the compression slider to specify how much compression you want to apply. Higher compression gives a smaller file size but lower image quality; lower compression gives a larger file size and higher image quality.

8. Click **OK** to close the Save Options dialog box, and then click **Save** to close the Save As dialog box. Paint Shop Pro saves the file as a progressive JPEG.

9. If you've finished working with Paint Shop Pro, click the **File** menu and then click **Exit**.

CREATE INTERLACED GIFS WITH OR WITHOUT TRANSPARENCY WITH PAINT SHOP PRO

To create an interlaced GIF, either with or without transparency, from an existing graphic with Paint Shop Pro:

1. Click the **Start** button, click **All Programs**, click **Jasc Software**, and then click **Paint Shop Pro**. Paint Shop Pro opens.

2. Click the **File** menu and then click **Open**. The Open dialog box appears. Select the graphic file you want to open, and then click **Open**. Paint Shop Pro opens the graphic.

3. Click the **File** menu and then click **Save As**. The Save As dialog box appears.

4. In the Save As Type drop-down list, select **CompuServe Graphics Interchange**.

5. Click **Options**. The Save Options dialog box for GIF files appears.

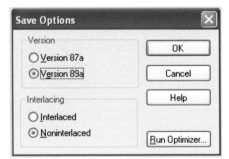

UNDERSTANDING GIF, JPEG, AND PNG *(Continued)*

Use JPEG when you want to make sure that all browsers can view the graphics on your web pages. (If a visitor has turned off the display of graphics in his or her browser, however, he or she will not see the graphics.)

For best performance, use *progressive JPEGs*, JPEG files created so that they can display a rough version of the graphic while downloading the rest of it. When a browser requests a progressive JPEG, the web server supplies first every eighth line of the JPEG, so that a rough version can be displayed, and then fills in the missing lines gradually. The result is that the visitor can get an idea of what the graphic looks like without waiting for the whole graphic to download.

GIF

GIF (Graphics Interchange Format) is a standard graphics format that has been widely used on the Web for many years. GIF uses lossless compression and maps the colors in a graphic to 256 colors and uses dithering to represent colors not included in those 256. GIF also lets you make parts of the graphic transparent. *Interlaced GIFs* work in the same way as progressive JPEGs, enabling the visitor to see a rough version of the graphic while the rest is being downloaded.

In general, GIF provides a good balance of picture quality with file size.

6. In the Interlacing area, select the **Interlaced** option button.

7. If you want to add transparency to the graphic (so that the web page's background is visible through parts of the graphic), click **Run Optimizer**. The GIF Optimizer dialog box appears (see Figure 4-2). Either click the **Use Wizard** button, and follow through the steps of setting up the GIF with the transparency you want, or work with the options on the Transparency tab. Then click **OK**.

8. Click **OK** to close the Save Options dialog box, and then click **Save** to close the Save As dialog box. Paint Shop Pro saves the file as an interlaced GIF. If Paint Shop Pro warns you that the saved file will be limited to a single layer and a maximum of 256 colors, click **Yes** to continue.

9. If you've finished working with Paint Shop Pro, click the **File** menu and then click **Exit**.

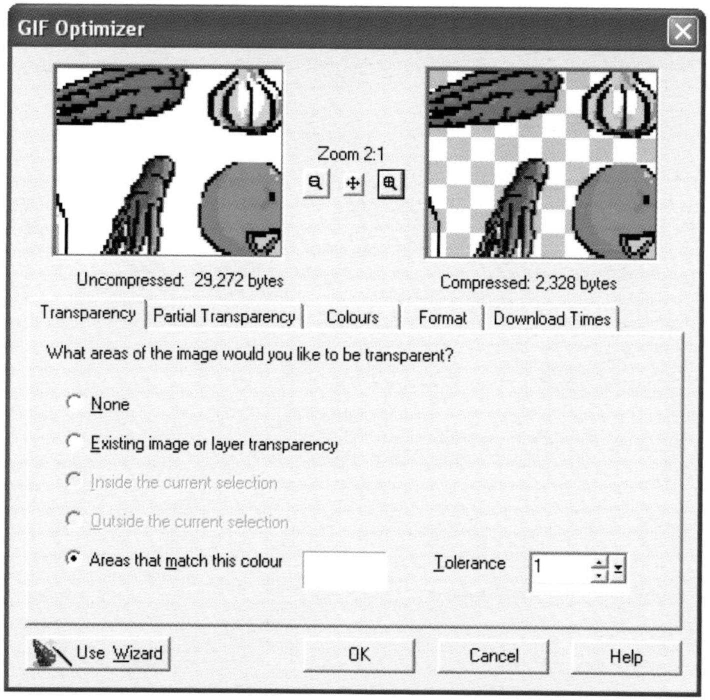

Figure 4-2: The Transparency tab of Paint Shop Pro's GIF Optimizer dialog box lets you make parts of a graphic transparent.

CREATE INTERLACED PNGS WITH TRANSPARENCY USING PAINT SHOP PRO

To create an interlaced PNG file with transparency from an existing graphic with Paint Shop Pro:

1. Click the **Start** button, click **All Programs**, click **Jasc Software**, and then click **Paint Shop Pro**. Paint Shop Pro opens.

2. Click the **File** menu and then click **Open**. The Open dialog box appears. Select the graphic file you want to open, and then click **Open**. Paint Shop Pro opens the graphic.

3. Click the **File** menu and then click **Save As**. The Save As dialog box appears.

4. In the Save As Type drop-down list, select **Portable Network Graphics**.

5. Click **Options**. The Save Options dialog box for PNG files appears.

6. In the Interlacing area, select the **Interlaced** option button.

7. If you want to add transparency to the graphic, click **Run Optimizer**. The PNG Optimizer dialog box appears. Either click the **Use Wizard** button, and follow through the steps of setting up the PNG with the transparency you want, or work with the options on the Transparency tab (see Figure 4-3). Then click **OK**.

8. Click **OK** to close the Save Options dialog box, and then click **Save** to close the Save As dialog box. Paint Shop Pro saves the file as an interlaced PNG.

9. If you've finished working with Paint Shop Pro, click the **File** menu and then click **Exit**. Look at the three pictures you saved, and see what the differences are.

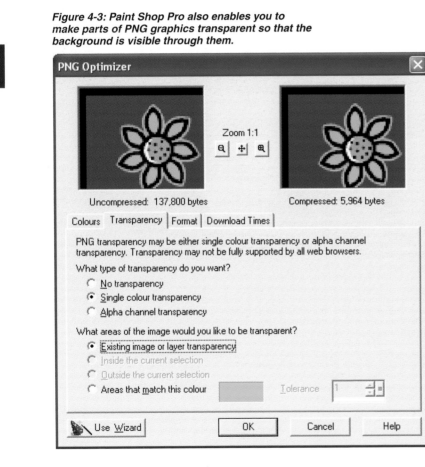

Figure 4-3: Paint Shop Pro also enables you to make parts of PNG graphics transparent so that the background is visible through them.

Download Pictures from Your Digital Camera

A digital camera offers a quick and easy way to create pictures of objects you want to include on your web pages. For example, if you're selling various products, you might photograph them with your digital camera. (You can also take photos with a film camera and scan the prints, but doing so involves more expense and effort, and loses quality, so it's seldom worthwhile.)

To import pictures from a digital camera to your PC:

1. Connect the digital camera or its memory card to your PC. Many digital cameras connect via USB (Universal Serial Bus). In others, you remove a storage card (such as a CompactFlash card or an SD card) and insert it in a card reader connected via USB to your PC.

2. When XP detects a storage device, it may display the Removable Disk dialog box (see Figure 4-4). If not, click the **Start** button, click **My Computer**, right-click the entry for the storage device, and click **AutoPlay** to display this dialog box.

3. Click **Open Folder To View Files**, select the **Always Do The Selected Action** check box, and click **OK**. XP opens a Windows Explorer window showing the pictures or the folder containing them.

4. Select the pictures you want to transfer, click the **Edit** menu, and click **Copy To Folder**. Select the destination folder in the Copy To Folder dialog box, and click **Copy**.

Figure 4-4: The easiest way to copy pictures from a digital camera or memory card to your PC is to use the Open Folder To View Files option in the Removable Disk dialog box.

Removable Disk (E:)

Windows can perform the same action each time you insert a disk or connect a device with this kind of file:

Pictures

What do you want Windows to do?

Copy pictures to a folder on my computer
using Microsoft Scanner and Camera Wizard

Print the pictures
using Photo Printing Wizard

View a slideshow of the images
using Windows Picture and Fax Viewer

Open folder to view files
using Windows Explorer

☐ Always do the selected action.

OK   Cancel

Safely Remove Hardware

Safely remove USB Mass Storage Device - Drive(E:)
My Computer   100NIKON   7:48 AM

4. Click the **Safely Remove Hardware** icon in the notification area, and then click the item for the removable disk drive on the resulting menu.

5. Detach the camera or remove the memory card from the card reader.

Scan Graphics from Documents or Pictures

To create graphics of hard-copy documents or pictures or of flat objects that are difficult to photograph with a camera, such as slides or jewelry, you will need a scanner.

For documents, pictures, and other flat objects, a scanner will give you a better picture than a camera will. To scan a document:

1. Place the document or object on the scanner, aligning it carefully with the guides.

2. Click the **Start** button, click **All Programs**, click **Accessories**, and then click **Scanners And Cameras Wizard**. The Scanners And Cameras Wizard starts. Click **Next**. The Choose Scanning Preferences page appears (see Figure 4-5).

TIP

The best type for general purposes is a flatbed scanner—one with a large glass surface on which you put the object you want to scan. Scanners that connect via USB typically offer the best value for computers running Windows XP. As with a digital camera, you don't need super-high resolution on your scanner provided that the resolution is high enough to produce a clear and recognizable picture. You will typically need to reduce the resolution of pictures so as to make them small enough for use on your web pages.

NOTE

If you have multiple scanners or cameras, the Scanners And Cameras Wizard lets you choose which device to use.

Figure 4-5: Click the Preview button to display a preview of the picture or document you're scanning, and select the appropriate Picture Type option button. Click the Custom Settings button if you need to adjust the default settings for that type.

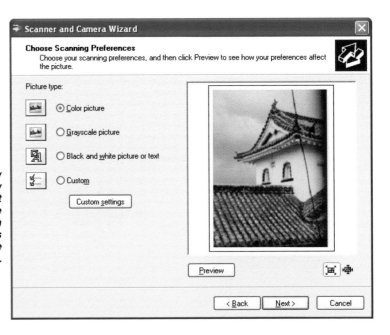

QUICKFACTS

KEEPING DOWN GRAPHIC SIZE TO MAKE PAGES LOAD FASTER

Unless you know that all visitors to your web site will be accessing it across a high-speed connection (for example, a corporate intranet), you should keep the size of your web pages small so that they load quickly across even a slow connection. In many cases, the key factor determining how quickly a page loads is how many graphics it contains and how large the file size of those graphics is.

To make your pages load faster:

* Reduce the number of graphics you use in your pages. Look at the web pages you visit most frequently and analyze their use of graphics. Some major sites, such as Google (www.google.com), use very few graphics indeed—and so load quickly even over dial-up connections.

* Reduce each graphic to the size at which it will be displayed, rather than using a larger graphic and displaying it at a smaller size.

* Reduce the number of colors used in your graphics. (If you use GIFs, you're automatically reducing the number of colors to 256 or fewer.)

* Compress each graphic by using a compressed file format (GIF, JPEG, or PNG). If you use JPEG, choose a degree of compression that provides adequate image quality with as small a file size as possible.

* Reuse graphics where possible so that the browser needs to download them only once. For example, use the same logo on each page rather than using variations on the logo.

3. Choose your scanning preferences and click **Next**. The Picture Name And Destination page appears.

4. Type the name for the group of pictures, select the file format (see the "Understanding GIF, JPEG, and PNG" QuickFacts in this chapter), and choose the folder in which to store the picture. Click **Next** to start the scan.

5. After scanning, choose whether to publish the picture to a web site, order prints online, or do nothing beyond saving the picture. Click **Next** and then click **Finish**. The wizard opens a Windows Explorer window showing you the results of the scan so that you can open it for viewing or editing.

Use Graphics in Your Web Pages

You can place graphics either with the text and other elements in the foreground of a web page or in the background behind the text and other elements.

Add an Inline Graphic

An *inline* graphic is one that appears in the same layer of a web page as the text—in other words, not in the background. You can control the size of graphics, specify alignment and alternative text, and apply borders, as needed.

TIP

The graphic file you add can be located either on the same computer as the web page or on another computer. To use a graphic on the same computer, use either an absolute path or a relative path. To use a graphic located on another computer, specify the full URL of the graphic file. Bear in mind that the graphic will have to be transferred from the server you specify, and that this server may respond more slowly than the main server you're using.

INSERT A GRAPHIC

To insert a graphic, you use an `<img>` tag. You must always use the `src` attribute to specify the source of the graphic—for example:

```
<img src="red_rose_14.jpg">
```

INCLUDE ALTERNATIVE TEXT FOR A GRAPHIC

It's a good idea to include alternative text explaining what the graphic is for any browser that has graphics turned off (as shown on the left in Figure 4-6) or a text-only browser or for someone using a screen reader. Some browsers, including Internet Explorer, display this text as a ScreenTip (as shown on the right in Figure 4-6) when the user hovers the mouse pointer over the graphic.

To include alternative text, use the `alt` attribute—for example:

```
<img src="red_rose_14.jpg" alt="A red rose in bloom">
```

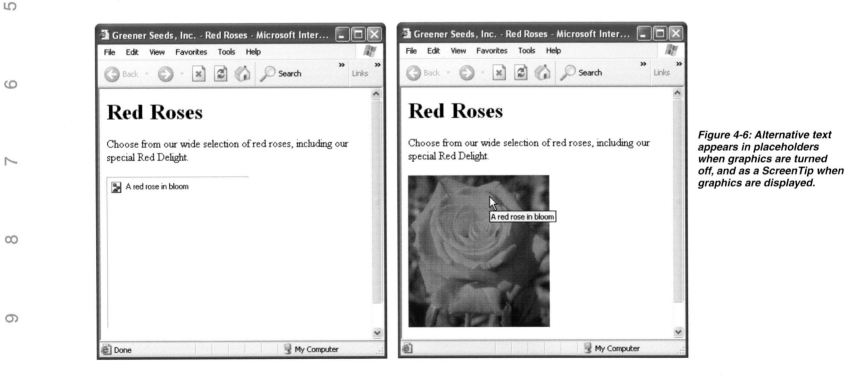

Figure 4-6: Alternative text appears in placeholders when graphics are turned off, and as a ScreenTip when graphics are displayed.

TABLE 4-1: VALUES FOR THE align ATTRIBUTE

align VALUE	ALIGNS THE GRAPHIC
top	With the top of the object
bottom	With the bottom of the object
middle	With the middle of the object
left	To the left of the object
right	To the right of the object

ALIGN A GRAPHIC

By default, most browsers align a graphic vertically with the baseline of any text or object on the same line. Figure 4-7 shows an example: the bottom of the rose is aligned with the base of the text (although the descenders on letter such as *y* and *g* go lower).

You can control horizontal alignment by using the align attribute (see Table 4-1).

The following example aligns the graphic to the left of the text. To ensure that this works, place the <img> tag before the text to whose left it should appear:

```
<img src="red_rose_14.jpg" alt="A red rose in bloom" align="left">
```

CHANGE THE SIZE OF A GRAPHIC

When you use an <img> tag without specifying the height or width of the graphic, the browser displays the graphic at its full size. This size might be too large or too small in the browser window, depending on the window's size and the screen resolution.

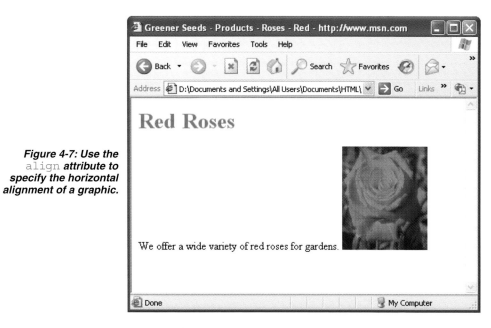

Figure 4-7: Use the align attribute to specify the horizontal alignment of a graphic.

<table><tr><td></td></tr></table>

NOTE

If you specify both dimensions for a graphic, most browsers can use the size as a placeholder that enables them to lay out the web page correctly before the graphic has fully downloaded. If, however, you don't specify the dimensions of the graphic, browsers aren't able to lay the page out correctly until the graphic has fully downloaded because they do not know how much space the graphic occupies.

To control the size at which the browser displays the graphic, use the `height` attribute and the `width` attribute of the `<img>` tag. Usually, you'll want to specify the exact number of pixels for these attributes, but you can also specify the percentage of the browser window that the graphic should occupy. The problem with specifying the percentage is that the graphic may be distorted depending on the proportions of the browser window—and if the user resizes the window, the graphic's proportions will change too.

The following example sets the height of the graphic to 150 pixels and its width to 125 pixels:

```
<img src="red_rose_14.jpg" alt="A red rose in bloom" height="150" width="125">
```

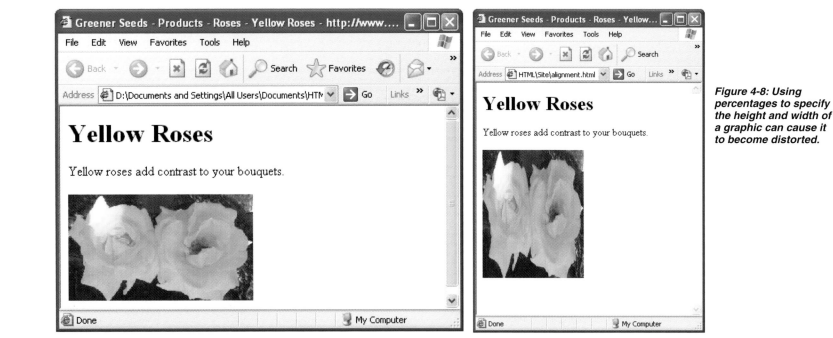

Figure 4-8: Using percentages to specify the height and width of a graphic can cause it to become distorted.

The following example displays the graphic at 60 percent of the height of the browser window and 50 percent of its width. Figure 4-8 shows how the graphic becomes distorted when the browser window is resized: in the left image, the graphic is compressed horizontally, whereas in the right image, its proportions are correct.

```
<img src="yellow_roses_3.jpg" alt="Two yellow roses" height="60%"
width="50%">
```

APPLY BORDERS TO A GRAPHIC

To apply borders to a graphic, add the border attribute to the <img> tag, and specify the appropriate properties. (See Table 3-4 in Chapter 3 for a list of border properties.) The following example applies a thick black border to the picture, as shown in Figure 4-9:

```
<img src="yellow_roses_3.jpg" style="border-style:solid;border-
color:black;border-width:thick">
```

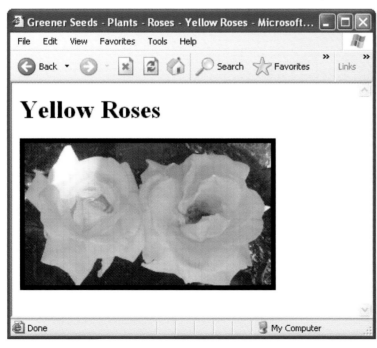

Figure 4-9: Apply borders to your graphics when you want to separate them further from the rest of the page.

QUICKSTEPS

USING GRAPHICS TO CONTROL HOW TEXT APPEARS

If a web page requires text to be displayed using exactly the font, size, and arrangement you specify rather than using the available fonts and current settings on the computer a viewer is using, use a graphic instead of text formatting.

1. Use a graphics application, such as Paint or Paint Shop Pro, to create a graphic that contains the necessary text in your desired arrangement. Save the graphic in your site's folder.

2. Use the techniques described in this chapter to position the graphic where you need the text to appear in your web page.

NOTE

The spacer graphic can be a much smaller size than the amount of space that you need it to occupy because you can use the `width` attribute and `height` attribute of the `<img>` tag to make it occupy more space.

POSITION A GRAPHIC WITH SPACERS

As discussed in Chapter 3, HTML enables you to specify the relative alignment of paragraphs and other items. If you need to align items precisely, however, you must either use styles (as discussed in Chapter 8) or work around the problem. One solution is to use *spacer images*—images that take up a certain amount of space but that don't display their physical presence on the web page because they're either transparent or the same color as the background.

To use a spacer image:

1. Use a graphics program (such as those discussed in the "Choosing Graphics Applications" QuickFacts, earlier in this chapter) to create a small graphic—just a few pixels (or even one pixel) in each direction.

2. Type an `<img src=>` tag that specifies the location of the graphic you want to use as a spacer—for example:

   ```
   <img src="images/spacer1.gif">
   ```

3. Use the `width` attribute and the `height` attribute to specify the size at which you want the spacer graphic to be displayed—for example:

   ```
   width="40" height="80"
   ```

4. If the spacer graphic isn't transparent, use the `border` attribute to set the border to a zero width:

   ```
   border="0"
   ```

5. Place the graphic you want to indent after the spacer graphic by using the `<img>` tag as usual—for example:

   ```
   <img src="yellow_roses_3.jpg" style="border-style:solid;border-
   color:black;border-width:thick">
   ```

6. Save the web page, switch to your browser, and refresh the display so that you can see the effect of using the spacer graphic.

Figure 4-10 shows an indent produced by using the spacer graphic specified in the following code:

```html
<h1>Yellow Roses</h1>
<img src="spacer1.gif" width="40" height="80" alt="A blank graphic
used for positioning">
<img src="yellow_roses_3.jpg" style="border-style:solid;border-
color:black;border-width:thick" alt="A picture of yellow roses">
<p><i>Add a splash of sun to your borders with these daffodil-
yellow roses!</i></p>
```

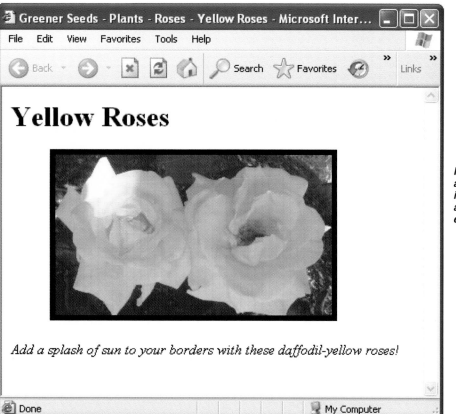

Figure 4-10: You can use an invisible graphic to indent an element, such as a graphic, as in the example here.

Add a Background Graphic

Instead of placing a graphic inline with the text, you may want to use it to form the background of a web page. A background graphic can make your web pages much more colorful and dramatic, but you must make sure that the graphic neither obscures the text of the page nor clashes with any graphics you place inline. In practice, this means that the background image should provide a considerable contrast with the content of the page. For example, you might use a subtle, light-toned image in your background that does not obscure black text.

To add a background image, add the `background` attribute to the `<body>` tag, and specify the file name (and, if needed, the path) in double quotation marks. The following example (shown in Figure 4-11) uses the file named peppers.jpg in the images folder:

```
<body background="images/peppers.jpg">
```

Figure 4-11: You can use a JPEG, GIF, or PNG file as a background graphic for a web page. Choose a contrasting text color to make sure that the text is legible.

Add a Horizontal Rule

To divide a web page into different horizontal areas, add one or more horizontal rules by using the `<hr>` tag. Used on its own, this tag creates a horizontal rule of the default color (black) and default width that is left-aligned and that spans the whole browser window. Often, you'll want to specify the alignment, color, thickness, or length of the horizontal rule. To do so, use the attributes listed in Table 4-2.

TABLE 4-2: ATTRIBUTES FOR THE `<hr>` TAG

ATTRIBUTE	VALUE
align	left, center, right
color	The name or hex code of a color
size	The thickness of the rule in pixels
width	The length of the rule in pixels
noshade	No value; if included, it prevents the rule from having a 3-D effect

> **TIP**
>
> Normally, when you put a background graphic in a web page, that image moves when the user scrolls through the web page. If you want the image to stay in place when the user scrolls so that it is always is the same position in the browser window and the text and other content scrolls over it, add `bgproperties="fixed"` to the `<body>` tag. This effect can be useful, but you must make sure that the page's content will be visible no matter which part of the background image it is displayed over.

> **TIP**
>
> HTML doesn't have a tag for a vertical line, but you can apply vertical lines by using a table. See Chapter 6 for more information.

The following example includes a plain horizontal rule (shown at the top of Figure 4-12) and a purple horizontal rule 400 pixels long by 10 pixels thick with the `noshade` attribute applied (shown at the bottom of the figure):

```
<p>Japanese maples are widely popular due to their beautiful
colors and their manageability.</p>
<hr>
<h2>Acer Palmatum Orange Dream</h2>
<p><i>One of our customers' all-time favorite trees!</i></p>
<img src="maple_1.jpg">
<br>
<ul>
 <li>Striking orange foliage; golden yellow in the fall</li>
 <li>Slow-growing: around 10' after 10 years</li>
 <li>Ideal for smaller yards</li>
</ul>
<hr color="#993399" width="400" size="10" noshade>
```

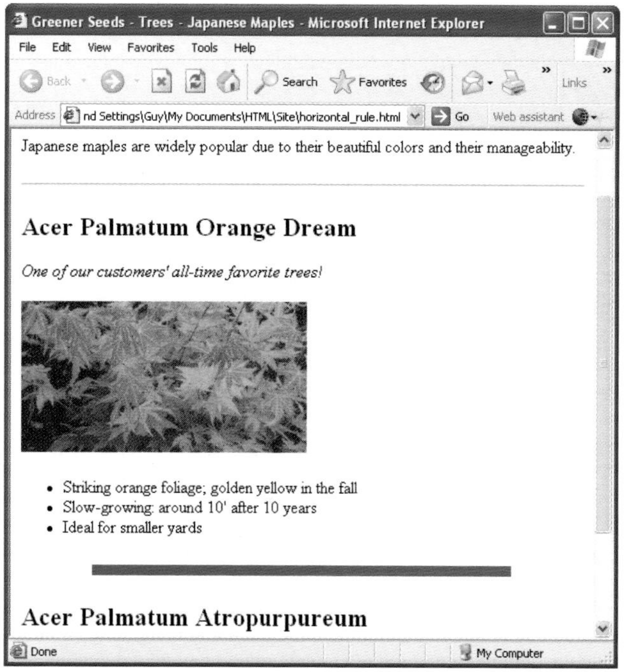

Figure 4-12: Use horizontal rules to break up a page into different areas. You can specify the alignment, color, length, and thickness of the rule for effect.

LAYING OUT YOUR WEB PAGES

As discussed in Chapter 2, people trying to view your web pages may be using any of a variety of browsers and operating systems, page sizes, connections, and operating systems.

Keep your web pages small so that they can be viewed in small windows if necessary. Even so, the only area of a page that you can be certain will be visible is the top-left corner—so this is where you should put all the vital information on the page. This crucial area is sometimes called "above the fold," a term taken from newspaper publishing: when the newspaper is folded, the most important information must be visible.

On most pages, the most important information is the site's name (and perhaps logo) and description, and primary means of navigation (perhaps including a Search tool), the page's name or description, and contact information. If your site carries advertising, above the fold is prime screen real estate, and you should charge accordingly.

You will probably also put a brief version of the site's name and the page's content in the page's title (using the <title> tag).

Create an E-Mail Signature Containing a Graphic

A *signature* is an item that most e-mail applications can automatically insert at the end of each outgoing message (if you choose to include it). A signature normally consists of text that identifies the sender—for example, by supplying the sender's full name, position and company (if applicable), physical address, phone numbers, and other relevant information, such as the URL of the sender's web site. Many signatures also include a short quote for the recipient's enjoyment or edification.

You can also add a graphic to your signature by creating a suitable page using HTML. This example shows you how to create a graphical signature and then apply it in Outlook Express, the e-mail application included with Windows.

CREATE AN HTML SIGNATURE FILE

To create an HTML signature file:

1. In your text editor (for example, Notepad), create an HTML file that contains the information you want. An example including a graphic follows:

```
<html>
<head>
<title></title>
</head>
<body>
<p>Anna Connor<br>Account Executive</p>
<br>
<img src="f:\site\images\acme.jpg" align="left">
<h3><b>Acme Heavy Industries</b></h3>
<p> Web site: <a href="http://www.acmeheavyindustries.com">
<tt>http://www.acmeheavyindustries.com</tt></a></p>
<p> E-mail: <a href=mailto:anna _ connor@acmeheavyindustries.com>
<tt>anna _ connor@acmeheavyindustries.com</tt></a></p>
<p> Office: 510-555-1298<br>
Mobile: 408-555-9823</p>
</body>
</html>
```

2. Make sure the file is correctly formed, with a starting `<html>` tag, a header section, a body section, and a closing `</html>` tag.

3. Create an `<img>` tag, add the `src` attribute, and specify the full path and file name of the graphics file. If necessary, use the `height` and `width` attributes to size the graphic.

4. Save the file and view it in your browser to make sure it looks the way you intend. Make any necessary adjustments and save the file again.

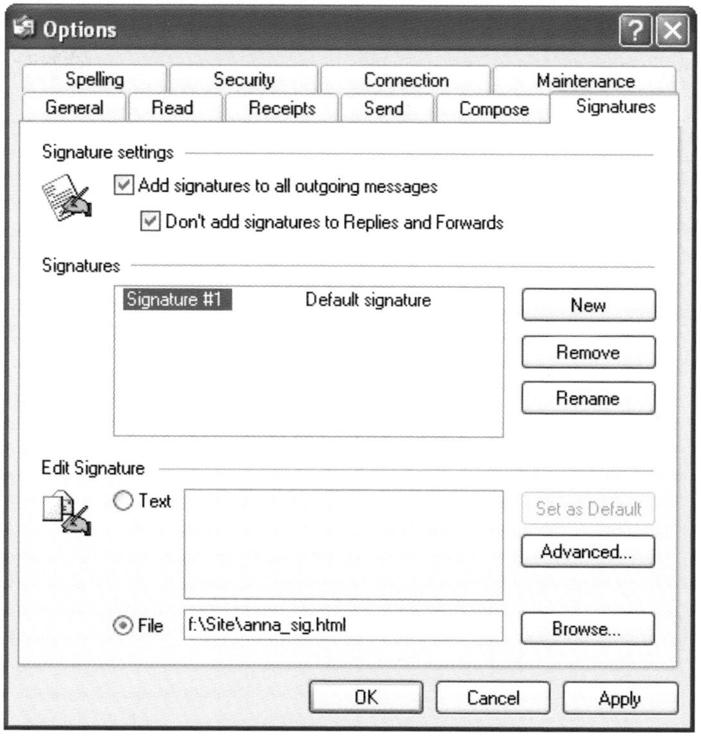

USE AN HTML SIGNATURE FILE IN OUTLOOK EXPRESS

To use an HTML signature file in Outlook Express:

1. If Outlook Express isn't already running, start it: click the **Start** button, click **All Programs**, and then click **Outlook Express**.

2. Click the **Tools** menu and then click **Options**. The Options dialog box appears. Click the **Signatures** tab (shown in Figure 4-13 with a signature applied).

3. Click **New**, click the **File** option button, and then click **Browse**. The Open dialog box appears. Select **HTML Files** in the Files Of Type drop-down list, select the signature file, and then click **Open**. Outlook Express closes the Open dialog box and enters the path and file name on the Signatures tab.

4. Select the **Add Signatures To All Outgoing Messages** check box if you want Outlook Express to add your signature automatically to all messages you send. Ensure that the **Don't Add Signatures To Replies And Forwards** check box is selected so that replies and forwarded messages you send do not receive a signature.

5. Click **OK**.

Figure 4-13: Define a signature on the Signatures tab of the Options dialog box in Outlook Express.

When you create a new message, Outlook Express automatically inserts the signature if you selected the **Add Signatures To All Outgoing Messages** check box. Otherwise, you can insert the signature manually when needed by clicking the **Insert** menu and then clicking **Signature**. Figure 4-14 shows the example signature in an Outlook Express message.

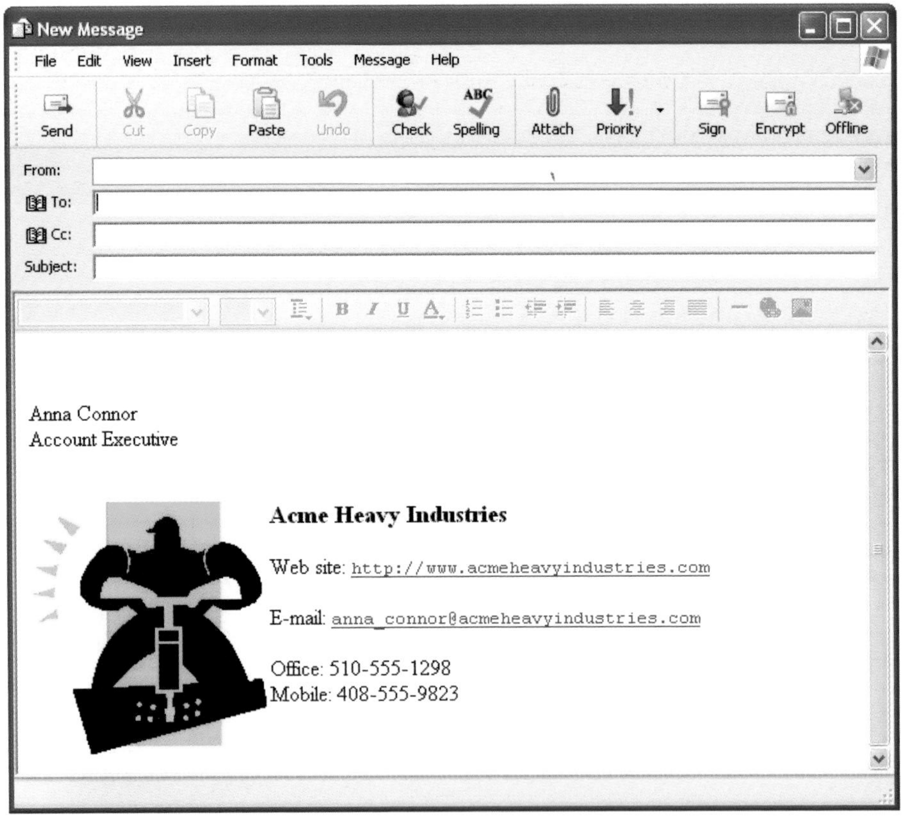

Figure 4-14: You can easily add signatures that contain graphics to your Outlook Express messages.

How to...

- Link to Another Web Page
- Understanding Absolute and Relative Links
- Link within a Web Page
- Making Your Site Navigable
- Link to a Particular Point on a Web Page
- Open a Link in a New Window
- Create a Link to Download a File
- Display a ScreenTip for a Link
- Create Links to Send E-Mail
- Making Useful Imagemaps
- Create Two or More Links in a Graphic
- Creating an Imagemap with Paint Shop Pro
- Add Audio and Video to Your Web Pages

Chapter 5

Adding Links

Hyperlinks—links that connect one web page to other pages—are one of the central components of the Web. This chapter shows you how to create links to other web pages and links to different locations on the same web page. You'll also learn how to create links that start e-mail messages for a specified address, links that use graphics rather than text, and links that download or play audio or video files.

Link to Another Web Page

A link consists of an anchor element (text or graphic) that defines how the link appears in the page that contains it and the URL of the destination to which the link leads. For example, many links appear as underlined text so that when the visitor clicks the text, the browser displays the page specified by the URL in the link. Other links appear as graphics that the visitor can click, or as buttons.

UNDERSTANDING ABSOLUTE AND RELATIVE LINKS

You can use either absolute links or relative links in your web pages.

ABSOLUTE LINKS

An *absolute link* is a link that includes the full address of the destination to which it links. The full address can be either a complete URL (for example, http://www.quicksteps.com/recipes/index.html) for a page on the Web or a complete file path (for example, \\acmeserver44\recipes\index.html) on a web server on your local network.

Complete URLs to web sites must always include the appropriate prefix, which tells the browser which protocol to use. When linking to a web site, you'll almost always use http:// to designate the HTTP protocol. Most browsers automatically supply this prefix if you omit the prefix when browsing, but you must include it in your absolute links.

RELATIVE LINKS

A *relative link* is a link that supplies just that part of the address needed to access the destination from the current page. For example, if the destination page is in the same folder as the current page, only the name of the destination page is needed—for example, `href="index.html"` to access the page named index.html in the current folder.

If the destination file is in a subfolder of the folder that contains the current page, specify the folder name, a forward slash, and the file name. For example,

Continued...

CREATE A TEXT LINK

To create a text link:

1. Position the insertion point in the element in which you want to create the link. For example, if you want to create the text link in a paragraph, create the paragraph and type any preliminary text.

2. Type the beginning of the anchor tag for the link:

   `<a`

3. Type the `href` attribute, an equal sign, the destination URL (within double quotation marks), and the closing angle bracket—for example:

   `href="http://www.quicksteps.com/products/seeds.html">`

4. Type the text that you want to have displayed as the anchor for the hyperlink—for example:

   `Seed Catalog`

5. Type the closing `</a>` tag for the anchor:

   `</a>`

The next example contains the entire link:

```
<p>You may also want to visit our <a href="http://
www.quicksteps.com/products/seeds.html">Seed Catalog</a>.</p>
```

CREATE A GRAPHIC LINK

To create a graphic link:

1. Position the insertion point where you want to place the graphic between other HTML elements.

2. Type the opening anchor tag, including the `href` attribute and the target address—for example:

   `<a href="http://www.quicksteps.com/products/squash.html">`

3. Type the `<img>` tag, including the `src` attribute and the graphic name (and, if needed, the file path)—for example:

   `<img src="squash.gif">`

4. Type the closing anchor tag:

   `</a>`

**UNDERSTANDING ABSOLUTE AND
RELATIVE LINKS** (Continued)

`href="products/index.html"` refers to the page named index.html in the subfolder named products contained in the same folder as the current page.

If the destination file is in a different part of the folder structure, enter two periods and a forward slash before the file name to instruct the browser to move up one level before traversing to the folder you specify. For example, `href="../webs/content/index.html"` causes the browser to move up one level, switch to the folder called webs, switch to the subfolder called content, and then open the file named index.html. To go up more than one level, use `../` as many times as necessary. For example, to go up two levels, use `../../`.

When creating the pages on your local computer, make sure that you don't include any drive letters (for example, C: or D:) or any backslashes (\) in your relative links. Neither will work after you transfer your web site to the web host.

WHEN TO USE ABSOLUTE AND RELATIVE LINKS

Relative links continue to work even if you move your entire web site from one location to another. For example, if you create your web site on your local computer and then transfer it to your web host, the links will continue to work. By contrast, if you use absolute links on your local computer, you will need to change all of the links to the correct URLs when you transfer your site to your web host.

Typically, you'll want to use relative links when linking to pages within your own web site. When linking to other web sites, use absolute URLs.

The complete tag looks like this:

```
<a href="http://www.quicksteps.com/products/squash.html">
<img src="squash.gif"></a>
```

When the user hovers the mouse pointer over the graphic, the pointer changes to a hand with a pointing finger to indicate the hyperlink, and the status bar displays the destination of the link (see Figure 5-1).

HTML displays a blue border around a linked graphic to draw the viewer's attention to the hyperlink. To prevent this border from being displayed, include the `border` attribute in the `<img>` tag and set it to zero:

```
<a href="http://www.quicksteps.com/products/squash.html">
<img src="squash.gif" border="0"></a>
```

Figure 5-1: By default, HTML displays a blue border around a linked graphic to indicate that it is a hyperlink. Specify a zero-width border if you want to remove the blue border.

http://www.htmlq.com/products/squash.html

Link within a Web Page

Instead of linking to a different web page, you can link to a different place on the same page by placing a named anchor at that point. This technique is useful for long pages that might otherwise be awkward for visitors to navigate. By providing at the top of the page a table of contents whose entries are linked to the relevant parts of the page, you can enable visitors to access those parts quickly. By also providing links from all regions of the page back to the top of the page, you can enable visitors to return to the table of contents easily.

To create a link within a web page:

1. Insert an anchor at the point within the page to which you want to be able to link. Type an anchor tag (`<a>`) and use the `name` attribute to specify the name for the anchor— for example:

```
<a name="Question_01"></a>
```

2. Create a link to the anchor you just inserted. Type an anchor tag (`<a>`) and use the `href` attribute to refer to the anchor, putting a hash symbol (#) before the name—for example:

```
<a href="#Question_01">How can I decide what to plant in my
garden?</a>
```

3. Save the file, switch to your browser, and test the link.

4. Add further anchors and links to the page as necessary. For example, insert an anchor named `Top` at the top of the page, and then insert links farther down the page to this anchor so that visitors can quickly return to the top of the page:

```
<p>Return to the <a href="#Top">top</a> of the page.</p>
```

The following code shows the beginning of a page that uses internal links for navigation between a list of questions at the top and answers to the questions farther down the page (see Figure 5-2). Note the anchor named `Top` in the first-level heading at the top of the page and the links to the anchors (`#Question_01` through `Question_09`) farther down the page.

```
<body>
<h1><a name="Top"></a>Greener Seeds Frequently Answered Questions
(FAQ)</h1>
<p>Customers often ask us similar questions about seeds and plants,
planting and gardening, and (of course) their orders. Please read
this list of questions before contacting us to see if we've already
answered your question.</p>
<h2>List of Questions</h2>
<ol>
<li><a href="#Question_01">How can I decide what to plant in my
garden?</a></li>
<li><a href="#Question_02">What are the advantages of organic
gardening?</a></li>
<li><a href="#Question_03">How do I make my garden organic?</a></li>
<li><a href="#Question_04">What is compost?</a></li>
<li><a href="#Question_05">What do I need to start making compost?
</a></li>
<li><a href="#Question_06">What is the best way of using compost?
</a></li>
<li><a href="#Question_07">What should and shouldn't I put in my
compost?</a></li>
<li><a href="#Question_08">How can I make my lawn grow better?</a></li>
<li><a href="#Question_09">Which natural fertilizers should I use?
</a></li>
```

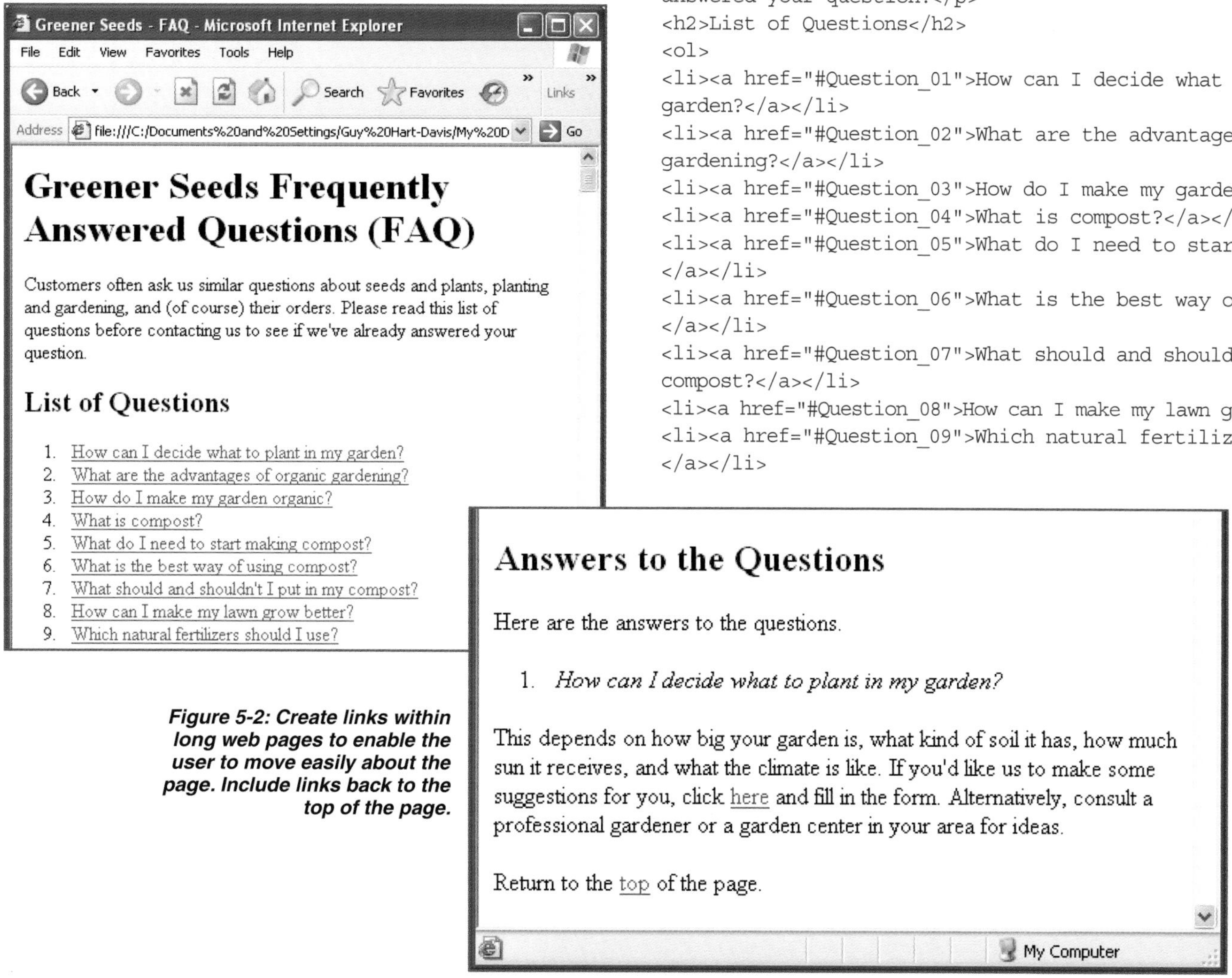

Figure 5-2: Create links within long web pages to enable the user to move easily about the page. Include links back to the top of the page.

MAKING YOUR SITE NAVIGABLE

To make your site easy for visitors to get around, you should provide effective navigation. You may also need to assign keyboard shortcuts to links so that links can be "clicked" using the keyboard, and change the tab order of links.

PROVIDE EFFECTIVE NAVIGATION

To provide effective navigation in your site:

- Include plenty of links on each page, including redundant links in different areas of long pages.
- Explain in text, in ScreenTips, or in both where the visitor will be taken if he or she clicks a link.
- Consider implementing a standard means of navigation across your entire site. For example, you might use a series of links across the top of each page to allow visitors to access the main areas of your site quickly.

ASSIGN A KEYBOARD SHORTCUT TO A LINK

To enable users without a mouse to click links, you can assign a keyboard shortcut to a link by adding the accesskey attribute and specifying the key. For example, add accesskey="h" to specify *h* as the access key for a hyperlink.

Most browsers display no indication of the access key, however, so you need to mark it to make it explicit. For example, you might use bold font on the access key letter in the text to indicate the access key.

CHANGE THE TAB ORDER OF LINKS

You can move from one hyperlink in a web page to the next hyperlink by pressing **TAB**; to move to the previous hyperlink, press **SHIFT+TAB**. Most browsers display a selection box or a highlight around the current link. To click the current link, press **ENTER**.

Continued...

Link to a Particular Point on a Web Page

You can use the anchor technique to create a link to a particular anchor on another web page. To do so:

1. Insert an anchor at the point on the destination page to which you want to be able to link. Type an anchor tag (`<a>`) and use the name attribute to specify the name for the anchor—for example:

   `<a name="shovels"></a>`

2. Save the destination page.

3. Switch to the page that will contain the link. Type the start of an anchor tag (`<a`), the href attribute, an equal sign, the absolute or relative address, a hash symbol (#), the anchor name, and the closing angle bracket—for example:

   `<a href="http://www.quicksteps.com/products/tools1.html#shovels">`

4. Type the text (or insert the graphic) that you want to use as the visible manifestation of the anchor and then the closing `</a>` tag—for example:

   `Shovels</a>`

5. Save the file, switch to your browser, and click the link. Make sure it takes you to the desired point on the other web page.

Open a Link in a New Window

When you click a link, most browsers open the linked page in the same window so that you can no longer see the page that contained the link. (You can configure some browsers to open linked pages in a new window or on a new tab.) To keep the previous page visible, you can create a link that opens in a new window by default. This technique is especially useful when your pages contain links to external web sites (as opposed to other pages in your site): you can enable visitors to access other sites without entirely leaving your site.

To make a link open a new window, include the target attribute with the value _blank in the link—for example:

```
<a href="http://www.quicksteps.com/products/tools1.html"
target="_blank">Gardening Tools</a>
```

5

MAKING YOUR SITE NAVIGABLE

(Continued)

The default order of the links is from the first to the last, top to bottom, and left to right. If you need to change this order, add the `tabindex` attribute to the links, using numbering to specify the desired order: add `tabindex="1"` to the link you want to be first, `tabindex="2"` to the second link, and so on.

For example, the following demonstrates `accesskey` and `tabindex` implemented with the list of questions described earlier in this chapter:

```
<h2>List of Questions</h2>
<ol>
<li><a href="#Question_01"
accesskey="p" tabindex="3">How
can I decide what to Plant in my
garden?</a></li>
<li><a href="#Question_02"
accesskey="o" tabindex="2">What
are the advantages of Organic
gardening?</a></li>
<li><a href="#Question_03"
accesskey="g" tabindex="1">How do
I make my Garden organic?</a></li>
```

NOTE

Even when you create a link that opens a page in a separate window, a visitor may be able to override the instruction by using a different type of click than a standard click. For example, the visitor might right-click and select Open from the shortcut menu to open the linked page in the same browser window.

Create a Link to Download a File

Depending on the content of your site, you may choose to provide files that visitors can download. For example, if you sell items, you might want to provide product manuals in a downloadable format rather than putting all the information on your web pages. If you sell computer hardware, you might need to provide updated drivers for your products.

To create a link that downloads a file, enter the absolute address or relative address of the desired file for the `href` attribute. For example, this code contains links to download two files (see Figure 5-3):

```
<h2>Files for Free Download</h2>
<p>We offer the following files for free download
(right-click and choose Save As):</p>
<dl>
<dt><a href="files/greener_composting_manual.pdf">
 <i>Greener Seeds Composting Guide</i></a></dt>
 <dd>A guide to creating compost that will reduce
 your garbage bill and boost your garden.
 (PDF file; requires Acrobat or Acrobat Reader)</dd>
<dt><a href="files/catalog.zip">
 <i>Greener Seeds Current Catalog</i></a></dt>
 <dd>Our current catalog, which contains details of
 all the products we offer, together with tips and
 special offers. (Zip file; requires Zip capability, such
 as that built into Windows XP or Mac OS X)</dd>
</dl>
```

Files for Free Download

We offer the following files for free download (right-click and choose Save As):

Greener Seeds Composting Guide
    A guide to creating compost that will reduce your garbage bill and boost your garden. (PDF file; requires Acrobat or Acrobat Reader)
Greener Seeds Current Catalog
    Our current catalog, which contains details of all the products we offer, together with tips and special offers. (Zip file; requires Zip capability, such as that built into Windows XP or Mac OS X)

Figure 5-3: When you provide files for download, it's a good idea to make sure the user knows how to download them rather than open them in the browser.

The exact name of the command for saving a file from a download link varies from one browser to another. For example, Internet Explorer 6 calls the command "Save Target As," while Mozilla Firefox and Netscape 6 call it "Save Link As." To cover both of these cases, and possibly others, we suggest that you tell the visitor to choose "Save As."

You can put e-mail links on as many pages as you like, but it's best to keep the number to a minimum so that you can easily change the links if you change your e-mail address (or if someone else takes over the responsibility for part of your site). Keeping all contact information together on a single page is often the simplest solution. Failing that, keep a list of each page that contains an e-mail link so that you can update them all when necessary.

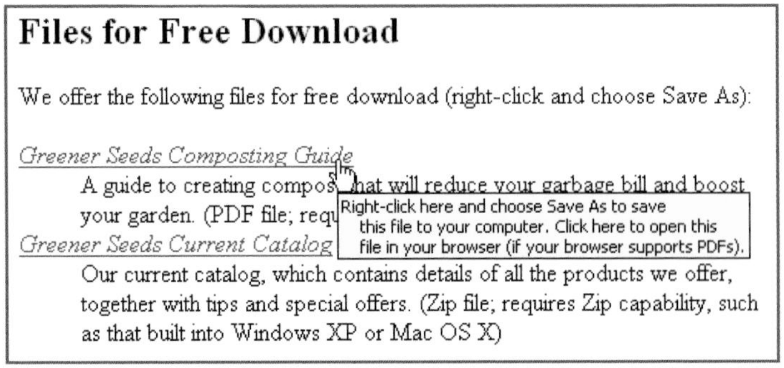

Display a ScreenTip for a Link

For some of your links, you may want to display extra information in a ScreenTip when the visitor hovers the mouse pointer over the link. To do so, add the `title` attribute to the link, and specify the text string that you want to display, as in the example shown here and in Figure 5-4:

```
<dt><a href="files/greener_composting_manual.pdf"
title="Right-click here and choose Save As to save
this file to your computer. Click here to open this
file in your browser (if your browser supports PDFs).">
<i>Greener Seeds Composting Guide</i></a></dt>
<dd>A guide to creating compost that will reduce
your garbage bill and boost your garden.
(PDF file; requires Acrobat or Acrobat Reader)</dd>
```

Create Links to Send E-Mail

To get feedback from visitors to your web site, you can simply list your e-mail address on your site (for example, on the Contact Us page, if you have one) and allow people to start messages manually using their e-mail clients as usual. Often, however, you can get better results by adding a link that automatically starts an e-mail message to the e-mail address you specify. This helps to ensure that the visitor gets the e-mail address right, eliminating the risk that he or she might mistype it. You can also include a subject line in the link. Provided that the user doesn't change the subject line in his or her e-mail client, you can then implement e-mail filters to pick out mail related to your web site.

Files for Free Download

We offer the following files for free download (right-click and choose Save As):

Greener Seeds Composting Guide
   A guide to creating compost that will reduce your garbage bill and boost your garden. (PDF file; requi~~Right-click here and choose Save As to save this file to your computer. Click here to open this file in your browser (if your browser supports PDFs).~~
Greener Seeds Current Catalog
   Our current catalog, which contains details of all the products we offer, together with tips and special offers. (Zip file; requires Zip capability, such as that built into Windows XP or Mac OS X)

USE TEXT OR A GRAPHIC TO SEND E-MAIL

A text link, such as that shown in the previous section, is the most straightforward means of enabling visitors to send you an e-mail. You can also add the `onClick` instruction to text or to a graphic if you choose. This example creates both a graphic e-mail link and a text link.

Figure 5-4: Use the `title` *attribute to display a* **ScreenTip of extra information when the visitor hovers the mouse pointer over a link.**

1. Enter some explanatory text for the graphic link so that the viewer knows he or she should click the link in order to start an e-mail message—for example:

```
<h3>Send Us a Customer Query</h3>
<p>Click the envelope icon to send us a customer query.</p>
```

2. Type an `<img>` tag that uses the `src` attribute to specify the graphic as usual, and specify `border="0"` to prevent the browser from displaying a blue border around the graphic to indicate the link—for example:

```
<img src="envelope1.gif" border="0">
```

3. Before the closing angle bracket of the `<img>` tag, add the `onClick` property with the details of the e-mail address and the subject (if desired)—for example:

```
onClick="location.href='mailto:customers@quicksteps.com?subject=
Customer Query'">
```

4. Add any explanatory text needed for the text link that will send e-mail, followed by the text hyperlink—for example:

```
<p>If you can't see the envelope icon,
<a href="mailto:customers@quicksteps.com?subject=Customer
Query">click here</a></p>
```

The complete code used in the example is as follows:

```
<h3>Send Us a Customer Query</h3>
<p>Click the envelope icon to send us a customer query.</p>
<img src="envelope1.gif" onClick="location.href='mailto:
customers@quicksteps.com?subject=Customer Query'"
 border="0">
<p>If you can't see the envelope icon,
<a href="mailto:customers@quicksteps.com?subject=Customer
Query">click here</a></p>
```

Figure 5-5 shows the icon and link created by the code.

Figure 5-5: When you use a graphic as a mailto hyperlink, it's a good idea to provide an alternate hyperlink in case the visitor is unable to see the graphic.

Send Us a Customer Query

Click the envelope icon to send us a customer query.

If you can't see the envelope icon, click here

CREATE AN E-MAIL BUTTON

To create an e-mail button, you create a button and set the `onClick` attribute's `location.href` property to send e-mail to the appropriate address. For example:

1. In the body of the web page, enter the opening tag for a button except for the closing angle bracket:

   ```
   <button
   ```

2. With the insertion point still placed after <button, type the `onClick` attribute with the `location.href` property:

   ```
   onClick="location.href=
   ```

3. Type a single quote, the `mailto` command, a colon, and the destination e-mail address:

   ```
   'mailto:webs@quicksteps.com
   ```

4. To add a subject line to the message, type a question mark, the word <u>subject</u>, an equal sign, and the text for the subject, as in the example here. (If you don't want to add a subject line to the message, skip this step.)

   ```
   ?subject=Address Change
   ```

5. Type a single quote, a double quotation mark, and the closing angle bracket:

   ```
   '">
   ```

6. Type the text you want to appear on the button—for example:

   ```
   Send an Address Change
   ```

7. Type the closing tag for the button:

   ```
   </button>
   ```

8. Save the page, switch to your browser, and refresh the display so that the button appears. The example button is shown at left.

9. Click the button to start a message in your default e-mail program (for example, Outlook Express or Outlook). Check that the address and subject are correct, and then close the message without sending or saving it.

```
Send an Address Change
```

MAKING USEFUL IMAGEMAPS

Should you need to, you can create highly complex imagemaps—but you must make sure that visitors to your site can immediately grasp the point of any imagemaps you put on your pages and that they can use them intuitively.

This depends both on the nature of the imagemaps and on how you use them. For example, if you needed visitors to choose which part of the world they were visiting from, you might use an image that showed the world and put in place imagemap coordinates that divided the map into the areas you required. Being familiar with maps, most users would quickly grasp that they should click the appropriate area of the map.

If, however, you displayed an image that showed different categories of merchandise, with an imagemap that linked each picture of a product to that product's page, visitors might have a harder time grasping the linkage unless the text made it explicit.

The full code for the sample button is as follows:

```
<button onClick="location.href='mailto:webs@quicksteps.com?subject=
Address Change'">Send an Address Change</button>
```

When this code is used and someone clicks it in a browser, the e-mail program will generate an e-mail message with the To and (if appropriate) the Subject line filled in and the body blank.

Create Two or More Links in a Graphic

Instead of linking a graphic to a single destination (such as another page or a `mailto` link), you can link different areas of the graphic to different destinations. A graphic with two or more different links is called an *imagemap*.

To create an imagemap, you place an image using the `<img>` tag as usual, and then use the `usemap` attribute to specify which imagemap to use. You then use `<map>` and `</map>` tags to define a map that consists of different areas, each of which is linked to a different page. The areas are defined by their coordinates from the upper-left corner of the image, which has coordinate 0,0. Each area can be a rectangle (`rect`), a circle (`circle`), or a free-form polygon (`poly`).

This example uses the graphic shown in Figure 5-6, which is 384 pixels wide by 254 pixels high. The graphic contains four distinct rectangular areas that are roughly the same size.

Figure 5-6: You can use a graphic with two or more distinct areas to create an imagemap with links to different pages from different parts of the graphic.

To create the imagemap:

1. Open the graphic in your graphics program, and use the program's selection tools to work out the coordinates of the areas you will need to define.

2. Type the `<img>` tag with the `src` attribute specifying the graphic file, the `alt` attribute specifying the alternative text (if desired), and the `usemap` attribute specifying the name of the map you'll create—for example:

```
<img src="veg2.jpg"
 alt="Picture of the vegetables (corn, split peas,
 chili peppers, and bell peppers) used in the recipe"
 usemap="#veg_map">
```

3. Type the opening `<map>` tag, and set the `name` attribute to the name you used for the `usemap` attribute of the `<img>` tag—for example:

```
<map name="veg_map">
```

4. Type an `<area>` tag with the `href` attribute specifying the destination page for the hyperlink, the `alt` attribute specifying the alternative text for the hyperlink (if desired), the `shape` attribute specifying the type of area (`rect`, `circle`, or `poly`), and the `coords` attribute specifying the coordinates of the area. For example, this code defines a rectangular area 192 pixels wide by 126 pixels high, starting at the upper-left corner of the graphic:

```
<area href="corn.html"
 alt="Corn"
 shape="rect"
 coords="0,0,192,126">
```

5. Enter `<area>` tags for the other areas in the graphic—for example:

```
<area href="chili_peppers.html"
 alt="Chili peppers"
 shape="rect"
 coords="0,126,192,254">
<area href="split_peas.html"
 alt="Split peas"
 shape="rect"
 coords="192,0,384,126">
<area href="bell_peppers.html"
 alt="Bell peppers"
 shape="rect"
 coords="192,126,384,254">
```

NOTE

You can also define areas in an imagemap by using the `shape` attribute and the `coords` attribute on the anchor (`<a>`) tag. In most cases, however, it is easier to use area tags to define the areas in an imagemap.

6. Type the closing `</map>` tag:

```
</map>
```

7. Save the page, switch to your browser, and then refresh the display so that you can see the change.

Figure 5-7 shows the page and imagemap produced by the sample code shown here:

```
<h1>Spicy Corn and Pepper Casserole</h1>
<p>This corn and pepper casserole is as tasty as it is colorful, not
to mention being great for you!</p>
<h2>Ingredients</h2>
<p>Click the picture to learn more about an ingredient:</p>
<img src="veg2.jpg"
 alt="Picture of the vegetables (corn, split peas,
 chili peppers, and bell peppers) used in the recipe"
 usemap="#veg_map">
<map name="veg_map">
<area href="corn.html"
 alt="Corn"
 shape="rect"
 coords="0,0,192,126">
<area href="chili_peppers.html"
 alt="Chili peppers"
 shape="rect"
 coords="0,126,192,254">
<area href="split_peas.html"
 alt="Split peas"
 shape="rect"
 coords="192,0,384,126">
<area href="bell_peppers.html"
 alt="Bell peppers"
 shape="rect"
 coords="192,126,384,254">
</map>
```

Figure 5-7: Using alternative text with your imagemaps gives visitors an idea of what they'll see if they click a particular part of the imagemap.

CREATING AN IMAGEMAP WITH PAINT SHOP PRO

Creating an imagemap manually takes some time and patience, not to mention some accurate typing of coordinates. You can automate the process by using a tool such as Paint Shop Pro. This automation is particularly valuable for creating complex imagemaps, such as those that use polygons.

To create an imagemap with Paint Shop Pro:

1. Click the **Start** button, click **All Programs**, click **Jasc Software**, and then click **Paint Shop Pro**. Paint Shop Pro opens.

2. Click the **File** menu, click **Open**, select the image that will serve as the backdrop for the imagemap in the Open dialog box, and then click **Open**.

3. Click the **File** menu, click **Export**, and then click **Image Mapper**. The Image Mapper dialog box appears (see Figure 5-8), showing the graphic at its top.

4. Either click the **Maximize** button to maximize the Image Mapper dialog box, or drag the dialog box's lower-right corner down and to the right to expand the dialog box so that you can comfortably see as much of the graphic as you need to.

5. Click the **Polygon** button (third from the left in the Tools toolbar), the **Rectangle** button, or the **Circle** button, and use the resulting cursor to define the appropriate area of the image. When creating a polygon, click to place the starting point, click to place each successive point, and then double-click to complete the polygon.

6. In the Cell Properties area, type the URL and any alternative text for the hyperlink.

7. Create further areas as needed by repeating steps 5 and 6.

8. In the Format drop-down list, select **GIF**, **JPEG**, or **PNG**, as appropriate.

Continued...

Add Audio and Video to Your Web Pages

As broadband becomes more widely available, the Web is an increasingly popular means of delivering audio and video to its potential audience. You can create links that allow users to download audio or video files, play audio or video files in a separate player, or play audio or video files within your web page.

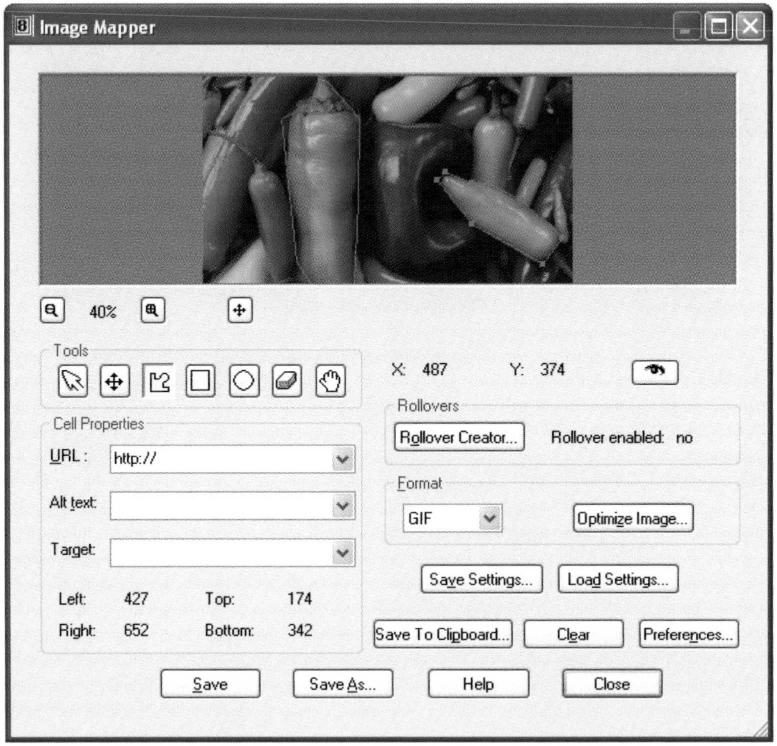

Figure 5-8: Paint Shop Pro's Image Mapper dialog box lets you quickly create complex imagemaps.

CREATING AN IMAGEMAP WITH PAINT SHOP PRO *(Continued)*

9. Click **Save**. The HTML Save As dialog box appears. Choose the folder in which you want to save the HTML code, type the file name, and then click **Save**. The Image Map Save As dialog box appears. Choose the folder in which you want to save the picture, type the file name, and click **Save**.

10. Click **Close** to close the Image Mapper dialog box, and then close Paint Shop Pro.

11. Switch to your text editor, open the HTML file you saved in step 9, copy the code for the imagemap, and paste it into its destination.

TIP

You can use Windows' built-in Sound Recorder application to save a WAV file to a compressed format that will take less time to download.

UNDERSTAND AUDIO AND VIDEO FORMATS

Computers use various audio and video formats, some of which are much more widely used than others. To make sure that as many visitors to your web site as possible can enjoy its audio or video, you must use a widely used format. You must also ensure that the file size of the audio or video is small enough that the file can be downloaded over even a dial-up connection.

Use compressed audio formats for all but the shortest audio files. Most computers can play MP3 files (which are compressed) and WAV files (which are not compressed). Also, consider reducing the complexity of the audio file—for example, by reducing it from a 16-bit sound to an 8-bit sound, or by using mono instead of stereo.

Video contains far more data than audio, so always use compressed formats for video—even for the shortest files. Most computers can play AVI (audio-video interleave) files, which offer modest compression, and MPEG files, which offer better compression. Most Windows computers can play Windows Media Video (WMV) files, which also use a compressed format.

Most digital video camcorders export video at VGA resolution (640 × 480 pixels). VGA gives great video quality but produces huge files. Reduce the resolution for video files you put on the web to 320 × 240 pixels for good quality, 240 × 160 pixels for medium quality, or 160 × 120 pixels for low quality.

UNDERSTAND AUDIO AND VIDEO DELIVERY METHODS

The easiest way to provide audio or video to visitors of your web site is to allow them to download entire files to their computers and play them when they want to. This approach has two advantages:

- People who download the files can listen to the audio or watch the video as many times as they like.

- Downloads work even over a slow connection (for example, a modem connection), provided the downloader has enough time and patience to download the whole file. By contrast, streaming video may require a broadband connection. (Some streaming technologies allow the client to download the entire stream before attempting to play it, while other technologies do not.)

Allowing downloads works well if you have full distribution rights for the audio or video files. If, however, you have only rights to play the files from your server, or to stream them, you will not be able to allow downloads.

CREATE A LINK FOR DOWNLOADING AN AUDIO OR VIDEO FILE

If you have audio or video files that you can legally offer for download (for example, music or movies that you have created yourself), create a link to the file, and instruct visitors to right-click the link and choose Save As (or the equivalent command, depending on the browser) from the shortcut menu to download the file. (If a visitor simply clicks the link, the audio or video file will probably play rather than be downloaded, although this depends on how the computer is configured.)

This example tells visitors how to download an MP3 file:

```
<p>To download Willa Moss' radio interview on choosing seeds,
right-click <a href="files/choosing_seeds.mp3"
title="Right-click this link and choose Save As to download the
file.">here</a>.</p>
```

CREATE A LINK TO PLAY AN AUDIO OR VIDEO FILE

To enable visitors to play an audio or video file, create a link to the file. This example links to the AVI video file named how_to_plant.avi in the files folder:

```
<p>Click <a href="files/how_to_plant.avi">here</a> to watch our How
to Plant video (AVI format, 2.4MB).</p>
```

When a visitor clicks the link, the default media player on his or her computer opens and plays the file. On a default configuration of Windows XP, the default media player for audio and video files is Windows Media Player.

TIP

You can use Windows Movie Maker, which is included with Windows Me and Windows XP, to change video resolution.

PLAY BACKGROUND AUDIO FOR A WEB PAGE

One popular use of audio is to play an audio file in the background when a visitor accesses the page. For example, if you create a web site for a rock band, you might use a short audio file of the band's music as a multimedia welcome to the site.

To play an audio file in the background:

1. Place the insertion point in the header of the desired page—for example, on a new line after the `</title>` tag.

2. Type the `<bgsound>` tag, including the `src` attribute and the absolute or relative address of the file—for example:

```
<bgsound src="files/welcome_to_site.mp3">
```

3. To make the audio file play more than once, add the `loop` attribute and specify the number of times—for example:

```
<bgsound src="files/welcome_to_site.mp3" loop="2">
```

4. Save the file, switch to your browser, load the page, and assess the effect.

EMBED AUDIO IN A WEB PAGE

Another option is to embed an audio player (as discussed in this section) or video player (as discussed in the next section) in a web page by using the `<embed>` tag. Doing this allows the visitor to control playback of the file and (for video) to view it in place on the page rather than viewing it in a separate application (such as Windows Media Player).

To embed audio in a web page:

1. Start typing the `<embed>` tag, and use the `src` attribute to specify the audio file you want to play—for example:

```
<embed src="files/choosing_seeds.mp3"
```

2. If desired, add the `width` attribute and the `height` attribute to specify the dimensions of the embedded player instead of letting it appear at its default size—for example:

```
width="350" height="40"
```

3. Type the `autostart` attribute and set its value to `true` if you want the file to start playing automatically when a visitor loads the page, or set it to `false` if you prefer to allow the visitor to start the file playing manually at his or her convenience—for example:

```
autostart="false"
```

4. Save the file, switch to your browser, and load the file to see the effect.

The following is a short example using an `<embed>` tag to embed audio in a web page:

```
<h3>Willa Moss Radio Interview: Choosing Seeds</h3>
<p>To listen to the radio interview, use the play controls below.</p>
<embed src="files/choosing_seeds.mp3" width="350" height="40"
 autostart="false">
```

Willa Moss Radio Interview: Choosing Seeds

To listen to the radio interview, use the play controls below.

If the computer is running Windows XP with Service Pack 2 applied and with default settings used, Internet Explorer automatically blocks pages with active content, such as embedded audio or video. When a visitor tries to access such a page, Internet Explorer displays a warning in the information bar. To see the active content, the visitor must click the information bar and click **Allow Blocked Content** on the resulting menu (as shown here) and then click **Yes** in the Security Warning dialog box.

EMBED VIDEO IN A WEB PAGE

To embed video in a web page:

1. Start typing the `<embed>` tag, and use the `src` attribute to specify the video file you want to play—for example:

```
<embed src="files/how_to_plant.avi" autostart=false">
```

2. If desired, add the `width` attribute and the `height` attribute to specify the dimensions of the embedded player instead of letting it appear at its default size. If you use these attributes, test them carefully to make sure that you've allowed space for the player's controls.

3. Type the `autostart` attribute and set its value to `true` if you want the file to start playing automatically when a visitor loads the page, or set it to `false` if you prefer to allow the visitor to start the file playing manually at his or her convenience. As with audio, you should specify `autostart="false"` if you don't want the video to start playing automatically.

4. Save the file, switch to your browser, and load the file to see the effect.

The following is an example using an `<embed>` tag to embed video in a web page (see Figure 5-9):

```
<h3>How to Plant Video</h3>
<p>To watch our <em>How to Plant</em> video,
 use the play controls below.</p>
<embed src="files/how_to_plant.avi"
width="320" height="280" autostart="false">
```

Figure 5-9: When you embed video in a web page, you can control the size of the video area and decide whether to start it playing automatically when the page is loaded.

How to...

- *Understand How Tables Work and When to Use Them*
- *Plan a Table*
- *Create the Table's Structure*
- *Add Rows and Columns to a Table*
- *Add Table Borders*
- *Group Cells by Rows and Columns*
- *Set Table and Cell Width*
- *Add Padding and Spacing*
- *Setting Table and Cell Height*
- *Align a Table, Row, or Cell*
- *Make a Cell Span Two Columns or Rows*
- *Apply a Background Color or Picture*
- *Create a Nested Table*
- *Create a Vertical Line*

Chapter 6
Creating Tables

Many technical books (including this book) use tables to lay out information in a clear and easily understandable format. You can use tables in this way in your web pages as well, but you can also use tables with invisible gridlines and borders for arranging the layout of the elements that make up pages. This chapter explains first how to create simple tables and then shows you how to use tables to create more complex page layouts.

Understand How Tables Work and When to Use Them

A table consists of cells made up of the intersections of rows and columns (see Figure 6-1):

- A *cell* is the basic unit of a table. A cell is formed by the intersection of a row and a column.
- A *row* is a line of cells running from left to right.
- A *column* is a stack of cells running up and down.
- The *border* is the rectangle that defines each cell and the outside of the table.

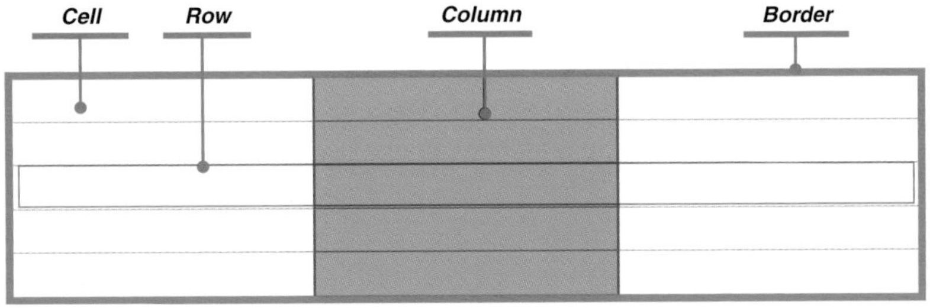

In a standard table, each row contains the same number of cells, and each column contains the same number of cells. Figure 6-2 shows an example of a standard table.

You can, however, change the layout of a table by *spanning*, or merging, cells together so that a single cell spans two or more columns, two or more rows, or both. Figure 6-3 shows an example of using a table for layout. The screen on the left, in which the table's borders are hidden, is how the page would normally be viewed. The screen on the right displays the borders so that you can see how the table is divided into cells.

Plan a Table

If you want to experiment with tables, you can start a table by entering table tags (discussed in the next section) in your HTML editor and placing content within the table cells. It's better, however, to start by planning how you want your table to look. Use any tool you find convenient—for example:

- Draw a rough sketch of the table on a sheet of paper.
- Use a graphical tool, such as Paint (click the **Start** button, click **All Programs**, click **Accessories**, and then click **Paint**), to create a mock-up of how the table will look.
- Use an HTML-capable word processor, such as Microsoft Word, to create a table; open the resulting file in a browser; and then copy the source code to your HTML editor for fine-tuning.

Figure 6-1: Each table has an outside border and rows and columns that create cells.

Code	Description	Type	Price	In Stock
4801	Eggplant, long green	Seeds	$2.99	Yes
4802	Eggplant, F1 Megadok	Seeds	$2.49	Yes
4803	Eggplant, F1 Bali	Seeds	$2.89	No
4804	Eggplant, F1 Green Ball	Seeds	$3.09	Yes

Figure 6-2: You can use a table to lay out information in a grid for easy reference.

Figure 6-3: Tables provide a way of controlling the placement of elements in a web page. When the table's borders are not displayed (left), it's not easy to see the table's structure (right).

Create the Table's Structure

To create a table, you use the following tags:

- The `<table>` tag marks the start of the table, and the `</table>` tag marks the end of the table. All the contents of the table go between these tags.

- The `<tr>` (table row) tag marks the start of each row, and the `</tr>` tag marks the end of each row. The number of pairs of `<tr>` and `</tr>` tags you use controls the number of rows in the table.

- The `<td>` (table data) tag marks the start of each cell within a row, and then the `</td>` tag marks the end of each cell. The number of pairs of `<td>` and `</td>` tags controls the number of cells in the row, and thus controls the number of columns.

To create a table, follow these general steps:

1. Open Notepad (or your HTML editor), and start a new web page. For example, if you have created a template file containing the basic structure of a web page, open that file and then click the **File** menu, click **Save As**, and use the Save As dialog box to save the file under a different name. Otherwise, create the basic structure of a web page manually:

```
<html>
<head>
<title></title>
</head>
<body>
</body>
</html>
```

2. Position the insertion point within the body section, and then type a starting `<table>` tag and a closing `</table>` tag:

```
<table>
</table>
```

3. Within the `<table>` and `</table>` tags, type the starting `<tr>` tag and a closing `</tr>` tag for each row. For example, to create two rows:

```
<table>
    <tr>
    </tr>
    <tr>
    </tr>
</table>
```

4. To create a cell, place the insertion point between the appropriate `<tr>` and `</tr>` tags, and then type a starting `<td>` (table data) tag, the contents of the cell, and a closing `</td>` tag. For example, to create two cells in the first row of the table:

```
<table>
    <tr>
        <td>Code</td>
        <td>Product Description</td>
        <td>Type</td>
    </tr>
    <tr>
    </tr>
</table>
```

5. Save the page, switch to (or start) your browser, and display the page. So far, you will see only the text of the table, as in this example.

6.

Code Product Description Type

Position the insertion point immediately before the closing angle bracket in the `<table>` tag, and then add the `border` attribute with the value `1` and the `border-color` attribute with the value `blue`:

```
<table border="1" bordercolor="blue">
```

7. Save the page, switch to your browser, and refresh the display. The cell borders are displayed, as shown in this example.

8. Using the technique described in step 3, create the cells in the remaining rows of the table. The following example shows the whole table with two further rows of cells added:

```
<table border="1" bordercolor="blue">
    <tr>
        <td>Code</td>
        <td>Product Description</td>
        <td>Type</td>
    </tr>
    <tr>
        <td>4801</td>
        <td>Eggplant, long green</td>
        <td>Seeds</td>
    </tr>
        <td>4802</td>
        <td>Eggplant, F1 Megadok</td>
        <td>Seeds</td>
    </tr>
    <tr>
        <td>4803</td>
        <td>Eggplant, F1 Bali</td>
        <td>Seeds</td>
    </tr>
</table>
```

9. Apply formatting to the cells, rows, and table, as discussed in the following sections, so that it looks the way you want it to look.

10. Optionally, add a table caption between an opening `<caption>` tag and a closing `</caption>` tag after the `<table>` tag:

```
<table>
<caption><b>Product Codes and Descriptions</b></caption>
```

Code	Product Description	Type
4801	Eggplant, long green	Seeds
4802	Eggplant, F1 Megadok	Seeds
4803	Eggplant, F1 Bali	Seeds

Product Codes and Descriptions

Code	Product Description	Type
4801	Eggplant, long green	Seeds
4802	Eggplant, F1 Megadok	Seeds
4803	Eggplant, F1 Bali	Seeds

TIP

To provide more information than the caption can accommodate, you can add a `<table summary>` tag to the table. The most convenient place is usually immediately before the `<caption>` tag. For example, `<table summary="This table provides the codes, product descriptions, and types of Greener Seeds' eggplant products.">`.

Add Rows and Columns to a Table

You can easily change the number of rows and columns in a table:

- To add another row, position the insertion point at the appropriate place (before, between, or after existing rows), and type another pair of `<tr>` and `</tr>` tags. Within these tags, type an opening `<td>` tag, the cell contents, and then the closing `</td>` tag for each cell you want to create.

- To add a column to a table, position the insertion point at the appropriate place (before, between, or after existing cells), and then type another pair of `<td>` and `</td>` tags with any content for the cell between them.

By default, each table has a grid pattern of rows and columns, so that each row has the same number of cells. For example, if you create two cells in the first row of a table, three cells in the second row, and one cell in the third row, as in the following example, the table will have three columns:

```
<table border="1" bordercolor="blue">
    <tr>
        <td>Cell 1</td>
        <td>Cell 2</td>
    </tr>
    <tr>
        <td>Cell 1</td>
        <td>Cell 2</td>
        <td>Cell 3</td>
    </tr>
    <tr>
        <td>Cell 1</td>
    </tr>
</table>
```

To change the grid, you make cells span two or more columns or rows. See "Make a Cell Span Two Columns or Rows," later in this chapter, for details.

NOTE

Use `border="0"` inside the opening `<table>` tag if you need to ensure that a table does not display a border—for example, when you are using a table to implement a precise layout in a web page. If you don't specify a zero-width border, some browsers may use an invisible two-pixel border, which can spoil the layout of your pages.

bordercolorlight   **bordercolordark**

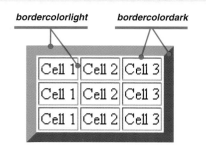

Figure 6-4: You can set different colors for the "dark" areas of table borders (shown here in blue) and for the "light" areas. Note that the dark and light positions are reversed for the cell borders.

TABLE 6-1: VALUES FOR THE frame ATTRIBUTE

VALUE	EFFECT
box	Displays the outside borders (same as `border`)
border	Displays the outside borders (same as `box`)
void	Hides all the outside borders
above	Displays the top border
below	Displays the bottom border
hsides	Displays the top and bottom borders
lhs	Displays the left border
rhs	Displays the right border
vsides	Displays both left and right borders

Add Table Borders

Each table has a border around its outside, and each cell has a border around it. You can set the border color for the table as a whole, and then set a different border color on particular rows or cells as necessary.

SET THE BORDER WIDTH

To set the border width for the outside border of a table, add the `border` attribute to the opening `<table>` tag, and specify the number of pixels for the width of the border. For example, to create a border five pixels wide around the table:

```
<table border="5">
```

SPECIFY THE BORDER COLOR

Specifying a border width without a border color makes the browser display the border in its default color, which is usually gray. To set the color, add the `bordercolor` attribute and specify the color to use. For example, to create a black border:

```
<table border="5" bordercolor="black">
```

Some browsers, including Internet Explorer version 5 and later, Mozilla, and Mozilla Firebird (after a fashion), support borders that use different colors for "dark" and "light" areas. To use different colors for dark and light areas, add the `bordercolordark` attribute and the `bordercolorlight` attribute to the opening `<table>` tag, specifying the appropriate color for each attribute. For example, to use the color blue for dark areas and the color cyan for light areas, as shown in Figure 6-4:

```
<table border="10" bordercolordark="blue" bordercolorlight="cyan">
```

CONTROL WHICH OUTSIDE BORDERS OF THE TABLE ARE DISPLAYED

To control which outside borders are displayed for a table, add the `frame` attribute to the opening `<table>` tag, and specify one of the values explained in Table 6-1.

TABLE 6-2: VALUES FOR THE `rules` ATTRIBUTE

VALUE	EFFECT
all	Displays rules around all cells.
none	Displays no rules.
groups	Displays rules around the horizontal or vertical groups that are defined. See "Group Cells by Rows and Columns," later in this chapter, for details.
rows	Displays all horizontal rules.
cols	Displays all vertical rules.

For example, to display only the top and bottom borders of a table:

```
<table border="10" frame="hsides"
 bordercolordark="blue" bordercolorlight="red">
```

To display only the outside border of a table:

```
<table border="10" frame="box"
bordercolor="silver">
```

CONTROL WHICH INSIDE BORDERS ARE DISPLAYED

To control which inside borders of a table are displayed, add the `rules` attribute to the opening `<table>` tag, and specify one of the values explained in Table 6-2. "Rules" are the lines or borders around the individual cells.

For example, to display only the horizontal borders within a table:

```
<table border="5" frame="box" rules="rows" bordercolor="green">
```

To display all the inside borders of a table but not the outside border:

```
<table border="5" frame="void" rules="all" bordercolor="purple">
```

Group Cells by Rows and Columns

The `frame` attribute and `rules` attribute of the `<table>` tag enable you to create many arrangements of borders in your tables. If you need more flexibility, however, you can use `rules="groups"` to put borders only on specific groups of rows and columns.

CREATE GROUPS OF ROWS

To create groups of rows, you split your table into a section of header rows, a body section, and a section of footer rows.

1. To create the header section, put an opening `<thead>` tag before the header rows and an ending `</thead>` tag after them.

2. Within the header section, you can use either `<th>` and `</th>` tags to create a table header or `<td>` and `</td>` tags to create standard table cells.

3. To create the body section, put an opening `<tbody>` tag before the body rows and an ending `</tbody>` tag after them.

4. To create the footer section, put an opening `<tfoot>` tag before the footer rows and an ending `</tfoot>` tag after them.

The next example shows a short table divided into header, body, and footer sections:

```
<table rules="groups"
    width="180"
    border="4"
    bordercolor="red">
    <thead>
    <tr>
        <td>Member #</td>
        <td align="right">First</td>
        <td>Last</td>
    </tr>
    </thead>
    <tbody>
    <tr>
        <td>1007</td>
        <td align="right">Jack</td>
        <td>Hobbs</td>
    </tr>
    <tr>
        <td>1008</td>
        <td align="right">Katja</td>
        <td>Mejia</td>
    </tr>
    </tbody>
    <tfoot>
    <tr>
        <td align="right">Member </td>
        <td>count:</td>
        <td>2</td>
    </tr>
    </tfoot>
</table>
```

Member #	First	Last
1007	Jack	Hobbs
1008	Katja	Mejia
	Member count: 2	

This HTML code produces the table shown here, with the `rules="groups"` statement producing borders across the rows in the groups defined.

To create groups of columns, you split your table by using the `<colgroup>` tag with the `span` attribute to specify which columns belong in each group. The following example shows a table with two two-column groups:

```
<table rules="groups"
    width="240"
    border="4"
    bordercolor="blue">
    <colgroup span=2></colgroup>
    <colgroup span=2></colgroup>
    <tr>
        <td>Employee</td>
        <td>Item</td>
        <td>Quantity</td>
        <td>Total $</td>
    </tr>
</thead>
<tbody>
    <tr>
        <td>Johns</td>
        <td>A384</td>
        <td align="right">48</td>
        <td align="right"> 480.00</td>
    </tr>
    <tr>
        <td>Bills</td>
        <td>C839</td>
        <td align="right">11</td>
        <td align="right">4492.00</td>
    </tr>
    <tr>
        <td>Acinth</td>
        <td>X420</td>
        <td align="right">88</td>
        <td align="right">6295.00</td>
    </tr>
</table>
```

Employee	Item	Quantity	Total $
Johns	A384	48	480.00
Bills	C839	11	4492.00
Acinth	X420	88	6295.00

This HTML code produces the table shown here, with the `rules="groups"` statement producing a vertical border between the groups of columns and no border between the columns that make up each group.

Set Table and Cell Width

If you don't specify the width of a table or the width of the cells in the table, browsers automatically fit the width of the cells to their contents (as in most of the examples shown so far in this chapter). The result is economical on space, but can produce crowded layouts, so it's often better to specify the table width, or the width of particular cells within the table, manually.

SPECIFY TABLE WIDTH

To specify the width of a table, add the `width` attribute to the opening `<table>` tag, and specify either the number of pixels (without a designation for pixels) or the percentage of the window width (with a percentage sign).

For example, to create a table 600 pixels wide:

```
<table width="600" border="1" bordercolor="gray">
```

To create a table that is 90 percent of the width of the browser window and that varies in width if the browser window's width is changed:

```
<table width="90%" border="1" bordercolor="blue">
```

SPECIFY CELL WIDTH

To specify the width of a cell, add the `width` attribute to the opening `<td>` tag, and specify either the number of pixels (without a designation for pixels) or the percentage of the window width (with a percentage sign).

The next example uses the `width` attribute of the `<table>` tag to set the width of the entire table to 90 percent of the width of the browser window. It then uses the `width` attribute of the `<td>` tags to set the width of the first cell to 200 pixels and the width of the second cell to 140 pixels. The `width` attribute is not specified for the third `<td>` tag, so the browser sets the width of this cell automatically to the remaining space (90 percent of the window width minus the space allocated to the first and second cells).

```
<table width="90%" border="1" bordercolor="blue">
    <tr>
        <td width="200">This cell is 200 pixels wide.</td>
        <td width="140">This cell is 140 pixels.</td>
        <td>This cell's width is set automatically.</td>
    </tr>
</table>
```

This cell is 200 pixels wide.	This cell is 140 pixels.	This cell's width is set automatically.

Add Padding and Spacing

Most of the example tables shown so far in this chapter have been tightly packed. This is because they haven't added any extra blank space between the contents of each cell.

HTML enables you to add extra space between cells in two different ways:

- You can use the `cellpadding` attribute to add padding between the walls of each cell and the cell's content. The default setting is 1 pixel. (You can also use a setting of 0 to remove all cell padding.)

- You can use the `cellspacing` attribute to change the width of the space between cells. Typically, you use `cellspacing` to increase the amount of space from its default setting, which is 2 pixels; you can also reduce the amount of cell spacing to 1 pixel or 0 pixels if you wish.

QUICKSTEPS

SETTING TABLE AND CELL HEIGHT

In addition to being able to set the width of a table or of the cells that constitute it, you may be able to set the height of the table or of its cells instead of letting the browser set the height automatically to accommodate the contents of the table or cells.

Most browsers (including Internet Explorer, Mozilla, and Mozilla Firefox) support setting the height of tables, but table height is technically not a part of the HTML standard, so you may find that some browsers do not support it. For this reason, it is best not to set the height of a table unless the design of a page absolutely requires a fixed height. Cell height *is* a part of the HTML standard and should work in all browsers, but setting it directly instead of using Cascading Style Sheets (CSS) is officially discouraged.

To set the height of a table, add the `height` attribute to the opening `<table>` tag, and specify the number of pixels. For example, to set the table height to 400 pixels:

```
<table width="300" height="400"
border="0">
```

To set the height of a cell, add the `height` attribute to the opening `<td>` tag, and specify the number of pixels. For example, to set the height to 100 pixels:

```
<td height="100">Tall cell</td>
```

You can also set the height of tables and cells by using CSS, which are discussed in Chapter 8.

For example, to create a table that uses 10 pixels of cell spacing and 10 pixels of cell padding:

```
<table border="1" cellspacing="10"
cellpadding="10">
```

Figure 6-5 shows the effect of changing cell spacing and padding on a table. 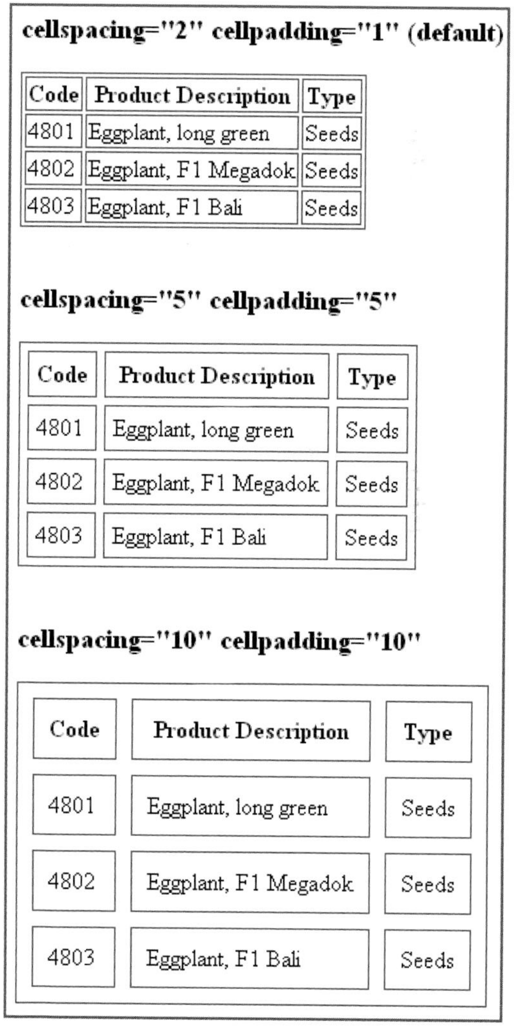

Figure 6-5: Cell spacing controls how far apart the cells are from each other. Cell padding controls how much blank space there is between the cell contents and the cell walls.

cellspacing="2" cellpadding="1" (default)

Code	Product Description	Type
4801	Eggplant, long green	Seeds
4802	Eggplant, F1 Megadok	Seeds
4803	Eggplant, F1 Bali	Seeds

cellspacing="5" cellpadding="5"

Code	Product Description	Type
4801	Eggplant, long green	Seeds
4802	Eggplant, F1 Megadok	Seeds
4803	Eggplant, F1 Bali	Seeds

cellspacing="10" cellpadding="10"

Code	Product Description	Type
4801	Eggplant, long green	Seeds
4802	Eggplant, F1 Megadok	Seeds
4803	Eggplant, F1 Bali	Seeds

Align a Table, Row, or Cell

To achieve the placement you want, you can align a whole table, a whole row, or the contents of individual cells.

ALIGN A TABLE HORIZONTALLY

You can align a table horizontally within a web page by adding the `align` attribute to the opening `<table>` tag and specifying `left`, `right`, or `center`, as needed. For example, to center a table on the web page that contains it (see Figure 6-6):

```
<table align="center" border="2" cellspacing="5">
```

ALIGN A ROW HORIZONTALLY

You can align the contents of a row within their cells by adding the `align` attribute to the opening `<tr>` tag and specifying `left`, `right`, `center`, or `justify`, as needed. For example, to apply justified alignment (where both the left and right edges of text are aligned) to a row:

```
<tr align="justify">
```

Figure 6-6: Instead of using the default left alignment, you can align a table horizontally on the page that contains it.

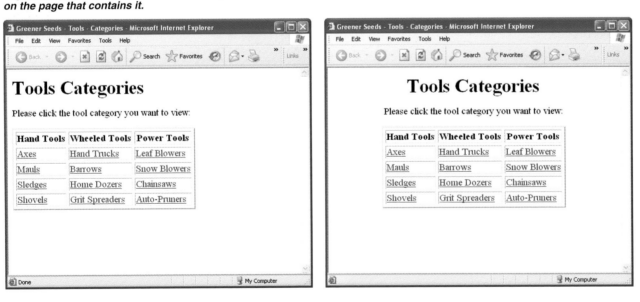

You can align a cell's contents horizontally by adding the `align` attribute to the opening `<td>` tag and specifying `left`, `right`, `center`, or `justify`, as needed. For example, the following code uses centered alignment in the third column and right alignment in the fourth column:

```
<table border="1" bordercolor="blue" cellspacing="2"
    cellpadding="4">
    <thead>
    <th>Code</th>
    <th>Product Description</th>
    <th>Type</th>
    <th>Price</th>
    </thead>
    <tr>
        <td>4801</td>
        <td>Eggplant, long green</td>
        <td align="center">Seeds</td>
        <td align="right">2.99</td>
    /tr>
    <tr>
        <td>4802</td>
        <td>Eggplant, F1 Megadok</td>
        <td align="center">Seeds</td>
        <td align="right">2.99</td>
    </tr>
    <tr>
        <td>4803</td>
        <td>Eggplant, F1 Bali</td>
        <td align="center">Seedlings</td>
        <td align="right">10.99</td>
    </tr>
    <tr>
        <td>4804</td>
        <td>Eggplant, F1 Assortment</td>
        <td align="center">Seed assortment</td>
        <td align="right">14.99</td>
    </tr>
</table>
```

Code	Product Description	Type	Price
4801	Eggplant, long green	Seeds	2.99
4802	Eggplant, F1 Megadok	Seeds	2.99
4803	Eggplant, F1 Bali	Seedlings	10.99
4804	Eggplant, F1 Assortment	Seed assortment	14.99

> **NOTE**
>
> The `baseline` value aligns the contents of the cells along the baseline, the imaginary line on which the bottom of a letter that does not have a descender rests.

> **NOTE**
>
> Vertical alignment applied to a cell overrides vertical alignment applied to the row that contains the cell.

ALIGN A ROW VERTICALLY

You can align a row's contents by adding the `valign` attribute to the opening `<tr>` tag and specifying `top`, `middle`, `bottom`, or `baseline`, as needed. For example, to apply top alignment to a row:

```
<tr align="top">
```

ALIGN A CELL'S CONTENTS VERTICALLY

Instead of applying the same vertical alignment to an entire row, you may need to apply different vertical alignment to the individual cells in a row. To do so, add the `valign` attribute to the opening `<td>` tag, and specify `top`, `middle`, `bottom`, or `baseline`, as needed.

The following example produces the table shown in Figure 6-7:

```
<table border="6" bordercolor="purple" cellspacing="2"
    cellpadding="2">
    <tr height="100">
        <td valign="top">Top alignment.</td>
        <td valign="middle">Middle alignment</td>
        <td valign="bottom">Bottom alignment</td>
    </tr>
    <tr height="50">
        <td valign="bottom">Bottom alignment</td>
        <td valign="baseline"><font size="+3">Baseline alignment
          </font></td>
        <td valign="baseline">Baseline alignment</td>
    </tr>
</table>
```

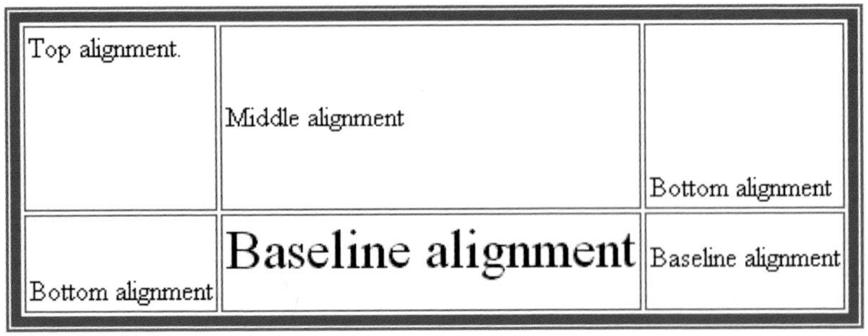

Figure 6-7: Use vertical alignment to control the vertical placement of text in a cell. Note how the two "Baseline alignment" examples are aligned on the baseline of the letters rather than on the bottom of the descender on the letter g.

Make a Cell Span Two Columns or Rows

Tables that use a regular grid are useful for presenting data in a tabular format, but to lay out a page with tables, you'll often need to remove some of the borders between rows and columns. To do so, you make a cell *span* two or more rows or columns—in other words, you merge the cells in two or more rows, or in two or more columns, into a single larger cell.

MAKE A CELL SPAN TWO COLUMNS

To make a cell span two or more columns, add the `colspan` attribute to the opening `<td>` tag of the cell in the leftmost of the columns involved, and specify the number of columns to span. If there are cells in the columns that will be spanned, delete them (if you don't, they will create extra columns in the table).

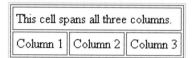

For example, to make a cell span three columns:

```
<td colspan="3">This cell spans all three columns.</td>
```

MAKE A CELL SPAN TWO ROWS

To make a cell span two or more rows, add the `rowspan` attribute to the opening `<td>` tag of the cell in the topmost of the rows involved, and specify the number of rows to span. If there are cells in the rows that will be spanned, delete them.

For example, to produce the cell containing the larger image in Figure 6-8 (shown with borders displayed), spanning two columns and two rows:

```
<td colspan="2" rowspan="2">
    <img src="images/logo_03.jpg" width="420" align="center">
</td>
```

Apply a Background Color or Picture

To make a table more colorful or distinctive, you can apply a background color or a background picture.

<td colspan="2" rowspan="2">

<td colspan="3">

Figure 6-8: You can span columns, rows, or both to create larger cells in order to produce the layout effects your web pages require.

APPLY A BACKGROUND COLOR TO A TABLE, ROW, OR CELL

To apply a background color to a table, add the `bgcolor` attribute to the opening `<table>` tag, and specify the color either by name or by hexadecimal code. For example, to apply yellow as the background color:

```
<table bgcolor="yellow">
```

To apply a background color to all cells in a row, add the `bgcolor` attribute to the opening `<tr>` tag. For example:

```
<tr bgcolor="black">
```

To apply a background color to an individual cell, add the `bgcolor` attribute to the opening `<td>` tag. For example:

```
<td bgcolor="blue">
```

APPLY A BACKGROUND PICTURE TO A TABLE, ROW, OR CELL

To apply a background picture to a table, add the `background` attribute to the opening `<table>` tag, and specify the path and name of the graphic file. For example, to use the graphic named gs_bg_01.gif in the folder named images stored in the same folder as the current web page:

```
<table background="images/gs_bg_01.gif">
```

To apply a background picture to a row, add the `background` attribute to the opening `<tr>` tag, and specify the path and name of the graphic file. For example:

```
<tr background="images/rowback1.jpg">
```

To apply a background picture to an individual cell, add the `background` attribute to the opening `<td>` tag, and specify the path and name of the graphic file. For example:

```
<td background="images/cauli_48.jpg">
```

Figure 6-9 shows part of a page that uses a background picture for the entire table and a smaller background picture for a cell in the final row.

TIP

When building a nested table, start by creating the table you'll nest as a separate table. When you've laid it out correctly and ensured that its size is right, cut it from its current position and paste it into the cell that will contain it. This approach is usually much easier than creating the nested table in its nested position.

Create a Nested Table

Spanning columns, spanning rows, or spanning both columns and rows gives you decent flexibility in laying out your tables; but if you must create a truly intricate table design, you may need to nest one table within another table.

To nest a table, enter the complete structure of the nested table within the `<td>` and `</td>` tags for the cell in which you want the nested table to appear. The next example creates the simple nested table shown here.

Table nested in a cell		Column 2	Column 3
Column 1		Column 2	Column 3

```
<font color="white" size="+2">
<table border="2" bordercolor="yellow" cellspacing="4"
    cellpadding="4" bgcolor="blue">
    <tr>
        <td bgcolor="green">
<table border="1" bordercolor="yellow" bgcolor="green"
cellspacing="2" cellpadding="2">
    <tr>
        <td>Table</td>
        <td>nested</td>
    </tr>
    <tr>
        <td>in a</td>
        <td>cell</td>
    </tr>
</table>
        </td>
        <td>Column 2</td>
        <td>Column 3</td>
    </tr>
    <tr>
        <td>Column 1</td>
        <td>Column 2</td>
        <td>Column 3</td>
    </tr>
</table>
</font>
```

Figure 6-9: You can apply a background picture to a table, a row, or a cell—or use different background pictures for different elements.

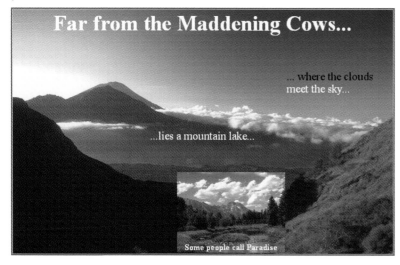

The next example shows part of the code for a nested table used to create the page shown in Figure 6-10, which includes a column of links on the left side for easy navigation.

Figure 6-10

```
<table border="0" cellpadding="3" cellspacing="4"
    bgcolor="#99CC00">
    <tr>
        <td><h1><font color="green">Greener Seeds</h1>
            </font></td>
        <td><h2 align="center"><font color="green" size="+3">
            Apple Varieties</font></h2></td>
        <td></td>
    </tr>
    <tr>
        <td valign="top">
<table border="0" cellpadding="3" cellspacing="3">
    <tr>
<th align="left">Name</th>
<th align="left">Type</th>
    </tr>
    <tr>
        <td><a href="apple_braeburn.html"> Braeburn</a></td>
<td>Eating</td>
    </tr>
    <tr>
        <td><a href="apple_bramley.html"> Bramley</a></td>
        <td>Cooking</td>
    </tr>
    <tr>
        <td><a href="apple_gem.html"> Winter Gem</a></td>
        <td>Eating</td>
    </tr>
</table>
        </td>
        <td><img src="images/cooking3.jpg" height="420"
            width="500"></td>
        <td></td>
    </tr>
</table>
```

Figure 6-10: This page uses a nested table to implement the Name and Type columns.

Greener Seeds	Apple Varieties
Name	**Type**	
Braeburn	Eating
Bramley	Cooking
Crispin	Eating
Cox's Orange Pippin	Eating
Egremont Russet	Eating
Jupiter	Eating
Katy	Eating
Lambourn	Cooking
Spartan	Eating
Sunset	Eating
Winter Gem	Eating

Create a Vertical Line

The `<hr>` tag (discussed in Chapter 4) lets you easily insert a horizontal line in a web page. To insert a vertical line, create a two-column table and specify `frame="void"` and `rules="cols"`, as shown in this example:

```
<table width="400" border="1"
  bordercolor="red"
  frame="void" rules="cols"
  cellspacing="0"
  cellpadding="10">
    <tr>
        <th valign="top" align="left"> Japanese</th>
        <th valign="top" align="left"> English</th>
    </tr>
    <tr>
        <td><i>Moshi moshi</i></td>
        <td>Hello (standard telephone greeting)</td>
    </tr>
    <tr>
        <td><i>Ohayo gozaimasu</i></td>
        <td>Good morning</td>
    </tr>
</table>
```

Japanese	English
Moshi moshi	Hello (standard telephone greeting)
Ohayo gozaimasu	Good morning

TIP

You can see that creating HTML tables can be laborious, especially when you nest tables within tables. A number of products, including Microsoft Office FrontPage, Adobe GoLive, and Macromedia Dreamweaver, allow you to create web tables directly in a What You See Is What You Get (WYSIWYG) environment, which is much easier. See *Microsoft Office FrontPage 2003 QuickSteps*, published by McGraw-Hill/Osborne, for details on Office FrontPage.

1 2 3 4 5 6 7 8 9 10

How to...

- *Understand How Frames Work*

- *Plan a Web Page That Uses Frames*

- *Deciding Whether to Use Frames in Your Web Pages*

- *Define Frame Height and Width*

- *Create the Component Documents*

- *Create the Frameset Document*

- *Lay Out the Frames*

- *Add the Component Documents to the Frameset*

- *Add Alternative Text*

- *Change a Frame's Borders and Margins*

- *Control Whether a Frame Scrolls*

- *Prevent Visitors from Resizing the Frame*

- *Nest One Frameset inside Another*

- *Create Inline Frames*

- *Create a Link That Changes the Contents of a Frame*

Chapter 7

Creating Frames

Frames provide a way of dividing the browser window into two or more separate rectangular areas whose contents you can supply separately. For example, you might create a frame in the left third of the window that contains navigation links, while the right two-thirds of the window display the content associated with the navigation link that the viewer clicks. By setting up the right frame's content to scroll independently of the left frame, you could enable the viewer to keep the links available on the screen all the time, even while scrolling down to the depths of the right frame.

Frames can make a powerful addition to your web tools, but they're not suitable for every page—or indeed for every browser. In this chapter you'll learn when to use frames (and when to avoid using them), how frames work, and how to create and use them in your web pages.

Understand How Frames Work

In the web pages shown so far in this book, the browser window contains a single rectangular frame, or area, that displays a single document. Frames enable you to divide the browser window to display different content in different areas of the browser window (see Figure 7-1), each of which displays a different document. Each frame can be either fixed in place or able to scroll independently of the other frames. Together, the frames used in a web page make up a *frameset*, a set of frames that are laid out so that they fit together.

Plan a Web Page That Uses Frames

A web page that uses frames consists of:

- A *frameset document* that specifies the frames involved in the frameset, how the frames are laid out and how they behave, and which document to display in each frame
- An HTML document for each frame in the web page

Begin the process of creating a web page that uses frames by planning how you will lay out the page:

- Decide how many frames you will use (for example, two frames, three, or more).
- Decide how to position the frames relative to each other. For example, a two-frame layout might have a shallow row at the top of the window with a deeper row below it, or a narrow column at the left side of the window and a wider column occupying the remaining space. A three-frame layout might have a shallow row at the top, a narrow column at one side, and a larger rectangle occupying the remaining space.
- Make a rough diagram, either on your computer (for example, in a graphics application, such as Paint, or a word processor, such as Word) or on paper, of your chosen layout. Include the dimensions that you will use for the frames (see the following discussion).

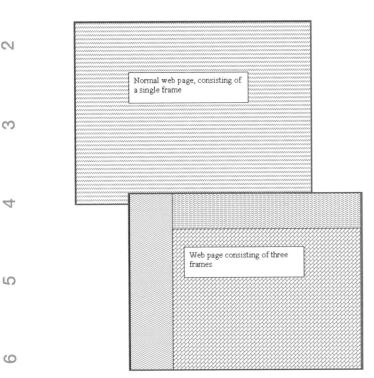

Figure 7-1: You can use frames within the browser window instead of displaying a single area.

The frameset document isn't displayed in the browser: it simply tells the browser which pages to display and how to lay them out. The title of the frameset document, however, is displayed in the browser's title bar as usual.

Define Frame Height and Width

You can define the height of a row and the width of a column. For either height or width, you can use either an *absolute* (fixed) dimension or a *relative* (variable) dimension. You can specify a dimension by using an exact number of pixels, by using a percentage of the width or height of the browser window, or by using wildcards to allocate any remaining space left after you've specified an exact width or height.

For most pages, your best choice is to use relative dimensions for your frames by specifying the percentage of space you want to devote to each row or column. For example, to create a two-column layout, you might allocate 25 percent of the space to the first column and the remaining 75 percent to the second column. If a visitor resizes the browser window, the columns resize so that they retain their proportions.

For some pages, you may want to allocate an exact amount of space to a particular frame and tell the browser to share out the rest of the available space among the other frames. To do so, specify the relevant dimension in pixels, and then use the * wildcard character to allocate the remaining space. The following example makes the first column in the frameset 200 pixels wide and then allocates all the remaining space to the second column:

```
<frameset cols="200,*">
```

CAUTION

Unless you know that all visitors to your web pages will be using a particular screen resolution (as might happen on a corporate intranet), avoid specifying exact dimensions for all the frames in a page. The danger is that visitors using different screen resolutions may have a hard time viewing your pages.

7

The next example makes the first row 150 pixels high and then allocates three-quarters of the remaining space to the second row and one-quarter to the third row:

```
<frameset rows="150,3*,*">
```

Figure 7-2 shows three examples using pixel measurements, percentages, and wildcards, respectively, to specify the width of columns.

200 (pixels)	200 (pixels)	400 (pixels)

Columns Using Fixed Widths in Pixels

25% (of the available space)	25% (of the available space)	50% (of the available space)

Columns Using Variable Widths in Percentages

200 (pixels)	* (1 share of the remaining space)	2* (2 shares of the remaining space)

Columns Using Fixed Widths and Wildcards

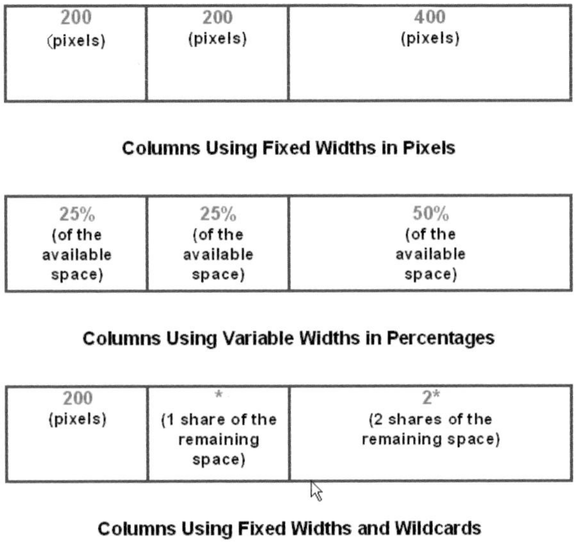

Figure 7-2: Using percentages (as in the middle example) or wildcards (as in the bottom example) gives greater flexibility to your frames than using absolute pixel dimensions (as in the top example).

Create the Component Documents

Create the component documents of the web page by using the techniques described in the other chapters of this book. Keep the following points in mind:

- Each component document should be a complete HTML page, starting with an `<html>` tag and ending with a `</html>` tag and containing a header section (within `<head>` and `</head>` tags) and a body section (within `<body>` and `</body>` tags).

- Design each component page to occupy the appropriate amount of space. For example, a column that will occupy only a narrow strip of the window should not contain any wide elements. Similarly, a row with a small height should not contain any tall elements.

- If the frame is resizable, it will usually be best to specify the size of any graphic as a percentage of the available space rather than using a fixed pixel size that may cause part of the graphic to be obscured when the size of the browser window changes.

- Although the titles of the component documents will not be displayed, you may want to add the `<title>` information anyway for the benefit of any search engines that visit your site.

Create the Frameset Document

To create a frameset document:

1. Open Notepad (or your HTML editor), and start a new web page:
   ```
   <html>
   <head>
   <title></title>
   </head>
   </html>
   ```

2. Position the insertion point between the opening `<title>` tag and the closing `</title>` tag, and then type the text you want to use as the title for the web page.

3. Instead of the opening `<body>` tag and closing `</body>` tag you would use for a standard web page, type an opening `<frameset>` tag right after the closing `</head>` tag and a closing `</frameset>` tag before the closing `</html>` tag:

```
<html>
<head>
<title></title>
</head>
<frameset>
</frameset>
</html>
```

4. Position the insertion point before the closing angle bracket of the opening `<frameset>` tag, and then type the details of the frameset. (See the next section for instructions on specifying the frameset.)

5. Position the insertion point between the `<frameset>` and `</frameset>` tags, and type a `<frame>` tag for each frame in the frameset, including the appropriate attributes for each frame. See the next section for instructions on specifying the frames.

Lay Out the Frames

You can create frame layouts that use rows, columns, or both.

CREATE FRAMES USING ROWS

To create frames using rows:

1. Create the skeleton of the frameset document as described in the previous section.

2. Position the insertion point before the closing angle bracket of the `<frameset>` tag.

3. Type the `rows` attribute; an equal sign; double quotation marks; the height of each row, separated by commas; and another set of double quotation marks.

For example, to create two frames, the first with a height of 200 pixels and the second occupying the remainder of the height of the browser window:

```
<frameset rows="200,*">
```

NOTE

Web pages that use frames are more difficult to troubleshoot than regular, single-frame web pages, because you must identify the component document that contains the error. If in doubt as to which component documents make up the frameset, open the frameset document, check its contents, and then open the appropriate component document.

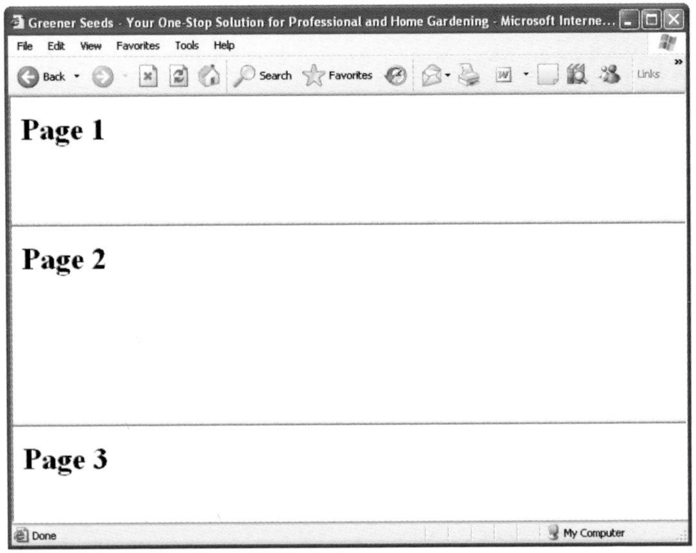

Figure 7-3: In a multirow frame layout, the component documents are arranged from the top to the bottom.

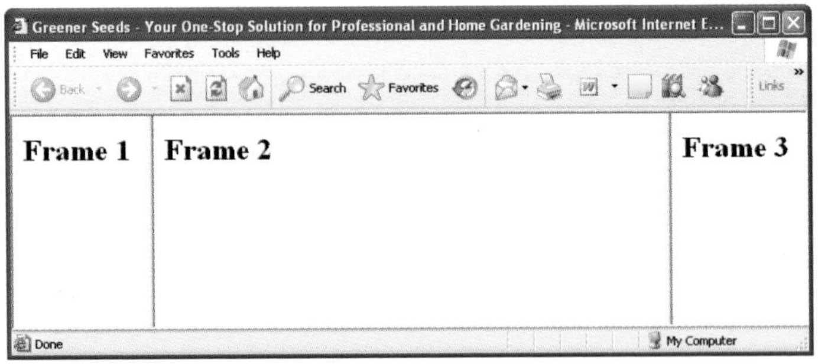

Figure 7-4: In a multicolumn frame layout, the component documents are arranged from left to right.

To create two frames, the first occupying one-quarter of the height of the browser window and the second occupying the remaining three-quarters:

```
<frameset rows="25%,75%">
```

To create three frames, the first with a height of 130 pixels, the third with a height of 100 pixels, and the second occupying the remainder of the height of the browser window (see Figure 7-3):

```
<frameset rows="130,*,100">
```

CREATE FRAMES USING COLUMNS

To create frames using columns:

1. Create the skeleton of the frameset document as described in "Create the Frameset Document" earlier in this chapter.

2. Position the insertion point before the closing angle bracket of the `<frameset>` tag.

3. Type the `cols` attribute; an equal sign; double quotation marks; the width of each column, separated by commas; and another set of double quotation marks.

For example, to create two frames, the first with a width of 175 pixels and the second occupying the remainder of the width of the browser window:

```
<frameset cols="175,*">
```

To create two frames, the first occupying approximately one-third of the width of the browser window and the second occupying the remaining two-thirds:

```
<frameset cols="33%,67%">
```

To create three frames, the first and third with a width of 125 pixels each and the second occupying the remainder of the width of the browser window (see Figure 7-4):

```
<frameset cols="125,*,125">
```

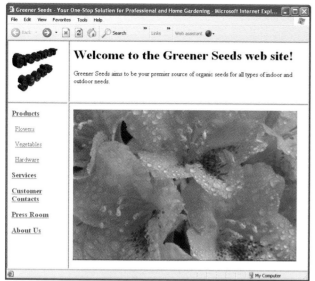

Figure 7-5: In a frame layout that uses multiple columns and multiple rows, the component documents are arranged from left to right and from top to bottom.

> The `name` attribute enables you to link other web pages directly to the frame rather than to the frameset document that contains it. If you will not need to link directly to the frame, you can omit the `name` attribute.

CREATE FRAMES USING BOTH ROWS AND COLUMNS

To create frames using both rows and columns, thus producing four, six, eight, nine, or more frames:

1. Create the skeleton of the frameset document as described in "Create the Frameset Document" earlier in this chapter.

2. Position the insertion point before the closing angle bracket of the `<frameset>` tag.

3. Type the `rows` attribute; an equal sign; double quotation marks; the height of each row, separated by commas; and another double quotation mark.

4. Type a space; the `cols` attribute; an equal sign; double quotation marks; the width of each column, separated by commas; and another set of double quotation marks.

For example, to create four frames in the arrangement shown in Figure 7-5:

```
<frameset rows="150,*" cols="150,*">
```

Add the Component Documents to the Frameset

To add the component documents to the frameset:

1. Position the insertion point after the end of the `<frameset>` tag, and press **ENTER** to start a new line. Type the beginning of the opening `<frame>` tag for the first frame:

```
<frame
```

2. Type a space, the `name` attribute, an equal sign, opening double quotation marks, the name for the frame, and closing double quotation marks. For example:

```
<frame name="page1"
```

3. Type a space, the `src` attribute, an equal sign, opening double quotation marks, the path (if necessary) and name of the web page to display in the frame, and closing double quotation marks. For example, to display the web page named page_1.html:

```
<frame name="page1" src="page_1.html"
```

4. Type the closing angle bracket for the `<frame>` tag:

```
<frame name="page1" src="page_1.html">
```

5. Press **ENTER** to start a new line, and then repeat steps 1 through 4 for each of the remaining frames.

NOTE

The alternative text does not appear when the web page is displayed in a browser that can handle frames, but a visitor can view the alternative text by displaying the source code for the web page.

Add Alternative Text

If a visitor is using a browser that does not support frames (for example, a browser on a handheld device or an old desktop browser), he or she won't be able to see the content of any page that contains a frameset. To let these visitors know what the problem is or to provide them with an alternative way of accessing the content, you should add alternative text to each frameset document.

To add alternative text, you place it between an opening `<noframes>` tag and a closing `</noframes>` tag between the `<frameset>` and `</frameset>` section of a frameset document. Figure 7-6 shows the example page produced by the following code in Opera with support for frames turned off:

```
<frameset rows="150,*" cols="150,*">
    <frame name="logo" src="logo.html">
    <frame name="mission" src="mission.html">
    <frame name="nav1" src="navigation1.html">
    <frame name="content" src="content.html">
    <noframes>
        <h1>Greener Seeds - Your One-Stop Solution
          for Professional and Home Gardening</h1>
        <p>This page uses frames, which either are not
          supported by your browser or are turned off
          in it.</p>
        <p>Click <a href="no_fr_home.html">here</a> to
          see a version of this page that does not use
          frames.</p>
    </noframes>
</frameset>
```

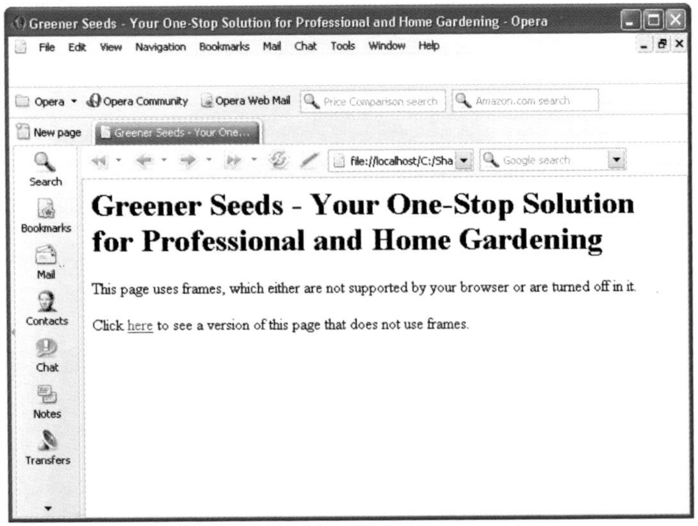

Figure 7-6: Most current and recent browsers support frames, but older browsers and some lightweight browsers do not. It's a good idea to include* `<noframes>` *text in your frameset pages to ensure that visitors without frames can learn what the pages contain.

The following code produces the complete frameset document with four frames shown in Figure 7-5 (earlier in this chapter). In the figure, the content fits within each frame and therefore doesn't display scroll bars. You can also prevent scroll bars from being displayed—see "Control Whether a Frame Scrolls" later in this chapter.

```
<html>
<head>
<title>Greener Seeds - Your One-Stop Solution for
    Professional and Home Gardening</title>
</head>
<frameset rows="150,*" cols="150,*">
    <frame name="logo" src="logo.html">
    <frame name="mission" src="mission.html">
    <frame name="nav1" src="navigation1.html">
    <frame name="content" src="content.html">
    <noframes>
        <h1>Greener Seeds - Your One-Stop Solution
          for Professional and Home Gardening</h1>
        <p>This page uses frames, which either are not
            supported by your browser or are turned off
            in it.</p>
        <p>Click <a href="no_fr_home.html">here</a> to
            see a version of this page that does not use
            frames.</p>
    </noframes>
</frameset>
</html>
```

TIP

When you use a frame to display a graphic, you'll often want to remove all the white space around the graphic. To do so, specify 0 for both the `marginheight` attribute and the `marginwidth` attribute.

Change a Frame's Borders and Margins

To make frames appear exactly as you want them, you can control whether they display borders and the width of their margins.

CHANGE A FRAME'S BORDERS

By default, a browser displays a border on each frame you create. (See Figure 7-5 for an example of a border.) Borders are convenient for when you want users to be aware that a web page consists of different frames—for example, when you use a frame to implement a navigation area that remains static while the contents of the other parts of the web page can move.

To remove borders from a frame, add the `frameborder` attribute to the appropriate `<frame>` tag, and set its value to `0`. For example:

```
<frame name="mission" src="mission.html" frameborder="0">
```

Figure 7-7 shows the sample page with all its frame borders hidden.

To ensure that borders are displayed on a frame, add the `frameborder` attribute to the appropriate `<frame>` tag, and set its value to `1`; however, because this is the default setting, there is no benefit to adding this to your code unless you want to make the code completely clear to anyone who needs to review or edit it.

CHANGE A FRAME'S MARGINS

To control the amount of space between a frame's contents and its margins, add the `marginheight` attribute and the `marginwidth` attribute to the `<frame>` tag, and specify a value in pixels for each attribute. For example:

- To set a margin of 10 pixels at the left and right sides of the frame:
  ```
  marginwidth="10"
  ```

- To set a margin of 15 pixels at the top and bottom of the frame:
  ```
  marginheight="15"
  ```

The following is a complete tag using `marginheight` and `marginwidth`:

```
<frame name="mission" src="mission.html" frameborder="0"
marginheight="10" marginwidth="10">
```

Figure 7-7: Hiding frame borders makes the layout of a frameset page less obvious.

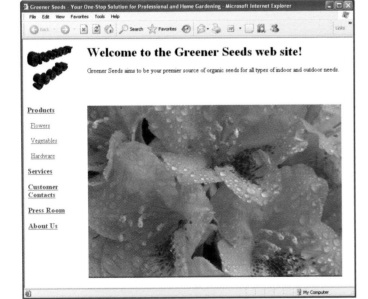

Bear in mind that the amount of space that the frame's contents occupy will vary depending on the settings that visitors have chosen in their browsers. If you prevent a frame from scrolling, the visitor will be able to view more of its contents by increasing the size of the frame—unless you prevent resizing as well (as described next).

NOTE

The `noresize` attribute for a frame does not take a value. Simply include `noresize` if you want to prevent a frame from being resized; otherwise, omit it.

Control Whether a Frame Scrolls

By default, each frame displays scroll bars if its contents are too large to fit in the frame at its current size; if, however, the contents will fit in the frame, the scroll bars are not displayed.

To control the scroll bars, add the `scrolling` attribute to the appropriate `<frame>` tag, and specify `yes` (to make the scroll bars always appear), `no` (to prevent the scroll bars from appearing, as in Figure 7-8), or `auto` (to apply automatic scrolling behavior). Given that there is little point in displaying scroll bars when they are not needed, you'll usually want to include the `scrolling` attribute only with a value of `no`; otherwise, the default setting (`auto`) is preferable.

Prevent Visitors from Resizing the Frame

By default, visitors can resize the frames on your web pages by moving the mouse pointer over the frame border. In most cases, leaving frames resizable is a good idea because it enables visitors to adjust any frames whose contents don't fit in the frame because of the settings on the visitors' web browsers. For precise layouts, however, you may want to prevent visitors from resizing one or more frames. To do so, add the `noresize` attribute to the `<frame>` tag—for example:

```
<frame name="logo" src="logo.html" noresize>
```

Figure 7-8: Should the need arise, you can set the scrolling *attribute to* no *to prevent visitors from scrolling a frame. In most cases, however, it is better to allow the default frame behavior, which is to display scroll bars when the frame content cannot be completely displayed in the frame.*

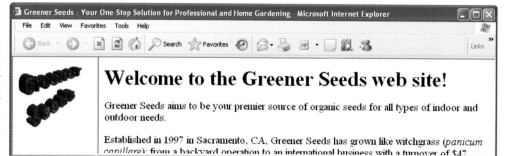

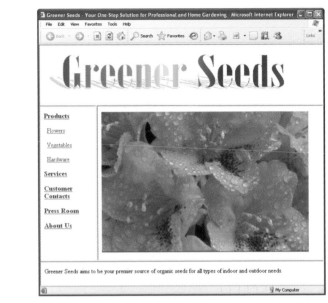

Figure 7-9: Nesting one frameset inside another enables you to produce frame layouts with varying numbers of rows and columns.

Nest One Frameset inside Another

To create more complex frame layouts, you can nest one frameset inside another. Figure 7-9 shows a nested frameset used to produce a three-row frameset in which only the second row is divided into columns.

The following example shows the code for the nested frameset that produces the layout shown in Figure 7-9. For conciseness, this example does not include the `<noframes>` information included in the previous examples; however, you would normally include `<noframes>` information in a frameset page:

```
<frameset rows="25%,*,10%">
    <frame name="contacts" src="logo_01.html">
    <frameset cols="150,*">
        <frame name="nav1" src="navigation1.html">
        <frame name="content" src="content2.html">
    </frameset>
    <frame name="mission" src="mission2.html">
</frameset>
```

Create Inline Frames

If you need to display a single frame within another web page, you can use an *inline frame*—one that appears as part of the page that contains it, without any other frames being involved. The advantage of the inline frame is that it enables you to place scrolling content within an otherwise static web page. For example, you might place a scrollable description in an inline frame alongside a product so that a visitor could scroll through the description without its occupying much space on the page. Similarly, you might place a series of graphics in an inline frame so as to let each visitor choose the graphic he or she wants (see Figure 7-10).

Figure 7-10: An inline frame lets you implement a scrolling box of content within an otherwise static web page.

CAUTION

Inline frames are suitable only for some purposes. One widespread use for which inline frames are *not* well suited is displaying an end-user license agreement for software: because the visitor can see only a small portion of the entire text at a time, the agreement becomes even harder to read than the smallest print of a tough contract.

TIP

If you want to center a frame horizontally and vertically in the web page, use align="middle" in the <iframe> tag, but also create the inline frame within a horizontally centered block of text (for example, by creating a center-aligned division using a <div align="center"> tag).

To create an inline frame:

1. Position the insertion point where you want to place the inline frame.

2. Type the beginning of the <iframe> tag:

   ```
   <iframe
   ```

3. Type the src attribute, an equal sign, double quotation marks, the URL of the web page that you want to display within the frame, and another pair of double quotation marks. For example:

   ```
   <iframe src="apples.html"
   ```

4. To specify the position of the inline frame relative to the next element in the page, type a space, the align attribute, and the appropriate value (see Table 7-1). For example, to align the inline frame to the left of the element in the page:

   ```
   <iframe src="apples.html" align="left"
   ```

5. To specify the height and width of the inline frame (rather than accepting default values, which may not suit your page), add the height attribute and a suitable value and the width attribute and a suitable value. Each value can be either a number of pixels or a percentage of the browser window's height or width. For example, to make the inline frame 150 pixels wide by 450 pixels high:

   ```
   <iframe src="apples.html" align="left" width="150" height="540"
   ```

6. To change the size of the inline frame's internal margins instead of accepting the default settings, add the marginheight attribute and a suitable value in pixels for the vertical margins, and add the marginwidth attribute and a suitable value in pixels for the horizontal margins. For example, to set horizontal and vertical margins of 5 pixels in the inline frame:

   ```
   <iframe src="apples.html" align="left" width="150"
        height="540" marginheight="5" marginwidth="5"
   ```

TABLE 7-1:
VALUES FOR THE
align **ATTRIBUTE**

VALUE	ALIGNS THE INLINE FRAME
left	With the left margin, allowing subsequent elements to flow to its right
right	With the right margin, allowing subsequent elements to flow to its left
top	With the top of the surrounding content
middle	With its center aligned vertically with the baseline of the surrounding content
bottom	With the bottom of the surrounding content

7. If you need to be able to refer to the inline frame using a hyperlink, add the `name` attribute and specify the name within double quotation marks—for example:

```
<iframe src="apples.html" align="left" width="150"  height="540"
marginheight="5" marginwidth="5" name="selector"
```

8. By default, each inline frame automatically displays scroll bars if its contents are too large to fit in the frame. If you want to suppress the scroll bars, add the `scrolling` attribute with the value `no`.

9. Type the closing angle bracket for the opening `<iframe>` tag and the closing `</iframe>` tag. The following example shows the complete code for the inline frame:

```
<iframe src="apples.html" align="left" width="150" height="540"
    marginheight="5" marginwidth="5" name="selector"></iframe>
```

Create a Link That Changes the Contents of a Frame

To create a link that changes the contents of a frame:

1. Open the frameset document that defines the frame, and then verify that the `<frame>` tag includes the `name` attribute. If it does not, add the `name` attribute—for example:

```
<frame name="mainframe" src="products.html">
```

2. If you made changes to the frameset document, save the changes. Then close the frameset document.

3. Open the component document that includes the link.

4. Add the `target` attribute and the name of the target frame to each link that should be opened within that frame. For example:

```
<h3><a href="content.html"
    target="mainframe">Products</a></h3>
<p>  <a href="flowers.html"
    target="mainframe">Flowers</a></p>
<p>  <a href="vegetables.html"
    target="mainframe">Vegetables</a></p>
```

5. Save the component document, switch to your browser, and test the links that you have just created.

How to...

- *Understand CSS Essentials*
- *Understanding the Style Cascade*
- *Create a Style Rule*
- *Understanding Other Ways of Creating Style Rules*
- *Create an Embedded Style Sheet*
- *Understanding CSS Versions*
- *Create and Apply an External Style Sheet*
- *Use Special Selectors*
- *Apply a Style to Part of an Element*
- *Override Style Sheets*
- *Control Font Formatting*
- *Set Alignment, Indents, Margins, and Line Height*
- *Overriding Style Sheets in Your Browser*
- *Prevent a Background Graphic from Being Tiled or Scrolling*

Chapter 8
Applying Formatting Using Style Sheets

Style sheets—known formally as Cascading Style Sheets, or CSS—are the preferred means of applying formatting consistently to your web pages. Unlike the HTML codes for direct formatting discussed so far in this book, which can be overridden by browser settings, CSS enable you to lay out web pages exactly as you want them: you can specify margins, indents, line spacing, font sizes, and more.

This chapter starts by discussing the basics of how CSS work and how you apply them. You will then learn how to write style rules, how to create style sheets, and how to use style sheets to implement widely useful effects.

8

NOTE

If you've created documents in a word-processing application, such as Microsoft Word, you've probably used document styles—a one-click means of applying a collection of formatting to a paragraph or another unit of text. For example, a style for a paragraph such as this might include 9-point sans-serif font with one-and-a-half line spacing and a yellow-shaded background. HTML styles work in much the same way.

TIP

Some older browsers don't support style sheets, and even current browsers don't all support style sheets in the same way. When creating style sheets, be careful to ensure that they're viewable on the vast majority of computers. This means not only checking them on Internet Explorer (the dominant browser, with more than 90 percent of the market), but also using a variety of screen resolutions and window sizes to make sure that all styled text is legible. No matter how attractive your site, few visitors will choose to return if they find the text too small, too faint, or the background too overpowering for comfortable reading and viewing.

Understand CSS Essentials

As discussed earlier in this book, much of the formatting that you can apply directly with HTML is either imprecise or can be overridden by the settings a visitor has chosen in his or her browser. For example, you can specify that a word or phrase be displayed in a font size two sizes larger than the default, but you do not usually know which size is being used as the default on a visitor's browser. Similarly, you can specify that a particular font be used, but it may not be installed on the visitor's computer—in which case, the browser will substitute a default font.

Styles enable you to apply consistent formatting to elements in your web pages. For example, by entering text between an opening `<h1>` tag and a closing `</h1>` tag, you apply the h1 style (or first-level heading style) to it. The browser displays all the instances of the h1 style using the same formatting. By defining different formatting for the h1 style, you can change all the instances of the h1 style in a web page.

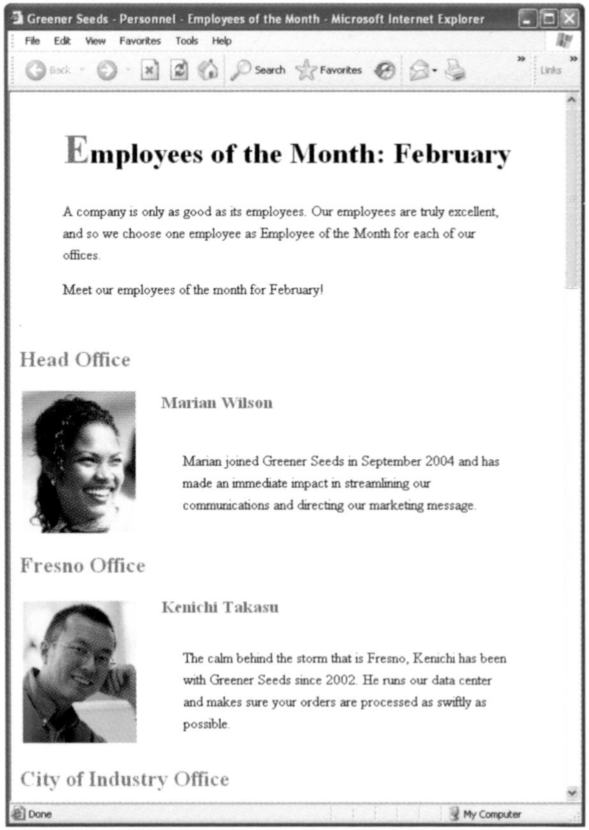

Greener Seeds - Personnel - Employees of the Month - Microsoft Internet Explorer

File   Edit   View   Favorites   Tools   Help

Back   •   ⌄   ×   🗘   🏠   🔍 Search   ⭐ Favorites   ⌄   🖉   •   🖨   »   Links   »

Employees of the Month: February

A company is only as good as its employees. Our employees are truly excellent, and so we choose one employee as Employee of the Month for each of our offices.

Meet our employees of the month for February!

Head Office

Marian Wilson

Marian joined Greener Seeds in September 2004 and has made an immediate impact in streamlining our communications and directing our marketing message.

Fresno Office

Kenichi Takasu

The calm behind the storm that is Fresno, Kenichi has been with Greener Seeds since 2002. He runs our data center and makes sure your orders are processed as swiftly as possible.

City of Industry Office

Done   My Computer

Figure 8-1: Style sheets not only simplify the layout and maintenance of your pages, but also enable you to create effects you cannot create via direct formatting.

UNDERSTANDING THE STYLE CASCADE

CSS are described as "cascading" because styles are applied at up to four different levels, with the properties flowing down from the top level and masking any duplicate properties in the lower levels. At the bottom of the cascade, the prevailing properties are applied to the web page:

1. The top level of the cascade is any style that is applied using the `style` attribute for a tag (see Chapter 3 for more information on the `style` attribute).

2. The second level is any style defined in a `<style>` element within the web page itself (considered an internal style sheet).

3. The third level is any style defined in the external style sheet (or style sheets) linked to the web page.

4. The fourth level is the settings that the visitor chooses in his or her browser.

These four levels give the following results:

- Formatting in an external style sheet overrides the visitor's browser settings.

- Formatting defined in an internal style sheet (a `<style>` element) overrides formatting in an external style sheet.

- Formatting applied to an element using the `style` attribute overrides formatting in both internal and external style sheets.

TIP

If you want an external style sheet to take effect and have the controlling influence, you cannot have internal style sheets (the `<style>` element) or use the `style` attribute in tags that conflict with those in the external style sheet.

Style sheets also enable you to apply some types of formatting—such as indents, line spacing, and precise positioning—that are either difficult or impossible to implement via direct formatting. Figure 8-1 shows a web page that uses a style sheet to implement indents and line spacing.

Style sheets enable you to specify exact formatting that overrides a browser's setting (unless the visitor has turned off style sheets or applied a style sheet of his or her own).

You can create a style sheet either as a part of a web page or as an external file that contains instructions. Using an external style sheet has the advantages of keeping the layout instructions separate from the content and enabling you to quickly apply style changes to all the web pages that use that style sheet; using an internal (or *embedded*) style sheet enables you to implement style effects only on that page, which can be useful in some circumstances. Even when you use an embedded style sheet, you save time on formatting: instead of needing to change every instance of a type of formatting throughout the page, you need change only the definition of the style, which appears at the beginning of the document.

The normal method is to create an external style sheet that you then apply to whichever pages need it; however, you can also create a style sheet within a web page in order to implement style effects only on that page.

NOTE

The *selector* is the part of a style rule that declares which markup element the style rule affects. For example, in a style rule that specifies that the h1 style have the color blue, h1 is the selector. The next part of the style rule, in this case, the color, is the *property* affected. The final part of the style rule is the *value* assigned to the property—in this case, blue.

NOTE

If the value includes spaces, you must put double quotation marks around it—for example, `font-family: "Arial Black"`. If the value does not include spaces, you do not need to put double quotation marks around it—for example, `font-family: Arial`.

TIP

You can place a semicolon at the end of the final value in a style declaration if you find doing so helpful for consistency. For example, the declaration `h2 { font-size: 20pt }` can also be written `h2 { font-size: 20pt; }` (with the final semicolon).

Create a Style Rule

Each internal or external style sheet consists of *style rules*, items that specify which markup element they affect and how that element should appear or behave. For example, a style rule might specify that the h1 (heading 1) style have the color blue and the font size 24 points.

To create a style rule:

1. Open the document in which you want to create the style rule:

   - For an internal style sheet, open the web page that contains it. Position the insertion point in the header area but not within a tag (see "Create an Embedded Style Sheet," later in this chapter, for more information).

   - For an external style sheet, open the style sheet, or create a new style sheet. (See "Create and Apply an External Style Sheet" later in this chapter.)

2. Type the selector:

   ```
   h1
   ```

3. Type a space, an opening brace, the name of the property you want to affect, and a colon:

   ```
   h1 {size:
   ```

4. Type a space and the value you want to assign to the property. For example, to make the font size 24 points:

   ```
   h1 {size: 24pt
   ```

5. If you want to specify another property for the same selector, type a semicolon, a space, the property, a colon, a space, and the value. For example, to make the font color blue:

   ```
   h1 {size: 24pt; color: blue
   ```

6. Repeat step 5 to add additional properties to the style rule. For example, to make the font Garamond:

   ```
   h1 {size: 24pt; color: blue; font-family: Garamond
   ```

7. End the style rule by typing a space and a closing brace:

   ```
   h1 {size: 24pt; color: blue; font-family: Garamond }
   ```

QUICK**FACTS**

UNDERSTANDING OTHER WAYS OF CREATING STYLE RULES

The section "Create a Style Rule" shows you what's usually the easiest way to create a style rule: specifying a single selector and then specifying each property you want to set for that selector and the value for the property, separating the property declarations with semicolons. You can, however, create style rules in two other ways.

SET ONE PROPERTY AT A TIME

If you choose, you can set a single property at a time. For example:

```
p { color: black }
p { font-size: 10pt }
```

The properties you set for a style are cumulative, so the style ends up with all the properties defined. The only advantage in setting properties like this is that your code is marginally easier to read even though it occupies more lines than if you had separated the properties with semicolons.

SET PROPERTIES FOR MULTIPLE SELECTORS AT ONCE

A technique you may sometimes want to use is to set properties for multiple styles in a single statement. To do so, separate each style from the previous style with a comma and a space. For example:

```
h1, h2 { color: blue ; font-family:
Arial }
```

This technique is most useful when you want to give two or more styles several of the same properties, but you can also use it to set a single property.

Create an Embedded Style Sheet

To create an embedded style sheet, you place the style declarations in the header of the web page.

1. In your text editor, open the web page to which you want to add the style.

2. Place the insertion point in the header section. Anywhere in the header section is acceptable provided that it is not within another element (such as the `<title>` and `</title>` tags), but your pages will be easier to edit if you use a consistent location—for example, directly after the closing `</title>` tag or immediately before the closing `</head>` tag.

3. Type the opening `<style>` tag. Include the `type` attribute and set its value to `text/css`:

```
<style type="text/css">
```

4. Press **ENTER** to start a new line, and then type the definition for the style. For example:

```
h1 { font-family: Garamond }
```

5. Repeat step 4 for each additional style rule you want to create.

6. Press **ENTER** to start a new line, and then type the closing `</style>` tag:

```
</style>
```

NOTE

You can use two or more pairs of `<style>` and `</style>` tags if you prefer, but in most cases it's easier and clearer to use only a single pair.

QUICKFACTS

UNDERSTANDING CSS VERSIONS

At this writing (fall 2004), version 2.1 of the CSS specification (CSS 2.1) is due to be released shortly. CSS 2.1 is an update to CSS 2, which added substantial capabilities to CSS 1:

- CSS 1 enables you to control major elements, such as the font (size, color, and type), how lists are displayed, margins and borders, alignment, line spacing, and background graphics and background colors.

- CSS 2 improves font support, provides more control over positioning objects, and enables you to control tables. CSS 2 also includes text-to-speech capabilities.

- CSS 3 is in development at this writing.

Most current and recent browsers can handle CSS 2 elements, but some browsers do not handle all CSS 2 elements properly. You do not need to specify the CSS version that you are using in your web pages, but you should be aware that elements added more recently to CSS may not work properly in all browsers. The easiest way to identify problems is to test your web pages in several browsers and make sure that they are displayed correctly. At a minimum, you must test every page using Internet Explorer, since it dominates the browser market.

NOTE

When saving a file for the first time with Notepad, remember to enclose the file name and extension within double quotation marks (for example, "standard.css") to prevent Notepad from adding its default .txt extension to the name.

Create and Apply an External Style Sheet

To use an external style sheet, you create it as a separate file in your text editor or HTML editor, and then link to it each web page for which you want to use the style sheet.

CREATE AN EXTERNAL STYLE SHEET

To create an external style sheet:

1. Open Notepad (or your HTML editor), and start a new document.

2. Optionally, on the first line of the style sheet, type a comment explaining what the style sheet is and what it is for. To create a comment in a style sheet, type a forward slash, an asterisk, a space, the text of the comment, another space, another asterisk, and another forward slash. For example:

   ```
   /* Greener Seeds standard style sheet, standard.css */
   ```

3. Type the definition for each style you want to include in the style sheet. For example:

   ```
   h1 { color: green; font-size: 24pt; font-weight: bold }
   h2 { color: olive; font-size: 18pt; font-weight: bold }
   h3 { color: #339900; font-size: 14pt; font-weight: bold }
   p {font-size:14pt ; color: black }
   ```

4. Click the **File** menu, click **Save**, and then save the style sheet with the .css extension. (You can also use other extensions, but using .css is clearest.)

5. Click the **File** menu and then click **Exit** to exit Notepad.

LINK A WEB PAGE TO AN EXTERNAL STYLE SHEET

After creating the external style sheet you want to use, link your web pages to it.

1. Open the web page that you want to link to the style sheet.

2. Position the insertion point within the header section of the web page. Anywhere in the header section will work, but your pages will be easier to edit if you use a consistent location—for example, immediately before the closing `</head>` tag.

3. Type the start of a `<link>` tag, specifying the `rel` attribute (which specifies the relationship of the link) with the value `stylesheet` and the `type` attribute with the value `text/css`:

   ```
   <link rel="stylesheet" type="text/css"
   ```

4. Type the `href` attribute and assign to it the path (if required) and file name of the external style sheet. For example:

```
href="styles/standard.css"
```

5. Finish the link by typing a space, a forward slash, and the closing angle bracket:

```
href="styles/standard.css" />
```

The following example shows the entire link in the header section of a web page:

```
<head>
<title>Greener Seeds - Corporate Information</title>
<link rel="stylesheet" type="text/css"
    href="styles/standard.css" />
</head>
<body>
```

Figure 8-2 provides a quick demonstration of the effect of linking a style sheet to a web page.

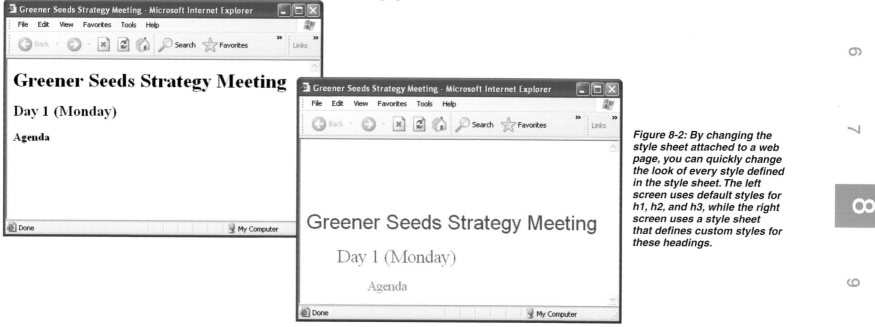

Figure 8-2: By changing the style sheet attached to a web page, you can quickly change the look of every style defined in the style sheet. The left screen uses default styles for h1, h2, and h3, while the right screen uses a style sheet that defines custom styles for these headings.

NOTE

This example assumes that the style sheet is on the same web server as the web page that is being linked to it. (The style sheet is in the /styles/ folder.) You can also link to a style sheet on another server if necessary; to do so, assign the full URL of the style sheet to the `href` attribute of the `<link>` tag. Bear in mind that keeping the style sheet on the same server as your web pages may help to avoid performance issues.

TIP

When you apply two or more style sheets to the same page, you must understand how the style cascade works so that you can achieve the style effects you want. (See the QuickFacts "Understanding the Style Cascade," earlier in this chapter, for details of the cascade.) When you're starting with style sheets, link only a single style sheet to a web page to avoid these complexities.

TIP

You can *validate*, or check the correctness of, an external style sheet by using the free W3C CSS Validation Service at http://jigsaw.w3.org/css-validator/.

Instead of linking a single style sheet to a web page, you can link two or more style sheets to the same page. Two common reasons for doing this are:

- The web page uses some styles that are contained in one of the style sheets and some styles that are contained in another style sheet. Instead of integrating all the styles into a third comprehensive style sheet, you can apply both the style sheets to achieve full coverage of the styles.

- The second style sheet redefines some of the styles used in the first style sheet to produce web pages with a similar yet slightly different appearance. For example, an organization or company might use a global style sheet that produces the general look for all web pages. Each office or department then might apply a second style sheet to adapt the global style sheet to meet their needs, producing a different look for each office's or department's pages.

The following example shows two style sheets applied to a document. The second style sheet (marketing.css) overrides the first style sheet (standard.css) because it is listed after the first style sheet:

```
<head>
<title>Greener Seeds - Corporate Information</title>
<link rel="stylesheet" type="text/css"
    href="styles/standard.css" />
<link rel="stylesheet" type="text/css"
    href="styles/marketing.css" />
</head>
```

Use Special Selectors

Up to this point, this chapter has used HTML tags as the selectors for style rules—for example, to create a style rule that applies to h1 elements. For flexibility, however, HTML also enables you to use other items—such as the `id` attribute, the `class` attribute, and the `<div>` and `<span>` types—as the selectors for style rules.

USE THE ID ATTRIBUTE AS A SELECTOR

If you need to pick out a single instance of an element from all the other instances, add the `id` attribute to it in the web page, and assign it a unique identifying value that starts with a letter. This example assigns the value `m41` to the heading:

```
<h2 id="m41">Breaking News</h2>
```

Once the item is marked with the `id` attribute, you can specify in the style sheet how to format the item. To do so, type a hash mark (#) followed by the ID value, a space, and the style information within braces. For example, to apply red formatting and 28-point font size to the m41 item created previously:

```
#m41 { font-size: 28pt; color: red }
```

USE THE CLASS ATTRIBUTE AS A SELECTOR

Sometimes, it can be useful to distinguish different types of items that are formatted as the same element. For example, your web pages might include various types of content formatted as paragraphs (entered between `<p>` and `</p>` tags) and various types of content formatted as second-level headings (entered between `<h2>` and `</h2>` tags).

To distinguish between different types of content formatted as the same element, you can use the `class` attribute to assign a particular description to the desired instances of the element. For example, you might create a class named "special_offers" so that you could apply different formatting to only the items in that class.

To create the class, on a new line in your style sheet, type a period, the name you want to assign to the class, and the style information for the class. For example, to make the special_offers class extra-large and a purple font:

```
special_offers {color: purple; font-size: x-large }
```

NOTE

A class can apply either to a single element or to multiple elements. By applying a class to multiple elements, you can use it to format disparate elements in a similar way. For example, you might want to display all the information related to the special_offers class in a bright color to increase its visibility.

Figure 8-3: By using the `class` attribute as a selector, you can apply formatting to different elements at the same time.

To apply the class to an element in a web page, add the `class` attribute to the element's opening tag, and specify the name of the class. For example:

```
<h2 class="special_offers">Latest Special Offers</h2>

<p class="special_offers">Here are our most popular special offers.</p>
<ol>
    <li class="special_offers">Aquatic Pumpkin</li>
    <li class="special_offers">200-Yard Garden Hose</li>
    <li class="special_offers">Collapsible Lean-To
Greenhouse</li>
    <li class="special_offers">Russet Delicious</li>
    <li class="special_offers">Broad-Leaf Cilantro</li>
</ol>
```

Figure 8-3 shows the effect of applying the `class` attribute with the previous formatting.

USE A SPAN AS A SELECTOR

A *span* is a flexible unit that you can use to select text within an element so that you can apply formatting to it. To create a span:

1. In your style sheet, create the class, if it does not already exist. For example:

   ```
   .special_offers {color: green; font-size: large;
       font-weight: bold }
   ```

2. In Notepad or your HTML editor, open the web page in which you want to create the span.

3. Position the insertion point before the desired text.

4. Type the opening `<span>` tag, including the `class` attribute and specifying the name of the class you want to apply to the span. For example, to apply the class named special_offers:

   ```
   <span class="special_offers">Special Offers
   ```

5. Position the insertion point at the end of the desired text, and then type the closing `</span>` tag:

   ```
   </span>
   ```

The following example shows the complete paragraph containing the span:

```
<p>For information about more of our
   <span class="special_offers">Special Offers</span>,
   click <a href="special_offers.html">here</a>.</p>
```

For information about more of our **Special Offers**, click <u>here</u>.

USE A DIVISION AS A SELECTOR

As discussed in Chapter 3, you can use the `<div>` and `</div>` tags to group paragraphs (or other elements) into a division so that you can manipulate them all together. You can apply styles to a division directly (by adding the style information to the opening `<div>` tag) or via either an internal style sheet or an external style sheet. Using an external style sheet gives the greatest flexibility because you can change the formatting of all the divisions in your web pages by simply changing the relevant style rules in your style sheets.

Instead of applying the `class` attribute to each of the elements to which you want to apply the special_offers formatting, you could create a division around the elements and apply the `class` attribute to the division. The following example (which also produces the effect shown in Figure 8-3) shows how to do this:

```
<div class="special_offers">
<h2>Latest Special Offers</h2>
<p>Here are our most popular special offers.</p>
<ol>
    <li>Aquatic Pumpkin</li>
    <li>200-Yard Garden Hose</li>
    <li>Collapsible Lean-To Greenhouse</li>
    <li>Russet Delicious</li>
    <li>Broad-Leaf Cilantro</li>
</ol>
</div>
```

TIP

You can use a span to apply font formatting to individual words or phrases in your documents without using the `<font>` tag. The advantage of using spans is that you can change them all centrally from your style sheet instead of having to change each instance of the formatting in the individual web pages.

NOTE

This example assumes that you have created the class named special_offers in the external style sheet attached to the web page, as described in "Use the Class Attribute as a Selector," earlier in this chapter.

Apply a Style to Part of an Element

You can apply a style to only part of an element rather than to a full element by using *pseudo-elements*, logically defined parts of elements. You don't need to tag the pseudo-element in your code: the browser identifies them on its own accord.

FORMAT THE FIRST LETTER OF AN ELEMENT

Sometimes you may find it useful to apply different formatting to the first letter in an element. To do so, define a style rule for the `first-letter` pseudo-element of the desired element.

1. In your style sheet, type the style name, a colon, and then <u>first-letter</u>. For example:

   ```
   h1:first-letter
   ```

2. Type a space and then the details of the style rule for the first letter. For example:

   ```
   h1:first-letter { font-size: 36pt; color: green}
   ```

Again, you do not have to make any changes on the web page itself, only in your style sheet. The following illustration shows an example of the effect produced.

We Care about Our Customers

FORMAT THE FIRST LINE OF AN ELEMENT

You can apply different formatting to the first line of an element by adding the `:first-line` pseudo-element to a style sheet. The following example, which you would place in either an internal style sheet or an external style sheet, makes the first line of each paragraph (p) green. Figure 8-4 shows the effect.

```
p {font-size:14pt ; color: black;}
p:first-line { color: green }
```

Figure 8-4: You can use the `:first-line` *pseudo-element to make the first line of each instance of an element pop out. The formatting applies to the first line no matter what size of browser window the page is displayed in.*

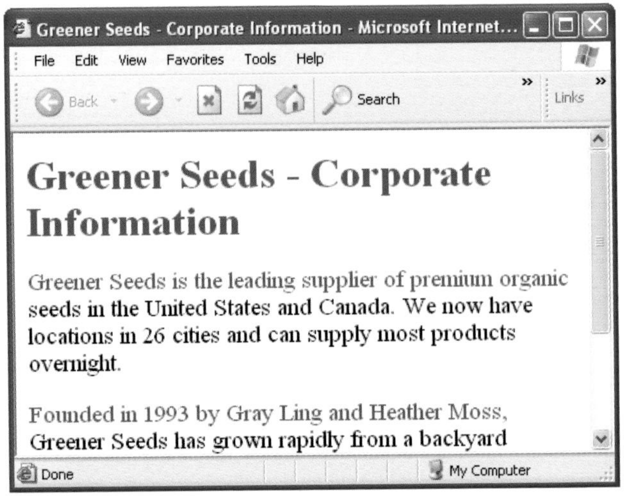

Override Style Sheets

If you're creating a web site and want to implement a consistent look across it, you should use external style sheets rather than internal style sheets. External style sheets will save you considerable time and effort in keeping your web pages up-to-date with your latest styles.

Sometimes, however, you may want to override an external style sheet by using an internal style sheet to apply one or more styles to a web page. You can use the external style sheet to implement the general look of your web site, and then use an internal style sheet to change one or more specific elements on a particular web page.

Beyond overriding the external style sheet by using an internal style sheet, you may sometimes need to override the internal style sheet as well. As discussed in Chapter 3, you can use the `style` attribute to apply formatting to an element. Any formatting you apply this way overrides any formatting applied using an internal style sheet, which in turn overrides any formatting applied using an external style sheet.

CAUTION

The `blink` value does not work in Internet Explorer and can quickly become irritating to visitors using those browsers that do support it. For this reason, it is best not to use `blink`.

Control Font Formatting

To control font formatting in style sheets, you can use either the individual properties explained in Table 8-1 or the all-encompassing `font` property.

TABLE 8-1: INDIVIDUAL FONT PROPERTIES FOR FORMATTING TEXT

PROPERTY	EXPLANATION	VALUES OR EXAMPLES
background-color	The background color to apply	navy, magenta, #CCFFFF
color	The font color to apply	red, blue, #993333
font-family	The name of the font family	Georgia, "Times New Roman"
font-size	A font size measured in points	12pt, 18pt
font-style	The style: normal, italic, or oblique (slanted)	normal, italic, oblique
font-variant	Whether to use normal letters or small caps	normal, small-caps
font-weight	How bold the font is	lighter, normal, bold, bolder
text-decoration	Whether to apply decoration to the text	none, blink, underline, overline, line-through
text-transform	Whether to apply consistent capitalization to the text	none, capitalize (initial capitals), lowercase, uppercase

1. *AQUATIC PUMPKIN*
2. *200-YARD GARDEN HOSE*
3. *COLLAPSIBLE LEAN-TO GREENHOUSE*
4. *RUSSET DELICIOUS*
5. *BROAD-LEAF CILANTRO*

1. *AQUATIC PUMPKIN*
2. *200-YARD GARDEN HOSE*
3. *COLLAPSIBLE LEAN-TO GREENHOUSE*
4. *RUSSET DELICIOUS*
5. *BROAD-LEAF CILANTRO*

For example, the following style, applied inline, produces text in 36-point boldface using small caps:

```
<p style="font-weight: bold; font-variant: small-caps;
    font-size: 36pt; color: blue">36-point Bold Small Caps</p>
```

The following style, entered in a style sheet, makes ordered (numbered) lists appear in maroon, italic uppercase:

```
ol { color: maroon; font-style: italic;
    text-transform: uppercase }
```

The font property has a fixed syntax that enables you to specify each of the values you want to set within a single property. The syntax, shown with vertical bars indicating the divisions between values, is as follows (the vertical bars are not used in the actual code):

```
font: style | weight | variant | size or line-height | font-family
```

The following style rule, entered in a style sheet, makes h3 elements appear in bold, italic, 24-point small capitals in the Times New Roman font:

```
h3 { font: italic bold small-caps 24pt "Times New Roman" }
```

Set Alignment, Indents, Margins, and Line Height

As discussed in Chapter 3, you can perform a basic alignment of individual items by using the align attribute, but you have little control over indents, margins, and line height via direct formatting. Style sheets offer far more control over these settings.

ALIGN, CENTER, OR JUSTIFY TEXT

Use the text-align property to left-align, right-align, center, or justify text. (Justified text is aligned with both margins.) Table 8-2 lists the values for the text-align property.

NOTE

When using the font property, you must specify the values in the correct order; however, you do not have to use every value, as HTML figures out which values you've omitted.

TABLE 8-2: VALUES FOR THE text-align PROPERTY

VALUE	EXPLANATION
left	Aligns the text with the left margin
right	Aligns the text with the right margin
center	Centers the text between the margins
justify	Aligns the text with both margins

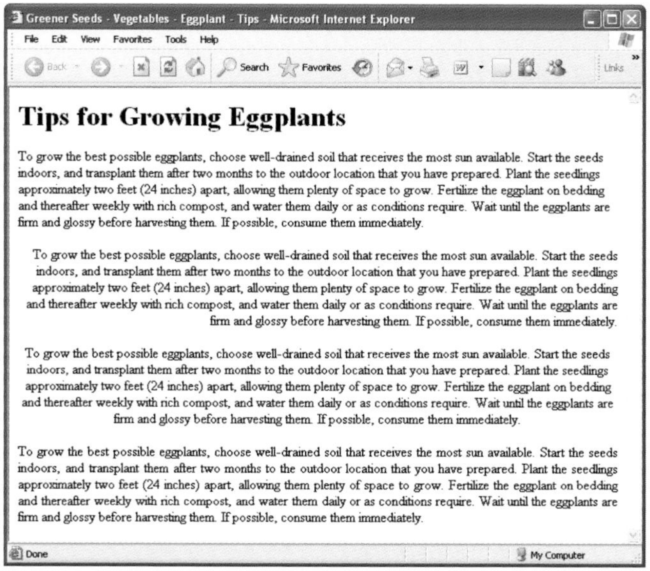

Tips for Growing Eggplants

To grow the best possible eggplants, choose well-drained soil that receives the most sun available. Start the seeds indoors, and transplant them after two months to the outdoor location that you have prepared. Plant the seedlings approximately two feet (24 inches) apart, allowing them plenty of space to grow. Fertilize the eggplant on bedding and thereafter weekly with rich compost, and water them daily or as conditions require. Wait until the eggplants are firm and glossy before harvesting them. If possible, consume them immediately.

To grow the best possible eggplants, choose well-drained soil that receives the most sun available. Start the seeds indoors, and transplant them after two months to the outdoor location that you have prepared. Plant the seedlings approximately two feet (24 inches) apart, allowing them plenty of space to grow. Fertilize the eggplant on bedding and thereafter weekly with rich compost, and water them daily or as conditions require. Wait until the eggplants are firm and glossy before harvesting them. If possible, consume them immediately.

To grow the best possible eggplants, choose well-drained soil that receives the most sun available. Start the seeds indoors, and transplant them after two months to the outdoor location that you have prepared. Plant the seedlings approximately two feet (24 inches) apart, allowing them plenty of space to grow. Fertilize the eggplant on bedding and thereafter weekly with rich compost, and water them daily or as conditions require. Wait until the eggplants are firm and glossy before harvesting them. If possible, consume them immediately.

To grow the best possible eggplants, choose well-drained soil that receives the most sun available. Start the seeds indoors, and transplant them after two months to the outdoor location that you have prepared. Plant the seedlings approximately two feet (24 inches) apart, allowing them plenty of space to grow. Fertilize the eggplant on bedding and thereafter weekly with rich compost, and water them daily or as conditions require. Wait until the eggplants are firm and glossy before harvesting them. If possible, consume them immediately.

Figure 8-5: Use the `text-align` *property to implement left (top), right (second), centered (third), or justified (bottom) alignment.*

TIP

If an element needs one border measurement for both the top and the bottom margins and one border measurement for both the left and right margins, you can specify only two values for the `margin` property. The browser uses the first value for the top and bottom borders and the second value for the left and right borders. For example, `{ margin: 10px 20px }` creates 10-pixel borders at the top and bottom and 20-pixel borders at each side.

The following example aligns the paragraph on the right. Figure 8-5 shows the effects of the four types of alignment.

```
<p style="text-align: right">To grow the best possible
eggplants, choose well-drained soil that receives the most sun
available. Start the seeds indoors, and transplant them after
two months to the outdoor location that you have prepared.
Plant the seedlings approximately two feet (24 inches) apart,
allowing them plenty of space to grow. Fertilize the eggplant on
bedding and thereafter weekly with rich compost, and water them
daily or as conditions require. Wait until the eggplants are
firm and glossy before harvesting them. If possible, consume them
immediately.</p>
```

SET INDENTS

Use the `text-indent` property to specify the indent you want to apply to the first line of a paragraph. Normally, the best option is to specify a fixed indent using a unit of measurement—for example, 0.5 inch—but you can also specify that the indent be a percentage of the line width if you want the indent to vary as the line width changes when the browser window is resized.

The following example uses an inline style to set a half-inch indent on the paragraph:

```
<p style="text-indent: 0.5in">
    Planting frames can make a huge difference to
    your winter gardening, especially in temperate
    climates and those in which frosts often occur or
    snow can be expected to fall.
</p>
```

How to Use a Planting Frame

Planting frames can make a huge difference to your winter gardening, especially in temperate climates and those in which frosts often occur or snow can be expected to fall.

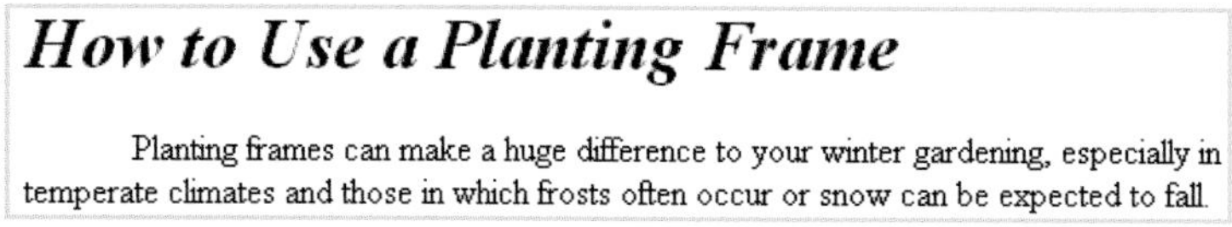

NOTE

If you don't specify line height using the `line-height` property, the browser automatically adjusts the line height so that it is large enough for the font size or for the object the element contains.

NOTE

You can also specify the line height as a percentage of the space normally allotted to the font size or object. For example, a setting of 150% makes the line height one-and-a-half times as large as usual; a setting of 25% makes the line height one-quarter of the normal height.

Figure 8-6: Applying a first-line indent and changing the line height can greatly change the appearance of an element.

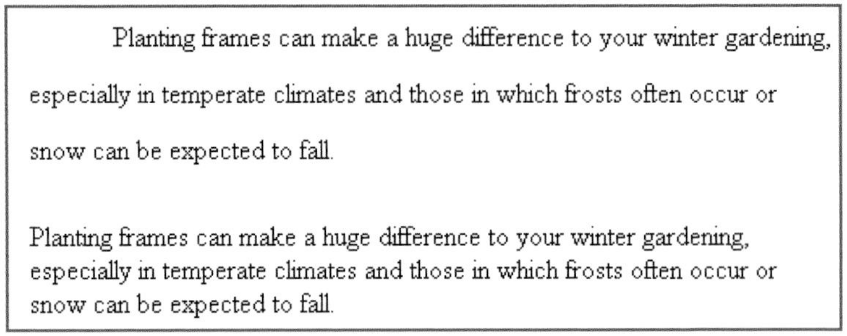

Planting frames can make a huge difference to your winter gardening, especially in temperate climates and those in which frosts often occur or snow can be expected to fall.

Planting frames can make a huge difference to your winter gardening, especially in temperate climates and those in which frosts often occur or snow can be expected to fall.

SET MARGINS

To control where an element appears on a web page, you can adjust the element's margins—the amount of space that appears between the element and the next element on the specified side.

To set a margin width, you use the `margin-left` property, the `margin-right` property, the `margin-top` property, or the `margin-bottom` property. You can specify the indent either as a percentage of the window size (which gives the best flexibility for when the window is resized) or as a number of pixels (px), inches (in), millimeters (mm) or centimeters (cm), points (pt), or picas (pc). For web pages, pixels are frequently used, although it may be easier to think in terms of inches or centimeters.

The following example, which you would use in a style sheet, sets all four margins for the `p` element:

```
p { margin-left: 0.5in; margin-right: 0.5in;
    margin-top: 0.25in; margin-bottom: 0.15in }
```

If you need to specify all the margins for an element, use the `margin` property and specify the margins in a clockwise order starting from the top: top, right, bottom, and then left. The following example sets a top margin of 0.75 inches, a right margin of 0.5 inches, a bottom margin of 0.25 inches, and a left margin of 0.5 inches:

```
h1 { margin: 0.75in 0.5in 0.25in 0.5in }
```

SET LINE HEIGHT

To control the amount of vertical space that an element occupies, you can set the line height (also called "leading") by using the `line-height` property and specifying the measurement in pixels (px), inches (in), millimeters (mm) or centimeters (cm), points (pt), or picas (pc).

The following example sets the line height to 24 points:

```
p { line-height: 24pt }
```

Figure 8-6 shows the effect of changing line height and applying a first-line indent.

QUICKSTEPS

OVERRIDING STYLE SHEETS IN YOUR BROWSER

Style sheets have many advantages, but with unsuitable desktop or browser settings, they may produce pages that are hard to read. Most browsers enable you to override some aspects of style sheets. You may want to use these techniques not only for easier viewing of some web pages you visit, but also to check how your own web pages look when your style sheets are not (or not fully) in effect.

APPLY YOUR OWN STYLE SHEET IN INTERNET EXPLORER

Internet Explorer lets you apply your own style sheet to all web pages you visit; this style sheet overrides any style sheet that each web page is using. You can also choose to ignore the colors, font styles, and font sizes specified on web pages.

1. Start Internet Explorer or switch to it.

2. Click the **Tools** menu and then click **Internet Options**. The Internet Options dialog box appears.

3. On the General tab, click **Accessibility**. The Accessibility dialog box appears.

Continued…

Prevent a Background Graphic from Being Tiled or Scrolling

As discussed in Chapter 4, you can add a background graphic to an element using the `background` attribute in the element's tag. If the graphic isn't large enough to occupy the entire background, however, the browser will *tile*, or repeat, the graphic automatically, so make it big enough. Tiling tends to spoil the effect of a background graphic (see Figure 8-7).

Figure 8-7: If the browser window is larger than the background graphic, the graphic will be tiled unless you specify that it should not be.

To prevent tiling, use the `background-image` property in the appropriate style to place the graphic, and then specify the `background-repeat` property with the value `no-repeat` to prevent the graphic from repeating. The following example, which uses an embedded style sheet, applies the graphic named sunset.jpg in the images folder as the background image and prevents it from being tiled:

```
<style>
     body {background-image: url(images/sunset.jpg);
     background-repeat: no-repeat }
</style>
```

To fix a background graphic so that it remains in the same position in the browser window even when the web page is scrolled, add the `background-attachment` property and specify the value `fixed`. The following example continues the previous example and fixes the background graphic in place:

```
<style>
     body {background-image: url(images/sunset.jpg);
     background-repeat: no-repeat;
     background-attachment: fixed }
</style>
```

TIP

Note the syntax for specifying the background graphic: `url` tells the browser that the parentheses contain the location of the graphic file.

How to...

- *Understanding How the Office Applications Use HTML*
- *Configure Web Options in the Office Applications*
- *Start a New Web Page in Word*
- *Create a Hyperlink*
- *Check How a Page Will Look*
- *Remove Personal Information from the File Properties*
- *Save Word Documents as Web Pages*
- *Choosing Suitable Web File Formats*
- *Remove Office-Specific Tags from a Word Document*
- *Using Word to Create HTML Elements*
- *Create Web Pages from Excel Workbooks*
- *Create Web Pages from PowerPoint Presentations*
- *Create Web Pages from Data-Access Pages in Access*

Chapter 9

Creating Web Pages Using Microsoft Office

If you have one of the versions of Microsoft Office 2003 (which is discussed in this chapter) or Microsoft Office XP (which has similar features), you can use the Office applications' built-in features for saving documents in web-page format. These features enable you to put Word documents, Excel spreadsheets, PowerPoint presentations, and data from Access databases on to a web site or an intranet site in a format in which they can be viewed using a browser.

Configure Web Options in the Office Applications

Before you start using the Office applications to create web pages, configure web options in each of the applications that you plan to use. These options control how the applications create web pages. Once you've specified the options you want for web pages, you probably won't need to change them. If you do need to change them for a particular file, you can do so when you're saving the file as a web page.

Each of the Office applications has a different set of web options, but Word, Excel, and PowerPoint have the same core set of options, which are discussed in this section. The options that are substantially different for one or another of the applications are discussed separately in the section for that particular application later in this chapter.

The General tab appears in the Web Options dialog box for Excel, PowerPoint, and Access; it doesn't appear for Word.

DISPLAY THE WEB OPTIONS DIALOG BOX

To configure web options, first display the Web Options dialog box.

1. If the application for which you want to configure web options is not already running, click the **Start** button, click **All Programs**, click **Microsoft Office**, and then click the item for that program (for example, click **Microsoft Office Word 2003** if you want to work with Word). The application opens.

2. Click the **Tools** menu and then click **Options**. The Options dialog box appears. Click the **General** tab if it is not automatically displayed, and then click **Web Options**. The Web Options dialog box for the application appears.

3. Choose options as discussed in the following subsections, click **OK** to close the Web Options dialog box, and then click **OK** to close the Options dialog box.

UNDERSTANDING HOW THE OFFICE APPLICATIONS USE HTML

(Continued)

Round-tripping enables you to create HTML documents instead of documents that use the standard Office file formats (for example, the Word Document format, the Excel Spreadsheet format, or the PowerPoint Presentation format). However, you must always remember that the Office-specific data is saved along with the HTML data. Any visitor to your web site can view the entire source code for a web page, including any Office-specific data, by using a View Source command.

Word enables you to remove the Office-specific tags from a web page you save (see "Remove Office-Specific Tags from a Word Document," later in this chapter). You may also choose to use Word to create specific HTML elements that you then paste into your standard HTML editor, where you can then integrate them with the code you create manually. (See the "Using Word to Create HTML Elements" QuickSteps, later in this chapter.)

CHOOSE GENERAL TAB OPTIONS FOR EXCEL

Choose options as follows on the General tab for Excel (see Figure 9-1).

1. Select the **Save Any Additional Hidden Data Necessary To Maintain Formulas** check box to make Excel save in the web page any hidden data that is required for maintaining the formulas in the worksheets shown in the web page. Excluding any relevant hidden data will prevent the formulas from working correctly.
2. Select the **Load Pictures From Web Pages Not Created In Excel** check box to make Excel include graphics from non-Excel sources in the web pages you create from Excel. Including such graphics helps to keep your worksheets complete. The usual reason for clearing this check box and omitting graphics from other sources is that the graphics will not be available in the web pages.

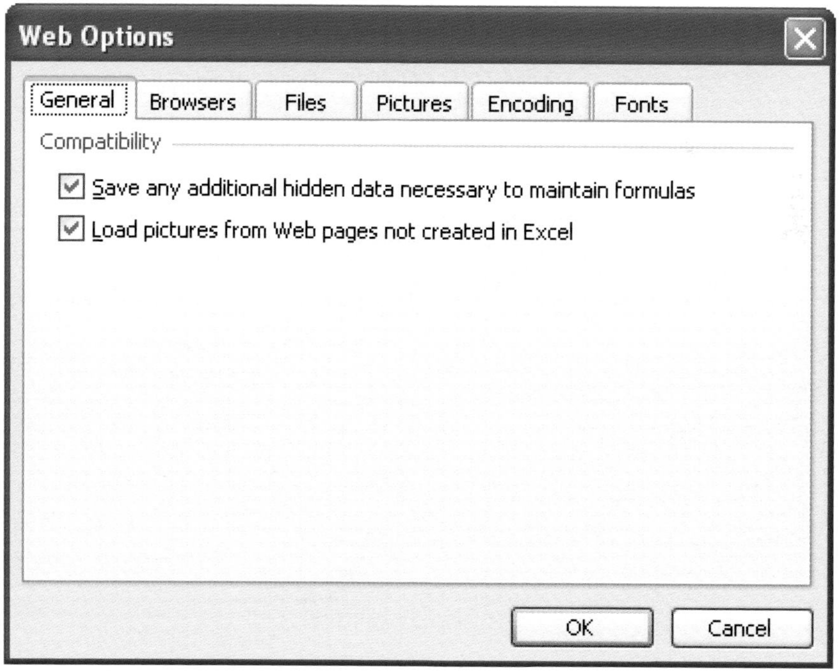

Figure 9-1: For most purposes, you should select both the options on the General tab of the Web Options dialog box for Excel.

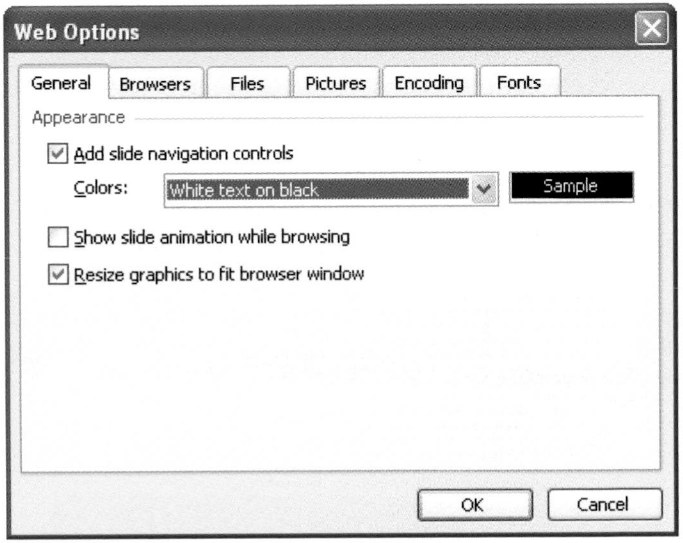

Figure 9-2: The General tab of the Web Options dialog box for PowerPoint enables you to add slide navigation controls, display slide animations while the viewer is browsing, and automatically resize graphics to fit the browser window.

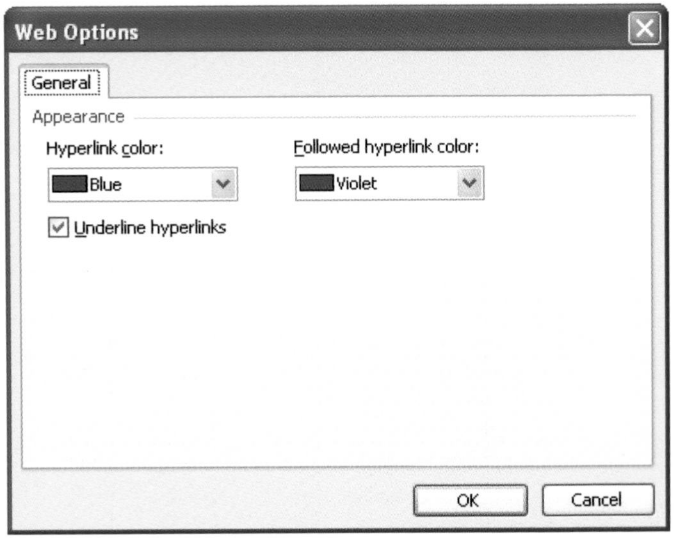

CHOOSE GENERAL TAB OPTIONS FOR POWERPOINT

Choose options as follows on the General tab of the Web Options dialog box for PowerPoint (see Figure 9-2).

1. Select the **Add Slide Navigation Controls** check box if you want the presentation to include controls for navigating among slides. Usually, having the controls is beneficial, but you may decide that your presentations don't need them; if so, clear this check box. If you include the controls, use the Colors drop-down list to choose the text color and background color you want for the controls

2. Clear the **Show Slide Animation While Browsing** check box unless you want the presentation to include animations when the viewer is browsing from slide to slide.

3. Select the **Resize Graphics To Fit Browser Window** check box to make the presentation automatically resize its graphics so that they fit within the browser window, which is usually a good idea.

CHOOSE GENERAL TAB OPTIONS FOR ACCESS

Choose options as follows on the General tab of the Web Options dialog box for Access (see Figure 9-3).

1. Choose your desired color for as-yet-unclicked hyperlinks in the Hyperlink Color drop-down list and the color for clicked hyperlinks in the Followed Hyperlink Color drop-down list.

2. Select the **Underline Hyperlinks** check box if you want the hyperlinks to be underlined. Otherwise, clear this check box. The Web's convention is to underline hyperlinks, so it's best to select this check box.

Figure 9-3: The Web Options dialog box for Access offers a far more limited set of options than for Word, Excel, and PowerPoint.

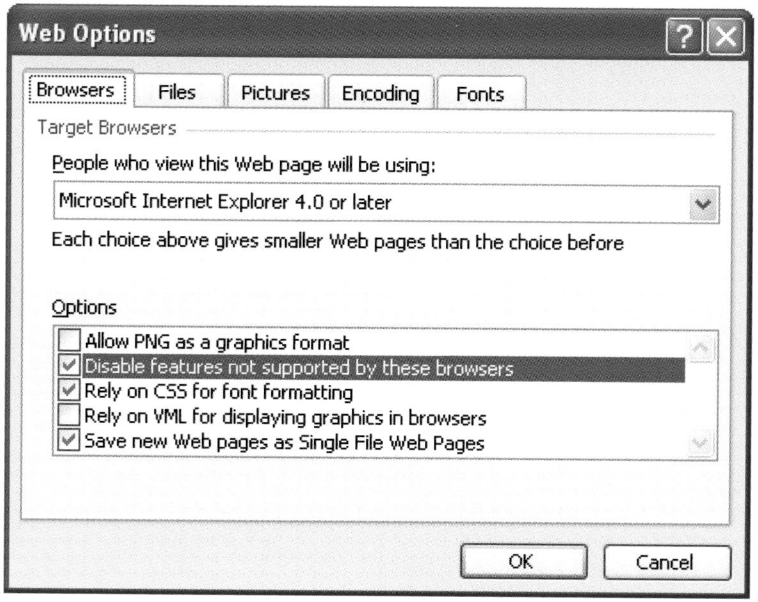

CHOOSE BROWSERS TAB OPTIONS

The Browsers tab appears in the Web Options dialog box for Word, Excel, and PowerPoint. Figure 9-4 shows the Browsers tab of the Web Options dialog box for Word, which offers one more option than for Excel and PowerPoint. Table 9-1 explains the options and shows for which browsers they're turned on (with the check box selected) or off (with the check box cleared).

Figure 9-4: The Browsers tab of Word's Web Options dialog box lets you specify the types of browsers for which you want your web pages to work correctly.

TABLE 9-1: OPTIONS ON THE BROWSERS TAB OF THE WEB OPTIONS DIALOG BOX

OPTION	EXPLANATION	IE 3, NAVIGATOR 3	IE 4, NAVIGATOR 4	IE 4 OR LATER	IE 5 OR LATER	IE 6 OR LATER
Allow PNG As A Graphics Format	Enables web pages to contain graphics in the PNG format. All current browsers can display PNG graphics.	Off	Off	Off	Off	On
Rely On CSS For Font Formatting	Uses Cascading Style Sheets for font formatting.	Off	On	On	On	On
Rely On VML For Displaying Graphics In Browsers	Uses Vector Markup Language for displaying graphics.	Off	Off	Off	On	On
Save New Web Pages As Single File Web Pages	Uses the Single File Web Page format for saving new files.	Off	Off	On	On	On
Disable Features Not Supported By These Browsers	(Word only.) Turns off HTML features the browsers don't support.	On	On	On	On	On

The best way to select the options is to click the **People Who View This Web Page Will Be Using** drop-down list and select the earliest browser version that you want to support. The choice you make in this drop-down list automatically selects the relevant check boxes in the Options group box. You can then select or clear check boxes manually to fine-tune the choices you've made:

- Choosing **Microsoft Internet Explorer 4.0, Netscape Navigator 4.0, Or Later** provides a reasonable baseline for most web sites.

- If you need maximum browser compatibility, choose **Microsoft Internet Explorer 3.0, Netscape Navigator 3.0, Or Later**.

- If your pages don't need support for Netscape Navigator, choose **Microsoft Internet Explorer 4.0 Or Later**.

- If your pages don't need support for Netscape Navigator but need to use features available only in a later version of Internet Explorer, choose **Microsoft Internet Explorer 5.0 Or Later** or **Microsoft Internet Explorer 6.0 Or Later**.

CHOOSE FILES TAB OPTIONS

On the Files tab of the Web Options dialog box, choose options for controlling how each Office application handles file names and file locations in the web pages you create, and specify whether to use Office as the default editor for web pages created by the Office applications. Figure 9-5 shows the Files tab of the Web Options dialog box for Excel, which has the most extensive set of options for files.

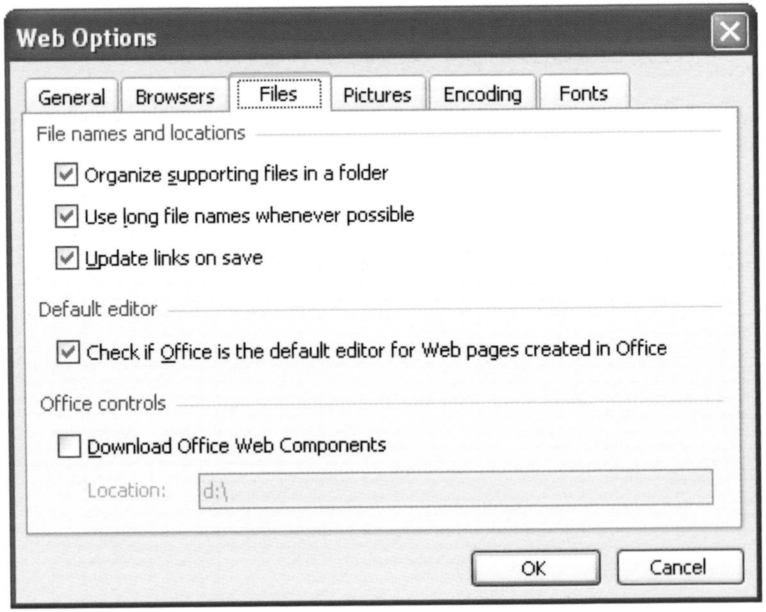

Web Options

| General | Browsers | Files | Pictures | Encoding | Fonts |

File names and locations

☑ Organize supporting files in a folder

☑ Use long file names whenever possible

☑ Update links on save

Default editor

☑ Check if Office is the default editor for Web pages created in Office

Office controls

☐ Download Office Web Components

Location: d:\

OK   Cancel

Figure 9-5: The Files tab of the Web Options dialog box contains a different set of options for Word, Excel, and PowerPoint. This is the Files tab for Excel.

NOTE

Word documents, Excel worksheets, and PowerPoint presentations keep all their text and embedded elements (such as graphics) in the same file. Linked items, such as graphics or Automation objects from other applications, are kept in separate files.

CAUTION

Keeping the supporting files together in a folder is usually helpful because you can move the web page and its supporting files easily to another folder. If you clear the Organize Supporting Files In A Folder check box, the Office applications save the graphics and other separate elements in the same folder as the web page. This behavior tends to make your folders harder to manage, as you cannot see at a glance which supporting files belong to which web page. However, if you do not have permission to create new folders in the folder in which you are saving your web pages, you may need to clear the Organize Supporting Files In A Folder check box so that the Office application does not attempt to create new folders for your web pages.

Word, Excel, and PowerPoint all include the following options:

- Select the **Organize Supporting Files In A Folder** check box if you want the application to save graphics and other separate elements in a folder that has the same name as the web page plus "_files"—for example, the web page named products.html receives a folder named products_files. The application automatically creates a file named filelist.xml that contains a list of the files required for the web page.

- Clear the **Use Long File Names Whenever Possible** check box to prevent the application from creating long file names that include spaces, which may not be compatible with the web server you're using. It's best to keep file names short and to use underscores instead of spaces when you need to separate parts of the file name.

- Select the **Update Links On Save** check box if you want the application to automatically check each link and update any information that has changed each time you save the file. In most cases, this automatic updating is helpful.

- Select the **Check If Office Is The Default Editor For Web Pages Created In Office** check box if you want Internet Explorer to check if the Office applications are your default HTML editors for web pages created by the Office applications when you click the Edit button in Internet Explorer. Clear this check box if you want to be able to use another application to edit the web pages you've created with the Office applications.

The Files tab in the Web Options dialog box for Word also includes the Check If Word Is The Default Editor For All Other Web Pages check box. Select this check box if you want to use Word as your default HTML editor for web pages created either using Word or using applications other than the other Office applications. (Excel will still be the default editor for web pages created using Excel, PowerPoint for web pages created using PowerPoint, and Access for web pages created using Access.) Clear this check box if you want to use another HTML editor as the default.

```
Default editor
  ☑ Check if Office is the default editor for Web pages created in Office
  ☑ Check if Word is the default editor for all other Web pages

                                              [ OK ]   [ Cancel ]
```

Office Web Components work both on intranets and on public web sites, but it is a good idea to warn visitors that they will need to download and install the Office Web Components on their computers (unless the components are already installed) in order to use the interactive spreadsheets. Otherwise, a visitor may be surprised to see a dialog box prompting him or her to install the Office Web Components in order to view your web pages.

Unicode is a scheme for representing characters on computers. For example, a capital A is represented by 0041 in Unicode, and a capital B is represented by 0042. *UTF-8* is the abbreviation for Universal Character Set Transformation Format 8-Bit. *ISO* is the short term used to denote the International Organization for Standardization.

Web Options

Browsers | Files | Pictures | Encoding | Fonts

Encoding

Reload the current document as:

Save this document as:

Western European (Windows)

☐ Always save Web pages in the default encoding

OK | Cancel

The Files tab in the Web Options dialog box for Excel includes the Download Office Web Components check box and Location text box. Office Web Components are controls (such as those needed to have an interactive worksheet in a browser) that you can insert in your web pages. If you're using these components in your web pages, select this check box and specify the path and folder containing the components in the Location text box.

CHOOSE PICTURES TAB OPTIONS

On the Pictures tab of the Web Options dialog box (shown here), choose options for the pictures you include in your web pages:

Web Options

Browsers | Files | Pictures | Encoding | Fonts

Target monitor

Screen size: 800 x 600

Pixels per inch: 96

- In the Screen Size drop-down list, select the minimum resolution that you expect most visitors to your web site to be using. For most web sites, the best choice is 800 × 600, a resolution that almost all monitors manufactured since 2000 support. If you're creating an intranet site whose visitors will all use monitors with a higher resolution than 800 × 600, you can choose a higher resolution.

- In the Pixels Per Inch drop-down list, select the number of pixels per inch (ppi) to use for pictures in your web pages. The default setting is 96 ppi, which works well for most pages. You can also choose 72 ppi or 120 ppi. This drop-down list does not appear in the Web Options dialog box for PowerPoint.

CHOOSE ENCODING TAB OPTIONS

The Encoding tab of the Web Options dialog box (shown here) lets you specify which character-encoding scheme to use for the characters in your web pages. The Office applications in North America and Western Europe use the Western European (Windows) encoding by default. This works well for most purposes, but you may prefer to choose Western European (ISO) for compliance with the ISO-8859-1 standard or Unicode (UTF-8) for compliance with the Unicode standard.

Select the encoding you want in the Save This Document As drop-down list. Then, if you always want to use this encoding, select the **Always Save Web Pages In The Default Encoding** check box. Selecting this check box disables the Save This Document As drop-down list.

CHOOSE FONTS TAB OPTIONS

The Fonts tab of the Web Options dialog box offers the following options:

- Use the Character Set list box to specify the character set you want to use for your pages. Use the English/Western European/Other Latin Script item unless you need to create pages in another character set, such as Hebrew or Arabic.

- Use the Proportional Font drop-down list and its Size drop-down list to specify the proportional font and font size to use for your pages.

- Use the Fixed-Width Font and its Size drop-down list to specify the monospaced font and font size.

After you finish choosing settings in the Web Options dialog box, click **OK** to close the dialog box, and then click **OK** to close the Options dialog box.

Start a New Web Page in Word

After choosing suitable web options, start a new web page in Word.

1. Start Word if it is not already running, or switch to Word.

2. Click the **File** menu and then click **New**. The New Document task pane opens.

3. In the New area, click **Web Page**. Word opens a new, blank web page.

4. Create content on the page by using standard Word techniques. For example:

   - To enter text, type it as usual.

   - To apply a style, click the **Style** drop-down list on the Formatting toolbar, and then click the desired style name.

   - To apply direct formatting (for example, bold or italic), select the text to which you want to apply it, and then click the appropriate button on the Formatting toolbar.

5. Save the document as described in the section "Save Word Documents as Web Pages," later in this chapter.

NOTE

Instead of starting a new web page from scratch in Word, you can also create a web page by opening an existing Word document, Excel workbook, or PowerPoint presentation, and then using the Save As Web Page command on the File menu to save it in a web format. See "Save Word Documents as Web Pages," "Create Web Pages from Excel Workbooks," "Create Web Pages from PowerPoint Presentations," and "Create Web Pages from Data-Access Pages in Access," all later in this chapter, for details.

Create a Hyperlink

The process of inserting a hyperlink is the same in each of the Office applications, so it is discussed here. The example shown is from Word. To insert a hyperlink, display the Insert Hyperlink dialog box by following these steps, and then follow the steps in the subsection that discusses the type of hyperlink you want to create.

1. Open the file in which you want to create the hyperlink. For example, start Word and then open the document.

2. Select the text or graphic, or otherwise position the insertion point where you want the hyperlink to appear.

3. Click the **Insert** menu, expand the menu if necessary, and then click **Hyperlink**. The Insert Hyperlink dialog box appears (see Figure 9-6).

4. Complete the hyperlink with one of the following sections, depending on whether you want to create a hyperlink to an existing file or web page, a place in the current document, a new document, or an e-mail address.

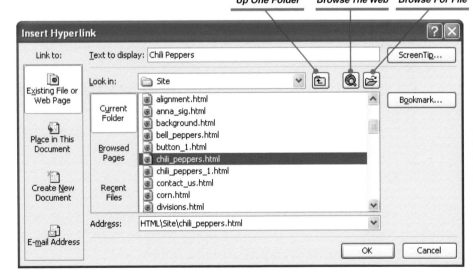

Figure 9-6: The Insert Hyperlink dialog box enables you to create hyperlinks to web pages, places within the same file, files, or e-mail addresses.

CAUTION

If Internet Explorer is not your default browser, the Browse The Web button will not work correctly. Clicking the button opens your default browser, but when you return to the Insert Hyperlink dialog box, the Office application tries to get the URL from Internet Explorer rather than from your default browser. Instead, browse to the web page in your default browser, copy the address from the address bar, and then paste it into the Address box in the Insert Hyperlink dialog box.

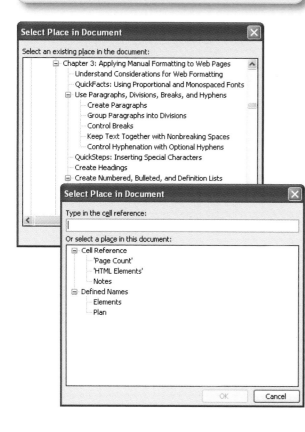

CREATE A HYPERLINK TO AN EXISTING FILE OR WEB PAGE

To create a hyperlink to an existing file or web page:

1. In the Link To column, click **Existing File Or Web Page** if it is not already selected.

2. Navigate to the file or web page in one of these ways:

- Use the Look In drop-down list (and, if necessary, the Up One Folder button) to browse to the folder.

–Or–

- Click the **Browse The Web** button to make Windows open an Internet Explorer window, browse to the desired page, and then switch back to the Insert Hyperlink dialog box. The Office application automatically enters the URL in the Address text box.

–Or–

- Click the **Current Folder** button to display the current folder. Click the **Browsed Pages** button to display a list of web pages you've browsed recently. Click the **Recent Files** button to display a list of local files you've worked with recently.

–Or–

- Select the address from the Address drop-down list.

3. Change the default text in the Text To Display text box to the text you want displayed for the hyperlink. (This is the text that the user clicks to access the linked page. If you have selected text on your web page, it will appear here.)

4. To add a ScreenTip to the hyperlink, click **ScreenTip**, type the text in the Set Hyperlink ScreenTip dialog box, and then click **OK**.

5. To make the hyperlink connect to a particular anchor in the document rather than simply to the beginning of the document, click **Bookmark** and choose the anchor item in the Select Place In Document dialog box (see Figure 9-7).

6. Click **OK**. The Office application inserts the hyperlink.

Figure 9-7: The Office applications enable you to link to a particular place in the destination document—for example, to a heading or bookmark in a Word document (upper left), a cell or range in an Excel worksheet (lower left), or a slide in a PowerPoint presentation.

CREATE A HYPERLINK TO A PLACE IN THE CURRENT DOCUMENT

To create a hyperlink to a place in the current document:

1. In the Link To column, click the **Place In This Document** button (see Figure 9-8).

2. Change the default text in the Text To Display text box to the text you want displayed for the hyperlink. (This is the text that the user clicks to access the linked page and is the text you first selected, if you did so.)

3. To add a ScreenTip to the hyperlink, click **ScreenTip**, type the text in the Set Hyperlink ScreenTip dialog box, and then click **OK**.

4. Click **OK**. The Office application inserts the hyperlink.

Figure 9-8: The Place In This Document area of the Insert Hyperlink dialog box enables you to quickly link to an anchor in the same document.

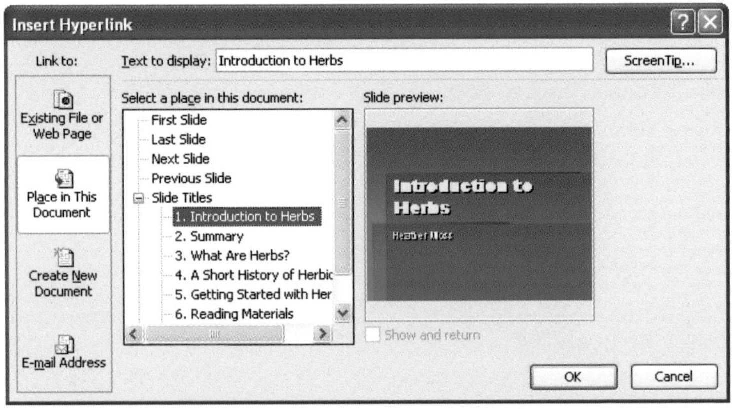

CREATE A HYPERLINK TO A NEW DOCUMENT

To create a hyperlink to a new document:

1. In the Link To Column, click the **Create New Document** button (see Figure 9-9).

2. Type the file name and extension in the Name Of New Document text box. Check the path in the Full Path area. If necessary, click **Change**; use the Create New File dialog box to specify the folder, file name, and extension; and then click **OK**.

3. Change the default text in the Text To Display text box to the text you want displayed for the hyperlink. (This is the text that the user clicks to access the linked page and is the text you first selected, if you did so.)

4. To add a ScreenTip to the hyperlink, click **ScreenTip**, type the text in the Set Hyperlink ScreenTip dialog box, and then click **OK**.

5. By default, the Office application selects the Edit The New Document Now option button. If you prefer not to open the new document for editing immediately, select the **Edit The New Document Later** option button.

6. Click **OK**. The Office application inserts the hyperlink.

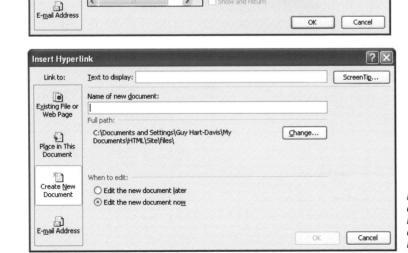

Figure 9-9: When you need to link to a new document, Office lets you create the new document immediately. This helps ensure that the new document is saved with the correct name and location, reducing the possibility of error.

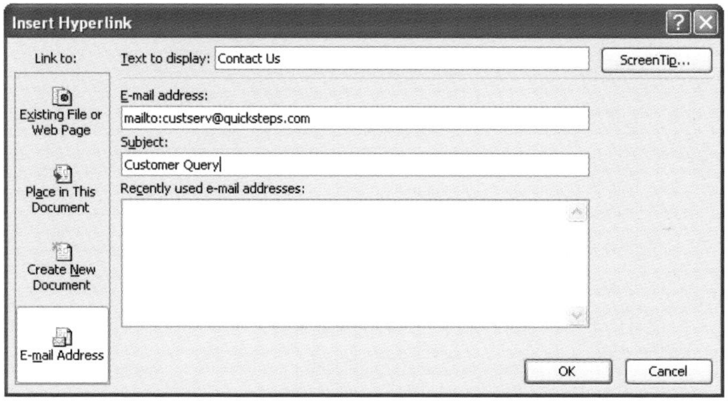

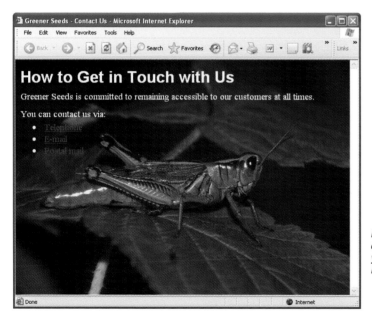

Figure 9-10: The Insert Hyperlink dialog box lets you quickly create a mailto hyperlink to a recently used e-mail address.

CREATE A HYPERLINK TO AN E-MAIL ADDRESS

To create a mailto hyperlink that starts a message to an e-mail address:

1. In the Link To column, click the **E-Mail Address** button (see Figure 9-10).

2. Type the e-mail address in the E-Mail Address text box (or click it in the Recently Used E-Mail Addresses list box), and type the subject for the message in the Subject text box.

3. Change the default text in the Text To Display text box to the text you want displayed for the hyperlink. (This is the text that the user clicks to access the linked page and is the text you first selected, if you did so.)

4. To add a ScreenTip to the hyperlink, click **ScreenTip**, type the text in the Set Hyperlink ScreenTip dialog box, and then click **OK**.

5. Click **OK**. The Office application inserts the hyperlink.

Check How a Page Will Look

Before you save an Office document as a web page, you may want to use Web Page Preview to check how it looks.

1. If the document is not already open, open it in the appropriate application. For example, open a Word document in Word.

2. Click the **File** menu, expand the menu if needed, and then click **Web Page Preview**. The application creates a temporary file containing the page in a web format and then displays the page in Internet Explorer. Figure 9-11 shows an example.

3. After viewing the web page, click the **File** menu and then click **Close** to close the Internet Explorer window.

Figure 9-11: Web Page Preview enables you to identify problems with your web pages before you save them in an HTML format.

NOTE

The Office applications automatically create a hyperlink when you type a URL, e-mail address, or a network path in a document and then press **SPACEBAR**, **TAB**, **ENTER**, or a punctuation key. If you find this behavior awkward, you can turn it off: click the **Tools** menu, expand the menu if needed, click **AutoCorrect Options**, click the **AutoFormat As You Type** tab, clear the **Internet And Network Paths With Hyperlinks** check box, and then click **OK**.

Remove Personal Information from the File Properties

When creating a web page that you will place on a web site (as opposed to a site on a local network), it's a good idea to remove the personal information that the Office applications automatically include by default in documents. To remove this information:

1. Start the application if it is not already running. Open the document that will become a web page if it is not already open.

2. Click the **Tools** menu and then click **Options**. The Options dialog box appears.

3. In Word, Excel, or PowerPoint, click the **Security** tab. Figure 9-12 shows the Security tab of the Options dialog box for Word. In Access, click the **General** tab.

4. Select the **Remove Personal Information From File Properties On Save** check box.

5. Click **OK**. Save the document as described in later sections of this chapter.

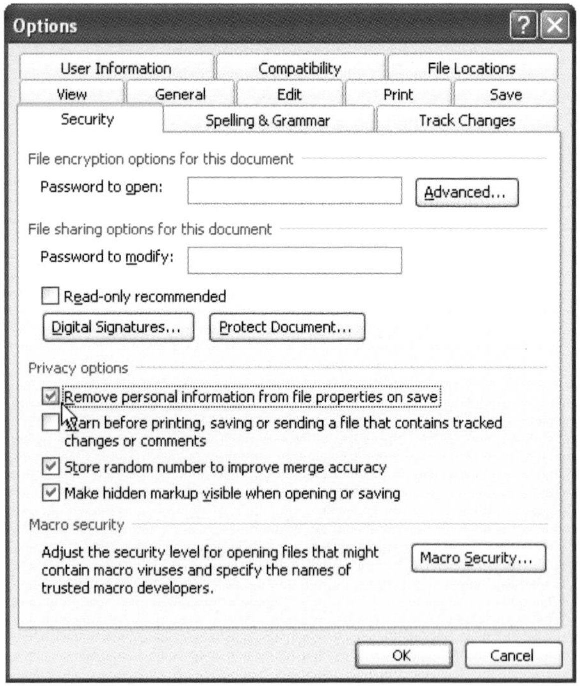

Figure 9-12: Select the Remove Personal Information From File Properties On Save check box in the Options dialog box to prevent the Office application from including personal information in the web pages you save.

Save Word Documents as Web Pages

To save an existing Word document as a web page:

1. Start Word if it is not already running, or switch to it.

2. Click the **File** menu, click **Open**, select the existing document you want to save as a web page, and then click **Open**. The document opens.

3. Click the **File** menu, expand the menu if needed, and then click **Save As Web Page**. The Save As dialog box appears (see Figure 9-13).

4. Use the Save In drop-down list and the main list box to specify the folder in which to save the web page.

5. In the Save As Type drop-down list, select the file format you want to use (see the "Choosing Suitable Web File Formats" QuickSteps in this chapter for a discussion of the available formats).

6. In the File Name text box, type the file name. If you want to use the .html extension instead of the .htm extension (for a file in either the Web Page format or the Web Page, Filtered format) or the .mhtml extension instead of the .mht extension (for a file in the Single File Web Page Format), type the extension as well.

Figure 9-13: Word's Save As dialog box for saving web pages includes the Page Title area and the Change Title button.

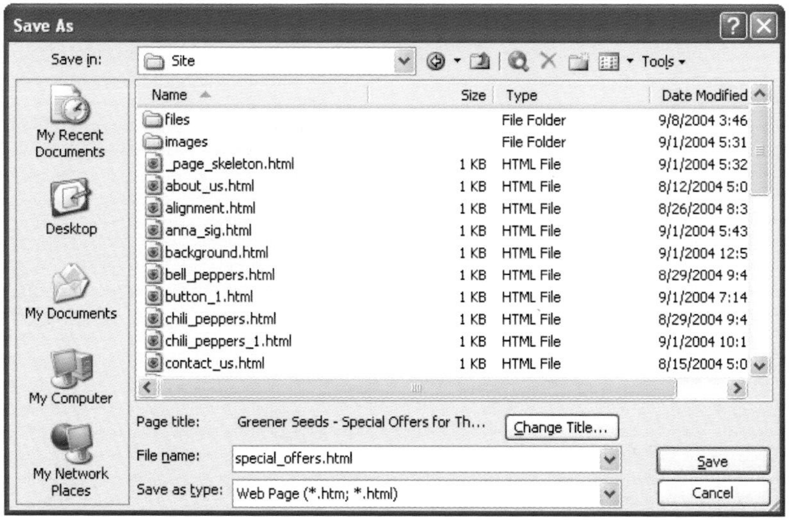

7. Check the title displayed in the Page Title area. To change it, click **Change Title**, type the new title in the Set Page Title dialog box, and then click **OK**.

8. Click **Save**. Word saves the document as a web page.

9. If you've finished working with the document, click the **File** menu and then click **Close**. If you've finished working with Word, click the **File** menu and then click **Exit**.

QUICKFACTS

CHOOSING SUITABLE WEB FILE FORMATS

Word, Excel, and PowerPoint each offer two or more HTML formats to choose from; so before you save a file in HTML, you should understand how the formats differ from each other and which format is suitable for which purposes.

Word, Excel, and PowerPoint each offer the Single File Web Page format and the Web Page format. Word also offers the Web Page, Filtered format.

WEB PAGE FORMAT

The Web Page format creates an HTML file that contains the text contents of the document along with a separate folder that contains the graphics for the document. This makes the web page's HTML file itself smaller, but the page as a whole is a little clumsy to distribute because you need to distribute the graphics folder as well. The folder is created automatically and assigned the web page's name followed by _files. For example, a web page named Products.html has a folder named Products_files.

Files in the Web Page format use the .htm and .html file extensions. These files also use Office-specific tags to preserve all of the information the file contains in an HTML format.

SINGLE FILE WEB PAGE FORMAT

The Single File Web Page format creates a web archive file that contains all the information required for the web page—all the text contents and all the graphics. Use the Single File Web Page format to create files that you can easily distribute.

Continued...

Remove Office-Specific Tags from a Word Document

As discussed earlier in this chapter, Word uses custom HTML tags to store the Office-specific data required to save the entire Word document in an HTML format. Saving this Office-specific data is good if you want to be able to edit the document in Word with all the features present, but you don't need this extra data when you're using Word on a one-time basis to create pages for your web site.

To remove the tags from a document:

1. Follow the steps in the previous section, but choose the **Web Page, Filtered** format in the Save As Type drop-down list.

2. When you click **Save**, the Microsoft Office Word dialog box shown here appears, telling you that Office-specific tags will be removed. Click **Yes**.

3. Depending on the browser settings you have chosen in the Web Options dialog box, you may also see warnings (see the dialog box next for an example) about features that will be removed from the Word document. Click **Continue** if you want to proceed anyway; click **Cancel** if you want to choose another format.

CHOOSING SUITABLE WEB FILE FORMATS *(Continued)*

Files in the Single File Web Page format use the .mht and .mhtml file extensions. These files use Office-specific tags to preserve all of the information the file contains in an HTML format.

WEB PAGE, FILTERED FORMAT

The Web Page, Filtered format is available only in Word. Like the Web Page format, this format creates an HTML file that contains the text contents of the document along with a separate, automatically named folder that contains the graphics for the document. However, this format removes Office-specific tags from the document. Removing these features reduces the size of the file, but the file uses items such as document properties and VBA code, so this format is not useful for round-tripping (being brought back into and edited with Word) complex documents.

Files in the Web Page, Filtered format use the .htm and .html file extensions.

Create Web Pages from Excel Workbooks

While Word creates only static web pages (pages that don't change), Excel enables you to create either static web pages or an interactive worksheet that users can manipulate using Internet Explorer 5.01 or later and the Microsoft Office 2003 Web Components. (Interactive worksheets don't work with browsers other than Internet Explorer.)

Excel lets you save a selected part of the workbook, a worksheet, or the entire workbook as a web page with or without interactivity. Usually, however, what you'll want to do is "publish" a copy of part of the workbook, of a worksheet, or of the entire workbook, because the Publish dialog box offers more features and flexibility for the web pages.

To save an Excel workbook, worksheet, or part of a worksheet as a web page:

1. Start Excel if it is not already running, or switch to Excel.

2. Open the existing worksheet, or create a new worksheet, add content, and save it.

3. If you want to save a worksheet rather than a workbook as a web page, select that worksheet. If you want to save a range from a worksheet as a web page, select that range.

4. Click the **File** menu and then click **Save As Web Page**. The Save As dialog box appears (see Figure 9-14).

Figure 9-14: Excel's Save As dialog box for saving web pages includes controls for adding interactivity and for publishing the workbook, worksheet, or selection.

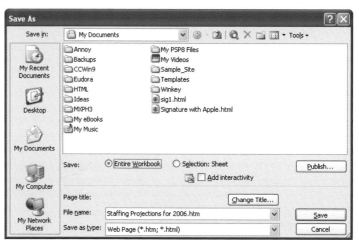

QUICKSTEPS

USING WORD TO CREATE HTML ELEMENTS

If you choose not to use Word as your main HTML editor, you may still want to use Word to create some HTML elements so that you can include them in your web pages.

1. Start Word if it is not already running.

2. Open an existing document or create a new document that contains the desired content.

3. Save the Word document in one of the HTML formats.

4. View the resulting page in your browser.

5. View the source code of the web page. For example, in Internet Explorer, click the **View** menu and then click **Source**.

6. Select the code for the element you want to copy, and then issue a Copy command (for example, press **CTRL+C**).

7. Switch to your HTML editor, position the insertion point, and then issue a Paste command (for example, press **CTRL+V**).

8. Close Word and your browser if you have finished working with them.

NOTE

Files saved in the Web Page format can use the .htm extension or the .html extension. Files saved in the Single File Web Page format can use the .mht extension or the .mhtml extension.

5. In the Save area, select the **Entire Workbook** option button if you want to save or publish the entire workbook. Select the **Selection** option button if you want to publish the active worksheet or the selected range. When a range is selected, the Selection option button lists the range (for example, "Selection: $A$1:$H$15"); if no range is selected, the Selection option button reads "Selection: Sheet."

6. If you want to make the web page interactive for visitors using Internet Explorer, select the **Add Interactivity** check box.

7. Use the Save In drop-down list and the main list box to specify the folder in which to save the web page.

8. In the Save As Type drop-down list, select the file format you want to use (see the "Choosing Suitable Web File Formats" QuickSteps in this chapter for a discussion of the available formats).

9. In the File Name text box, type the file name. If you want to use the .html extension instead of the .htm extension or the .mhtml extension instead of the .mht extension, type the extension.

10. Click **Publish**. The Publish As Web Page dialog box appears (see Figure 9-15).

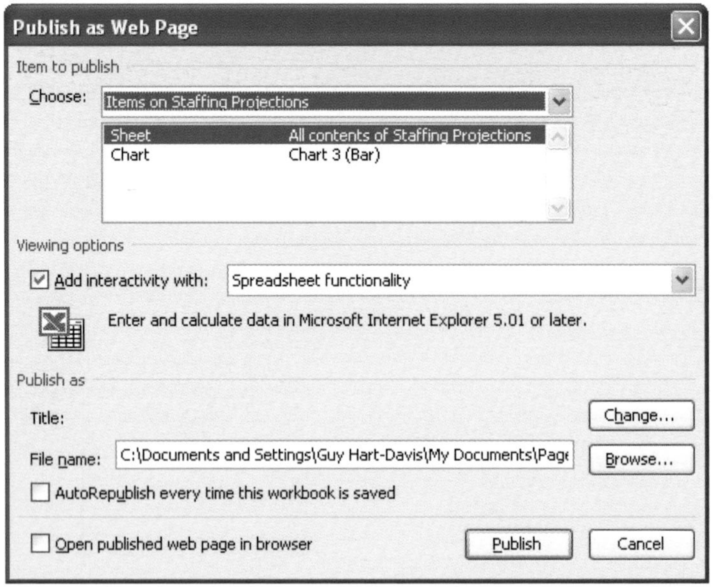

Figure 9-15: Excel's Publish As Web Page dialog box enables you to choose which form of interactivity— spreadsheet functionality or PivotTable functionality—to add to your web page for Internet Explorer users.

NOTE

A PivotTable is an interactive report in which you can rearrange the rows and columns into a different layout. You can *pivot*, or rotate, the columns in the PivotTable so they become rows to display data summarized in different ways; and you can collapse and expand the level of detail displayed.

NOTE

The AutoRepublish Every Time This Workbook Is Saved option is convenient for making sure the web page is always up-to-date, but use it only if you have a permanent and fast connection to the site on which you're publishing the web page.

11. Use the Choose drop-down list and list box in the Item To Publish section to specify which item to publish. If necessary, change the item selected in the Choose drop-down list. If you select the **Range Of Cells** item, Excel displays a Collapse Dialog button. Click this button (as shown here) to collapse the dialog box to its title bar, select the range in the worksheet, and then click the **Collapse Dialog** button again to restore the dialog box.

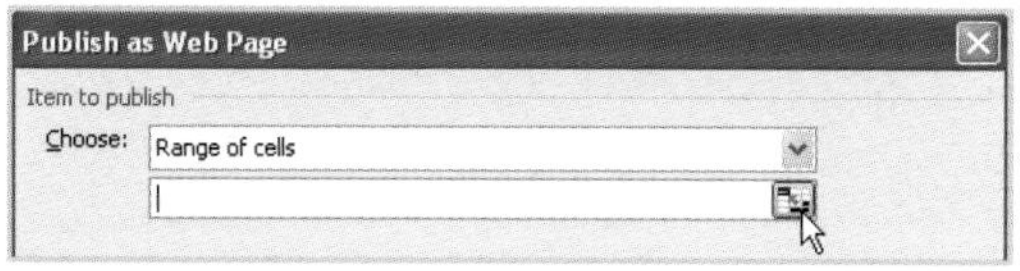

12. In the Viewing Options section, if the Add Interactivity With check box is not selected and you want to add interactivity, select it. In the drop-down list, select **Spreadsheet Functionality** or **PivotTable Functionality**.

13. Check the title displayed in the Title text box. To change it, click **Change**, type the new title in the Set Title dialog box, and then click **OK**.

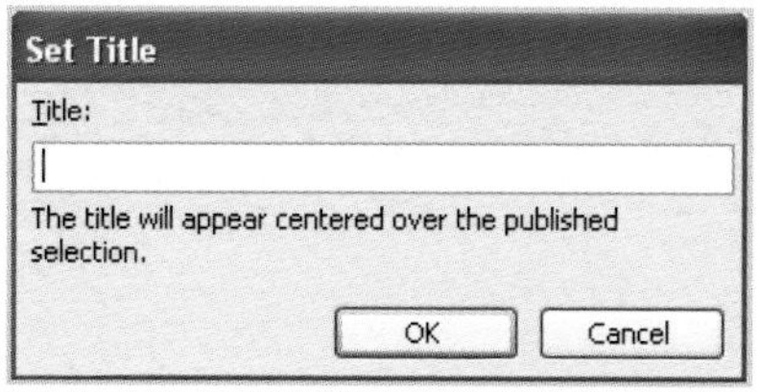

14. Check the path and file name in the File Name text box. If necessary, type a change, or click **Browse**, specify the folder and file name in the Publish As dialog box, and then click **OK**.

15. Select the **AutoRepublish Every Time This Workbook Is Saved** check box if you want Excel to automatically publish this web page again each time you save the file.

16. Select the **Open Published Web Page In Browser** check box if you want Excel to display the web page in Internet Explorer so that you can check it, which is usually a good idea.

17. Click **Publish**. Excel publishes the web page and (if necessary) displays it in Internet Explorer (see Figure 9-16).

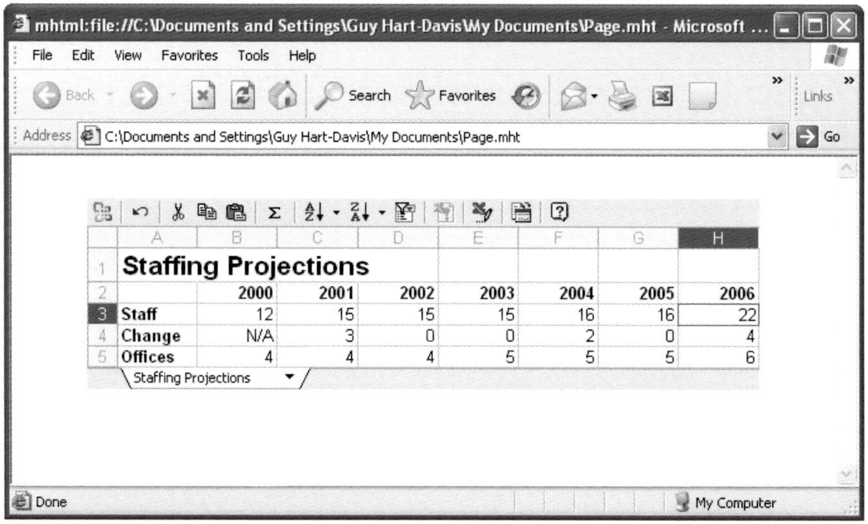

Figure 9-16: You can use and edit interactive web pages directly in Internet Explorer 5.01 or a later version. To change from one worksheet to another, click the single tab that appears, and then select the desired worksheet from the pop-up list.

Create Web Pages from PowerPoint Presentations

To save a PowerPoint presentation as a web page:

1. Start PowerPoint if it is not already running, or switch to PowerPoint.

2. Open the existing presentation, or create a new presentation, add content, and save it.

3. Click the **File** menu and then click **Save As Web Page**. The Save As dialog box appears (see Figure 9-17).

4. Click **Publish**. The Publish As Web Page dialog box appears (see Figure 9-18).

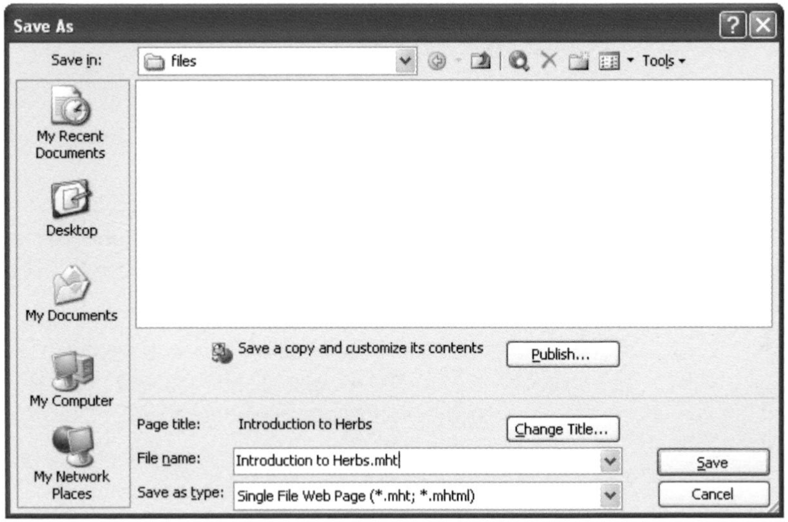

Figure 9-17: PowerPoint's Save As dialog box for saving web pages includes a Publish button and a Page Title text box.

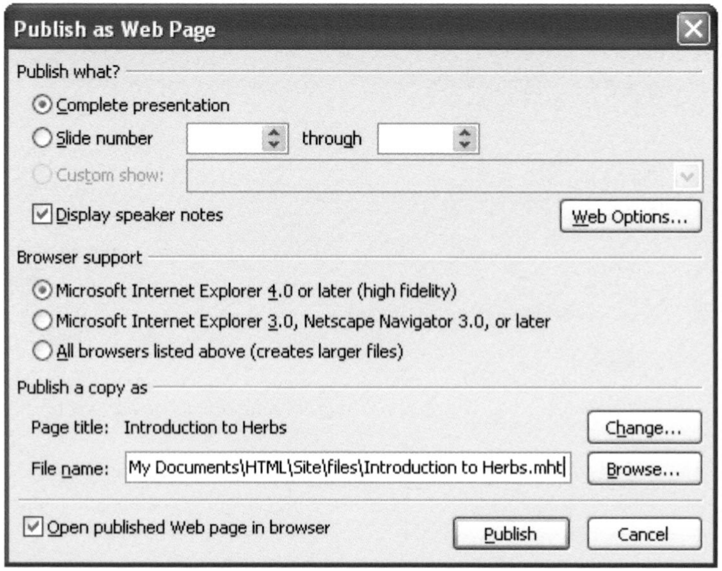

Figure 9-18: The Publish As Web Page dialog box lets you choose which parts of the PowerPoint presentation to publish and which browsers to support.

Web presentations created with the Microsoft Internet Explorer 4.0 Or Later setting work for Mozilla and Mozilla Firefox, making them accessible to nearly 98 percent of the browsers in use in summer 2004.

If your PC has XP with Service Pack 2 or a later Service Pack, Internet Explorer displays the information bar, telling you that it has restricted the file from showing active content that could access your computer and prevented the presentation from being displayed. To view the presentation, click the information bar, click **Allow Blocked Content**, and then click **Yes** in the Security Warning dialog box.

PowerPoint presentations tend to include many graphics for elements, such as background, bullets, or lines, as well as any graphics that you include manually. If a graphic is missing, the presentation may display no image, a blank placeholder for the image, or a red X.

5. In the Publish What? section, choose which part of the presentation to publish: the complete presentation, a range of slides, or a custom show that you've defined. (If the presentation contains no custom shows, the Custom Show option button is unavailable.) Select the **Display Speaker Notes** check box if you want to include speaker notes with the slides.

6. In the Browser Support section, select the **Microsoft Internet Explorer 4.0 Or Later** option button, the **Microsoft Internet Explorer 3.0, Netscape Navigator 3.0, Or Later** option button, or the **All Browsers Listed Above** option button.

7. Check the title displayed in the Page Title field. To change it, click **Change**, type the new title in the Set Page Title dialog box, and then click **OK**.

8. Check the path and file name in the File Name text box. If necessary, type a change, or click **Browse**, specify the folder and file name in the Publish As dialog box, and then click **OK**.

9. Select the **Open Published Web Page In Browser** check box if you want PowerPoint to display the web page in your default browser so that you can check it.

10. Click **Publish**. PowerPoint publishes the page and (if necessary) displays it in Internet Explorer (see Figure 9-19).

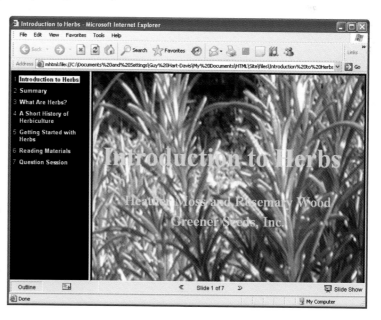

Figure 9-19: Internet Explorer displays a control bar at the bottom of the presentation for moving from slide to slide and for starting the slide show. Most other browsers can display the presentation but do not provide these controls.

Create Web Pages from Data-Access Pages in Access

To create web content from Microsoft Access, you use a *data-access page*, which is a live page bound to a database. When you publish a data-access page to the Web, users of Internet Explorer 5.01 or later can access and manipulate the database through the web page. Users of other browsers can usually view the web page successfully but cannot manipulate the data it contains.

To create a web page from a data-access page:

1. Start Access (if it is not already running), or switch to it.
2. Open the appropriate database, select the **Pages** item, and then double-click the data-access page. The data-access page opens.
3. Click the **File** menu and then click **Save As**. The Save As dialog box (shown here) appears. 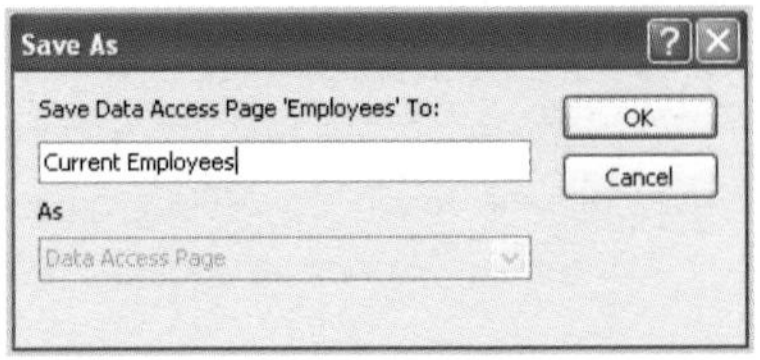
4. Type the name for the data-access page, and then click **OK**. The Save As Data Access Page dialog box appears.
5. Choose the folder in which to save the file, type the file name (include the .html extension if you do not want to use the default .htm extension), and then click **Save**.
6. If you have finished working with Access, click the **File** menu and then click **Exit**.
7. Open Internet Explorer (for example, click the **Start** button and then click **Internet**), click the **File** menu, click **Open**, click **Browse**, select the file you just saved, click **Open**, and then click **OK**. The file opens in Internet Explorer. Figure 9-20 shows an example.

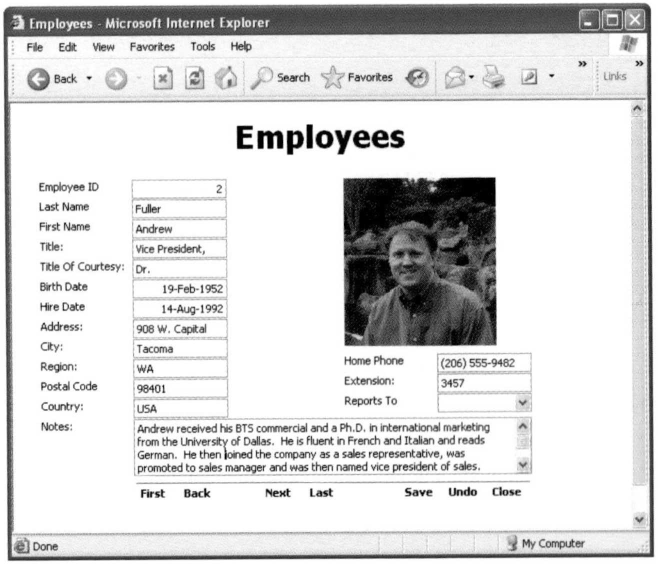

Figure 9-20: Using Access, you can create data-access pages that you can open in Internet Explorer and use to browse and edit a database.

How to...

- *Understand the Basics of Forms*
- *Define the Form Structure*
- *Understanding the Method Attribute*
- *Add Fields to the Form*
- *Complete a Form*
- *Letting Visitors Upload Files*
- *Create a Form That E-Mails Its Contents to You*
- *Understand the Different Categories of User Events*
- *Dealing with Script Threats*
- *Show When a Page Was Last Updated*
- *Redirect the Browser to Another Page*
- *Display a Pop-Up Window*
- *Verify That a Form Is Filled In*
- *Develop Your "About Me" Page on eBay*
- *Understanding Item-Level Tags and Page-Level Tags*
- *Use Blogger.com Tags*

Chapter 10

Using Forms, Scripts, and Special Tags

This chapter shows you how to create forms to collect information from visitors to your web site, either using a script on a web server or (more simply) via e-mail.

You'll also learn how to perform some useful actions—such as redirecting the browser to another page, displaying a pop-up window with additional information, or verifying that the visitor has completed the required fields on a form—with easy-to-implement scripts and how to use special tags for eBay and Blogger.com.

Create Forms

To enable visitors to your web pages to provide you with information, you create a form that the visitors can fill in. For example, you might:

- Implement a logon form to ensure that all visitors to certain parts of your web site have registered (and perhaps paid a subscription)
- Provide a signup form for an e-mail newsletter or a hard-copy catalog
- Allow visitors to upload pictures or other files to you

Understand the Basics of Forms

A web form is a web page that contains *fields*, areas in which a visitor can enter information or select from a set of predefined options. When a visitor accesses the form, the browser displays the web page as usual, including the form's fields. The visitor can interact with the fields—for example, by typing text into a text field, by selecting a check box or an option button from a group of option buttons, or by choosing an item from a drop-down list.

When finished with the form, the visitor then clicks a command button that submits the form, usually by running a Common Gateway Interface, or CGI, script written in a programming language such as Perl.

For a form to work, you must:

- Create a form that contains the appropriate fields for your purpose
- On the web server, set up a script that will handle the information the visitor enters in the form
- Include in the form the appropriate HTML instructions for the script that will process the form

This process is much more complex than simply creating a web page and copying it to your web host's server, but most web hosts provide easy-to-use scripts for a variety of common form uses.

TIP

Before you start to plan or create any forms, check which script capabilities your Internet service provider (ISP) or web host provides for your type of account. (Different types of user accounts have different levels of scripts available—usually, the more you pay, the more scripts you get.)

10

Define the Form Structure

Before starting to create your form as described in this section, decide the purpose of the form and establish which information it will collect. Divide that information into suitable fields. For example, if you plan to create a database using the information the form gathers, you should keep first and last names separate rather than placing them together in a single field. Similarly, you should separate address information into several fields, as in the example shown later in this chapter. Separating both the name and address allows you to sort by each of the components—for example, you can sort by last name or by ZIP code.

To start a form:

1. Open Notepad or your HTML editor, and start a new web page. For example, if you have created the skeleton of an HTML document, as suggested earlier in this book, open that file and then save it under a different name. Otherwise, create the following document skeleton, and then save it under a name of your choice:

```
<html>
<head>
<title></title>
</head>
<body>
</body>
</html>
```

2. Type the beginning of the opening `<form>` tag:

```
<form
```

3. Type the `action` attribute and specify the name (and, if necessary, the location) of the script that you want to use for returning or processing the data that the visitor enters in the form. The following example uses the script named register.php stored in the /cgi-bin/ folder:

```
<form action="cgi-bin/register.php"
```

4. Type the `method` attribute and specify the value `get` or `post`, as needed. (See the "Understanding the Method Attribute" QuickFacts for an explanation of the difference between `get` and `post`.) For example:

```
<form action="cgi-bin/register.php" method="get">
```

NOTE

For the `action` attribute, you will need to enter the name and location of a script that is available to you—a script that your web host provides for you, a script that you have downloaded from another location on the web and have installed on your web site, or a script that you have developed yourself. If you simply follow the example shown in this section, your form will not work unless you just happen to have a script of the same name in the same folder.

UNDERSTANDING THE METHOD ATTRIBUTE

For the `method` attribute, you will need to specify either `get` (to send the form data to the script specified by `action`) or `post` (to send the form data in the HTTP header). Whether you need to specify `get` or `post` depends on the script you're using.

`get` assembles the content of the form into a text string called a *querystring*, which is added after a question mark to the URL in the address bar of the next page loaded in the browser.

Each field in the querystring is separated by an ampersand (`&`), each space is replaced by a plus sign (`+`), and the name of each field is followed by a space and the field's value.

For example, if you were to visit the (hypothetical) site http://www.quicksteps.com/form1.html, type <u>Jane Ramirez</u> in the text box named textbox1, and click the **Submit** button, the querystring `?textbox1=Jane+ Ramirez&mybutton=Submit` would be added to the URL in the address bar.

The advantage of `get` is that if the visitor bookmarks the page, the querystring is saved in the bookmark, so he or she can return directly to the result of the form. The disadvantage is that displaying the form contents in the address bar can present a security problem.

`post` does not add the querystring to the address bar, so it avoids the potential security problem. The disadvantage of `post` is that the visitor cannot bookmark the result of the form.

5. Optionally, type the `name` attribute and specify the name you want to assign to the form. The name is not necessary unless you want to be able to access your forms via scripts, but you may find that assigning names to your forms helps you to distinguish one from another:

   ```
   <form action="cgi-bin/register.php" method="get"
       name="registration"
   ```

6. Type the closing angle bracket to complete the `<form>` tag:

   ```
   <form action="cgi-bin/register.php" method="get"
       name="registration">
   ```

7. On a new line, type the closing `</form>` tag:

   ```
   </form>
   ```

8. Between the `<form>` and `</form>` tags, enter the text and fields for the form, as discussed in the following sections.

Add Fields to the Form

After creating the basic structure for the form and specifying the action and method to take, add text boxes, drop-down lists, check boxes, and command buttons to the form as needed. Also add any text or other objects (for example, graphics) that the form needs using tags as usual.

ADD A SINGLE-LINE TEXT BOX

To add a single-line text box:

1. Place the insertion point at the appropriate position between the `<form>` and `</form>` tags, and press **ENTER** to create a new line.

2. Type a label for your field to identify it to the user. For example, type <u>Full Name</u>.

3. Type the beginning of an `<input>` tag, a space, the type attribute, an equal sign, double quotation marks, text, and double quotation marks:

   ```
   <input type="text"
   ```

4. Type a space, the `name` attribute, an equal sign, double quotation marks, the name that you want to assign to the text box, and double quotation marks:

   ```
   <input type="text" name="fullname"
   ```

TIP

Setting the `type` attribute to `text` makes the `<input>` tag display a single-line text box.

NOTE

You do not need to use double quotation marks when specifying numeric values, such as those for the `size` attribute and the `maxlength` attribute.

TIP

If the text box is for the visitor to enter a password or other information that should be shielded from prying eyes, use `type="password"` instead of `type="text"` for the `<input>` field. When a visitor types in the box, it displays an asterisk or bullets for each character rather than the character itself. Don't assign a default value to a password text box because it will appear as asterisks or bullets rather than as text.

Login Name: psmith449

Password: ●●●●●●●●●

5. Type a space, the `size` attribute, an equal sign, double quotation marks, the desired width for the text box, and double quotation marks. This is the number of characters that can be displayed in the text box (the user can enter more than this number; see the `maxlength` attribute described in the following text):

```
<input type="text" name="fullname" size=40
```

6. If you want to display default text in the text box, type a space, the `value` attribute, an equal sign, double quotation marks, the default text, and double quotation marks:

```
<input type="text" name="fullname"
    size=40 value="Please type your full name here"
```

Name:
Please type your full name here

7. If you want to limit the amount of text that the visitor can enter, type a space, the `maxlength` attribute, an equal sign, double quotation marks, the maximum number of characters, and double quotation marks:

```
<input type="text" name="fullname"
    size=40 value="Please type your full name here"
    maxlength=25>
```

ADD A MULTILINE TEXT BOX

Single-line text boxes are convenient for getting short pieces of information from your visitors, but if you want them to be able to express themselves more freely, use a multiline text box instead.

To add a multiline text box:

1. Place the insertion point between the `<form>` and `</form>` tags, and press **ENTER** to create a new line.

2. Type the beginning of a `<textarea>` tag:

```
<textarea
```

3. Type a space, the `cols` attribute, an equal sign, and the number of columns that the text box should occupy. This is roughly the number of characters that will appear across the width of the text box (this is equivalent to the `size` attribute for the `<input>` tag):

```
<textarea cols="40"
```

4. Type a space, the `rows` attribute, an equal sign, and the desired number of rows for the text box:

   `<textarea cols=40 rows=10`

5. Type the closing angle bracket for the `<textarea>` tag, any default text you want to appear in the text box, and the closing `<textarea>` tag:

   `<textarea cols=40 rows=10>Please type your message here.</textarea>`

ADD A DROP-DOWN LIST

If you need to enable visitors to select one item from a number of items, use a drop-down list. To add a drop-down list:

1. Place the insertion point at the appropriate position between the `<form>` and `</form>` tags, and press **ENTER** to create a new line.

2. Type the beginning of the `<select>` tag:

   `<select`

3. Type a space, the `size` attribute (which specifies the number of lines visible in the list), an equal sign, double quotation marks, 1, and double quotation marks:

   `<select size="1">`

4. Press **ENTER** to start a new line.

5. Type the beginning of the `<option>` tag, a space, the `value` attribute, an equal sign, double quotation marks, the identifying number that will signify that the visitor chose this item, and double quotation marks. For example, to create the first item:

   `<option value="1"`

6. Type the closing angle bracket of the `<option>` tag, the text that you want to appear for the item in the drop-down list, and the closing `</option>` tag. For example, to create the list item AL:

   `<option value="1">AL</option>`

7. Repeat steps 4, 5, and 6 to create as many list items as you need. The following code shows an abbreviated example (the ellipses indicate that lines have been omitted):

```
<option value="1">AL</option>
<option value="2">AK</option>
<option value="3">AR</option>
<option value="4">AS</option>
<option value="5">AZ</option>
<option value="6">CA</option>
<option value="7">CO</option>
<option value="8">CT</option>
...
<option value="58">WI</option>
<option value="59">WY</option>
```

8. Type the closing `</select>` tag to end the drop-down list. When the user clicks the down arrow of the drop-down list, the entire list will be displayed.

ADD A CHECK BOX

For presenting options that are not mutually exclusive, use check boxes. To add a check box:

1. Place the insertion point at the appropriate location between the `<form>` and `</form>` tags, and press **ENTER** to create a new line.

2. Type the beginning of an `<input>` tag, a space, the `type` attribute, an equal sign, double quotation marks, <u>checkbox</u>, and double quotation marks:

```
<input type="checkbox"
```

3. Type a space, the `name` attribute, an equal sign, double quotation marks, the name that you want to assign to the check box, and double quotation marks:

```
<input type="checkbox" name="Catalog"
```

4. Type a space, the `value` attribute, an equal sign, double quotation marks, the identifying text that will signify that the visitor chose this item, and double quotation marks.

5. If you want the check box to be selected by default, type a space followed by <u>checked</u>:

```
<input type="checkbox" name="Catalog" value="Catalog" checked
```

TIP

By default, the browser displays the first item in the drop-down list. To make the browser display another item, add the `selected` attribute to the opening `<option>` tag for the relevant item—for example, `<option value="3" selected>United States </option>`. Setting the default item is particularly useful when you have a long list of items in which the item the visitor is most likely to choose does not appear first. (Alternatively, you can rearrange the list to put the most likely item or items first.)

NOTE

If you do not specify text for the `value` attribute of a check box, it receives the value "on" if it is selected.

State: AL

AL
AK
AR
AS
AZ
CA
CO
CT
DC
DE
FL
FM
GA
GU
HI
IA
ID
IL
KS
KY

6. Type the closing angle bracket for the `<input>` tag, the text that you want the check box to display, and the closing `</input>` tag:

```
<input type="checkbox" name="Catalog" value="Catalog" checked>Send a
Catalog</input>
```

☑ Send a Catalog ☐ Add to Mailing List

ADD OPTION BUTTONS

Option buttons enable a visitor to choose between two or more mutually exclusive options. Only one option button in a group of option buttons can be selected at any one time; selecting an option button clears all the other option buttons in the group.

To add a group of option buttons:

1. Place the insertion point at the appropriate location between the `<form>` and `</form>` tags, and press **ENTER** to create a new line.

2. Type the beginning of an `<input>` tag, a space, the `type` attribute, an equal sign, a pair of double quotation marks, <u>radio</u>, and another pair of double quotation marks:

```
<input type="radio"
```

3. Type a space, the `name` attribute, an equal sign, a pair of double quotation marks, the name for the group of option buttons, and another pair of double quotation marks:

```
<input type="radio" name="customertype"
```

4. Type the closing angle bracket for the `<input>` tag, the text that you want to appear for the option button, and then the closing `</input>` tag:

```
<input type="radio" name="customertype">Existing Customer</input>
```

5. Repeat steps 1 through 4 to add each of the other option buttons to the group.

6. Optionally, to make one of the option buttons selected by default, add the `checked` attribute to it:

```
<input type="radio" name="customertype" checked>New Customer</input>
```

○ Existing Customer ◉ New Customer

NOTE

To create a reset button, follow these steps but use `type="reset"` instead of `type="submit"`, and assign the button a value, such as <u>Reset the Form</u> or <u>Clear All Fields</u>.

ADD COMMAND BUTTONS

The controls discussed so far in this chapter let visitors interact with your forms, but to enable them to take an action, you must add one or more command buttons. At the very least, you must add a button for submitting the form. It's often a good idea to include a button that resets the form, clearing all the data chosen or entered in its fields.

To add a submit button:

1. Place the insertion point at the appropriate position between the `<form>` and `</form>` tags, and press **ENTER** to create a new line.

2. Type the beginning of an `<input>` tag, a space, the `type` attribute, an equal sign, a pair of double quotation marks, <u>submit</u>, and another pair of double quotation marks:

   `<input type="submit"`

3. Type a space, the `value` attribute, an equal sign, a pair of double quotation marks, the name for the button, another pair of double quotation marks, and the closing angle bracket for the `<input>` tag:

   `<input type="submit" value="Submit Feedback">`

Complete a Form

The following listing shows the complete code for the sample form shown in Figure 10-1; the list of states and possessions is omitted for conciseness:

```
<h1>Customer Feedback</h1>

<form action="feedback.php" method="get">
<p>Full Name: <input type="text" name="fullname"
    size=40 value="Please type your full name here"
    maxlength=40>
</p>
<p>Address 1:
<input type="text" name="address1"
    value="Address line 1" size="40">
</p>
<p>Address 2:
<input type="text" name="address2"
    value="Address line 2" size="40">
</p>
```

Figure 10-1: Include a reset or clear button on your forms so that visitors can easily clear the information they've entered in the form if necessary.

```
<p>City:
<input type="text" name="addresscity"
    value="City" size="17">
 State:
<select size="1">
    <option value="1">AL</option>
    <option value="2">AK</option>
    <option value="3">AR</option>
    ...
    <option value="58">WI</option>
    <option value="59">WY</option>
</select>
 Zip:
<input type="text" name="addresszip"
    value="Zip" size="5" maxlength=5>
</p>
<p>E-mail:
<input type="text" name="email"
    value="Type your e-mail address here" size="40">
</p>
<p><input type="radio" name="customertype">Existing Customer
</input>  
<input type="radio" name="customertype" checked>
New Customer</input></p>
<p><input type="checkbox" name="Catalog"
    value="Catalog" checked>Send a Catalog</input>
      
<input type="checkbox" name="MailList"
    value="MailList">Add to Mailing List</input></p>
<p>Your message for us:<br>
<textarea cols=40 rows=10>Please type your message here.
</textarea></p>
<p><input type="submit" value="Submit Feedback"
    name="submit">
<input type="submit" value="Clear the Form" name="clear"></p>
</form>
```

LETTING VISITORS UPLOAD FILES

Depending on the types of forms you create, you may sometimes need to let visitors upload files to you. For example, if you accept visitor input for your site, you might need to let visitors upload pictures; if you sell software, you may need to allow visitors to upload configuration files so that you can diagnose problems.

1. Place the insertion point at the appropriate position between the `<form>` and `</form>` tags, and press **ENTER** to create a new line.

2. Type the beginning of an `<input>` tag, a space, the `type` attribute, an equal sign, a pair of double quotation marks, file, and another pair of double quotation marks:

   `<input type="file"`

3. Type a space, the `name` attribute, an equal sign, a pair of double quotation marks, the name for the upload controls, and another pair of double quotation marks:

   `<input type="file" name="upload"`

4. Type a space, the `size` attribute, an equal sign, a pair of double quotation marks, the approximate width of the text box in the upload controls, another pair of double quotation marks, and the closing angle bracket for the tag:

   `<input type="file" name="upload" size=60>`

Figure 10-2 shows the resulting upload controls in a form. No matter which types of files you receive, check them for viruses before opening them by using an antivirus program, such as Norton AntiVirus (http://www.symantec.com) or McAfee VirusScan (http://www.mcafee.com), with up-to-date virus definitions. Even files as apparently harmless as JPEGs can contain malware (malicious software).

Create a Form That E-Mails Its Contents to You

If your web host doesn't supply an easy-to-use script that fulfills your needs, you can easily create a form that e-mails its contents to you. This is a quick and easy method of returning the contents of the form, but you have to expose an e-mail address, which may be gathered by either live visitors or spiders crawling the Web. Either way, the e-mail address may end up on a spam list so it is best to use an address that you can abandon if necessary without disrupting your main lines of communication.

To create a form that e-mails its contents to you:

1. Type the beginning of the opening `<form>` tag:

   `<form`

2. Type the `action` attribute, an equal sign, a pair of double quotation marks, the `mailto:` attribute and the e-mail address, and another pair of double quotation marks:

   `<form mailto:"customers@quicksteps.com"`

3. Type a space, the `method` attribute, an equal sign, a pair of double quotation marks, post, another pair of double quotation marks, and the closing angle bracket for the `<form>` tag:

   `<form mailto:"customers@quicksteps.com" method="post">`

4. Create the remainder of the form as described earlier in this section.

Show Us Your Prize Vegetables

To send us a picture file, click the **Browse** button, use the resulting **Choose File** dialog box to select the file, and then click the **Open** button to enter the path and file name in the text box. Click the **Submit** button to submit the form, including the picture file.

[   ] [Browse...]

Figure 10-2: Use an `<input>` tag with `type="file"` to create upload controls in a form. The visitor clicks the Browse button to display a Choose File dialog box that makes it easy to select a file on a local drive.

NOTE

The `type` attribute `file` gives you a text box field with a Browse button. The user can enter a path and file name in the field or click the Browse button, which opens the standard Windows dialog box used to locate and select a file, which, in either case, will be uploaded to the server running your web page.

NOTE

As with the simple text box, the `size` attribute does not limit the number of characters the user can enter; it only specifies the size of the text box that displays them.

NOTE

Scripts can run either on the server (*server-side scripts*) or on the web browser (*client-side scripts*). This section discusses client-side scripts.

If the visitor is using Internet Explorer, clicking the command button to submit an e-mail form may display a warning (such as that shown here) that the form will be submitted via e-mail and without encryption, revealing the visitor's e-mail address to you. The visitor can choose whether to proceed with submitting the data or canceling the submission.

> **Microsoft Internet Explorer** ⊠
>
> ⚠ This form is being submitted using e-mail.
> Submitting this form will reveal your e-mail address to the recipient, and will send the form data without encrypting it for privacy.
>
> You may continue or cancel this submission.
>
> [OK]   [Cancel]

Visitors using one of the Mozilla browsers will typically see a message started automatically in their default e-mail application and will be able to choose between sending it manually and canceling it without sending it. The message will not be sent automatically.

Use Scripts in Your Web Pages

A script is a list of commands written in a scripting language (a type of programming language) that is used to automate activity. Various scripting languages can be used on web pages, but the most widely used at this writing is JavaScript.

Scripting can be highly complex—but you can also use short and straightforward scripts to add interactivity to your web pages and make them perform actions that HTML alone cannot accomplish. This section introduces you briefly to scripts and shows you examples of some simple actions that you can perform with JavaScript without having to learn much of the language. If you find these actions useful, you may choose to learn more about JavaScript so that you can use it more fully.

To tell the browser that you're using a script rather than HTML codes, you enclose the script between an opening `<script>` tag and a closing `</script>` tag. Inside the opening `<script>` tag, you use the `language` attribute to specify the language in which the script is written—in this case, JavaScript:

```
<script language="JavaScript">
</script>
```

Understand the Different Categories of User Events

A script runs because it is triggered by the visitor (or the visitor's browser) taking an action. Such an action is called an *event*, simply meaning that something definable happened. Table 10-1 explains the most common user events that you can employ in your scripts, divided into categories. The following events are usually the most useful:

- The `onclick` event is useful for performing actions when the visitor clicks an element on a web page—for example, a link.
- The `onsubmit` event is useful for checking that all required fields in a form have been completed before it is sent for processing.
- The `onmouseover` and `onmouseout` events are used for implementing effects such as an image rollover: as the mouse moves over it, an existing graphic is replaced by another graphic; when the mouse moves off the graphic's area, the original graphic is restored.
- The `onselect` event can be used to automatically select, clear, or make available other check boxes, option buttons, or menu items affected by the current choice.

NOTE

The `onload` and `onunload` events are widely used by unscrupulous web sites to display pop-up windows containing material that most visitors would probably not have chosen to view. Because of this usage, many browsers enable users to block the display of such automatically generated windows. Even if these windows are not blocked, you will do well to avoid using them, as they frequently produce negative reactions from visitors.

TABLE 10-1: USER EVENTS FOR SCRIPTS

EVENT NAME	EVENT OCCURS WHEN
BROWSER-GENERATED EVENTS	
onload	The browser starts to load a web page.
onunload	The browser starts to leave the web page (because the visitor has told it to load another web page).
onerror	An error occurs in a script that the browser is trying to run.
onabort	The visitor stops the current page from being loaded (for example, by clicking the Stop button).
MOUSE EVENTS	
onmousemove	The visitor moves the mouse pointer in the browser window.
onmouseover	The visitor moves the mouse pointer so that it is over a particular element—for example, the visitor moves the mouse pointer over a graphic.
onmouseout	The visitor moves the mouse pointer so that it leaves the element in question—for example, the visitor moves the mouse pointer off the graphic again.
onclick	The visitor clicks an element on the web page.
ondoubleclick	The visitor double-clicks an element on the web page.
onmousedown	The visitor clicks the mouse button on an element and keeps the mouse button pressed down.
onmouseup	The visitor releases the mouse button that he or she has been holding down.
KEYBOARD EVENTS	
onkeypress	The visitor presses and releases a key (in other words, performs a normal keystroke action).
onkeydown	The visitor presses a key and holds it down.
onkeyup	The visitor releases a key that he or she has been holding down.
FORM FIELD EVENTS	
onsubmit	The visitor clicks the submit button on a form.
onreset	The visitor clicks the reset button on a form.
onselect	The visitor selects an option button, a check box, or a menu item.
onchange	The visitor types in a text box or selects a different option button, check box, or menu item.
onfocus	The visitor moves the focus to a form field—for example, by clicking in a text field before typing in it.
onblur	The visitor moves the focus away from the form field in question.

QUICKFACTS

DEALING WITH SCRIPT THREATS

JavaScript can be used to perform malicious actions against the will of the visitor to a web page, so some people prevent their browsers from executing JavaScript. Some browsers also block scripts by default on the grounds that they might be malicious.

With Windows XP Service Pack 2 installed, Internet Explorer displays the information bar to warn a visitor about active content such as JavaScript. To use the script, the visitor must click the information bar, and then click **Allow Blocked Content**, as shown here.

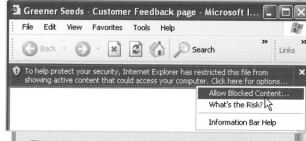

The visitor must then click **Yes** in the Security Warning dialog box that appears.

If your pages rely on JavaScript and the visitor's browser doesn't execute it, the pages will not work properly. Consider warning users that they will need to enable JavaScript in order to view your pages successfully. Alternatively, provide a version of your site that doesn't use JavaScript so that users can view your site without it.

Show When a Page Was Last Updated

Some of the pages on your site are likely to change frequently. If they do, you may want to show visitors when the pages were last updated so that they will know whether the pages contain new information since their last visit. While you can include the date as text and change it manually each time you change the page, it's much easier to use a short script that inserts the date and time on which the page was last modified—or, more accurately, when it was last saved to the web server.

The following example uses the `document.lastModified` statement to provide the date and time the page was saved and the `document.write` statement to add explanatory text before and a period after:

```
<script language="JavaScript">
    document.write("This page was last modified on")
    document.write(document.lastModified)
    document.write(".")
</script>
```

> This page was last modified on 10/03/2004 16:10:33.

Redirect the Browser to Another Page

You can use JavaScript to redirect the browser to another page:

```
<script language="JavaScript">
    window.location="http://www.quicksteps.com"
</script>
```

Display a Pop-Up Window

Instead of creating a link that opens in the same browser window (or on the same tab of a tabbed browser, such as Mozilla Firefox), you can create a link that opens in a separate window. This technique is useful for displaying more detail about an item without the browser leaving the main page. For example, you might use a pop-up window to display detailed product information.

You can also use the `document.write` statement to display other information in a web page. For example, `document.write(document.title)` displays the page's title; `document.write(location.href)` displays the file name of the active web page; and `document.write(document.referrer)` displays the name of the web page that referred the browser to the current web page.

You can also redirect the browser by using an `http-equiv` meta tag, as discussed in Chapter 1. The advantage of the meta tag is that it will not trigger a script warning; however, some browsers enable you to block meta refreshes, which prevents such redirection from working. If you use a meta tag to redirect the browser, provide a link that the visitor can click manually if the meta refresh is disabled.

Don't display pop-up windows automatically by using events such as `onload`, `onunload`, or `onmouseover`, because windows springing up apparently spontaneously may make visitors feel that their browser has been hijacked. (Many disreputable web sites open large numbers of pop-up windows.) Instead, allow visitors to open pop-up windows manually by clicking the links that interest them.

To open a pop-up window, use the `onclick` event for the appropriate link.

1. Place the insertion point at the appropriate location in the web page (not in the header), and type any necessary element tags. The example described here is contained in a table cell for placement.

2. Type the opening anchor tag, a space, the `href` attribute, a pair of double quotation marks, a hash symbol (#), and another pair of double quotation marks:

```
<td><a href="#"
```

3. Type a space, a pair of double quotation marks, the `window.open` command (which instructs the browser to open a new window), and an opening parenthesis:

```
<td><a href="#" onclick="window.open(
```

4. Type a single quote, the path (if necessary) and file name of the desired web page for the link, another single quote, and a comma:

```
<td><a href="#" onclick="window.open('bramley.html',
```

5. Type a space, a single quote, the name you want to assign to the pop-up window, another single quote, and a comma:

```
<td><a href="#" onclick="window.open('bramley.html',
    'bramleypop',
```

6. Type a space, a single quote, and then each of the properties you want to specify for the pop-up window (see Table 10-2) with an equal sign and the appropriate value. Separate the property-and-value pairs from each other with a comma and a space. For example, to specify that the window display any scroll bars that are needed, be resizable, and be 400 pixels wide by 400 pixels high:

```
<td><a href="#" onclick="window.open('bramley.html',
    'bramleypop', 'scrollbars=1, resizable=1, width=400,
    height=400'
```

7. Type the closing parenthesis, a pair of double quotation marks, the closing angle bracket, the text that you want displayed for the hyperlink, the closing anchor tag, and any closing element tag that is needed:

```
<td><a href="#" onclick="window.open('bramley.html',
    'bramleypop', 'scrollbars=1, resizable=1, width=400,
    height=400'">Bramleys</a></td>
```

Figure 10-3 shows the link on the page and the resulting pop-up window.

The `href="#"` statement indicates that the URL for the web page will be specified in the following script command rather than directly within the double quotation marks as usual.

Unless the pop-up window contains only a graphic of a fixed size, it's best to allow the display of the scroll bars and make the window resizable in case the visitor's browser settings make the contents too big for the initial window size.

The name you assign to the pop-up window enables the browser to identify the window. If the visitor clicks the link again when the pop-up window is still open, the browser can activate the existing pop-up window instead of opening a new pop-up window.

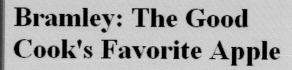

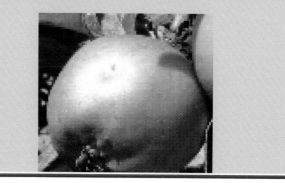

Figure 10-3: A pop-up window can be a convenient way of displaying additional information without causing the visitor to leave the current page.

TIP

You can add a command button to enable the visitor to close a pop-up window even more easily than by clicking the close button in the window's title bar.

You can do so by adding a statement, such as `<button onclick="window.close();">Close This Window</button>`, at the relevant point in the form. If the visitor is using Internet Explorer with XP SP2, however, he or she will need to permit the script to run (by clicking the information bar, clicking Allow Blocked Content, and then clicking Yes in the Security Warning dialog box) before the close button will work. This rigmarole makes the close button not worth the

wide variety of apple dishes.

Close This Window

Verify That a Form Is Filled In

If you create forms, you may need to verify that the required fields are filled in before you allow a visitor to submit the form. You can use a script to check the contents of the fields.

TABLE 10-2: PROPERTIES FOR A POP-UP WINDOW

PROPERTY	EXPLANATION
width	Sets the browser window's width in pixels (for example, `width=400`).
height	Sets the browser window's height in pixels (for example, `height=500`).
left	Specifies the offset of the new window from the left edge of the existing window, in pixels. For example, `left=100` places the left edge of the new window 100 pixels to the right of the left edge of the existing window.
top	Specifies the offset of the new window from the top edge of the existing window, in pixels. For example, `top=50` places the top edge of the new window 50 pixels below the top edge of the existing window.
resizable	Allows (`resizable=1`) or prevents (`resizable=0`) the resizing of the browser window.
menubar	Displays (`menubar=1`) or hides (`menubar=0`) the browser window's menu bar.
toolbar	Displays (`toolbar=1`) or hides (`toolbar=0`) the browser window's toolbar.
location	Displays (`location=1`) or hides (`location=0`) the browser window's address bar.
scrollbars	Displays (`scrollbars=1`) or hides (`scrollbars=0`) the browser window's scroll bars.

The following example shows the code for a web page (see Figure 10-4) that includes a short script that performs basic validation on the two text boxes, ensuring that neither is empty:

```html
<html>
<head>
<title>Greener Seeds - Preferred Customer Login</title>
<script language="JavaScript">
    function verify(loginform)
        {if (loginform.login.value=='')
            {alert('Enter your login name.'); return false;}
        if (loginform.password.value=='')
            {alert('Enter your password.'); return false;}
        return true}
</script>
</head>
<body background="images/leaves_1.jpg"
    style="color:white; font-weight:bold">
<h1>Preferred Customer Login</h1>
<p>Please log in to access the Preferred
    Customer options.</p>
<form method="post" action="login.cgi"
    onsubmit="return verify(this);">
<table border=0>
    <tr>
        <td>Login Name:</td>
        <td colspan="2"><input type="text"
          name="login" size=20></td>
    </tr>
    <tr>
        <td>Password:</td>
        <td><input type="password" name="password" size=10></td>
        <td><input type="submit" value="Log In"></td>
    </tr>
</table>
</form>
<p>If you are not yet a Greener Seeds customer,
    click <a href="new_cust.html"
    style="color:orange">here</a>.</p>
</body>
</html>
```

Figure 10-4: This page uses a short script to check that the Login Name text box and Password text box contain entries before the form is submitted.

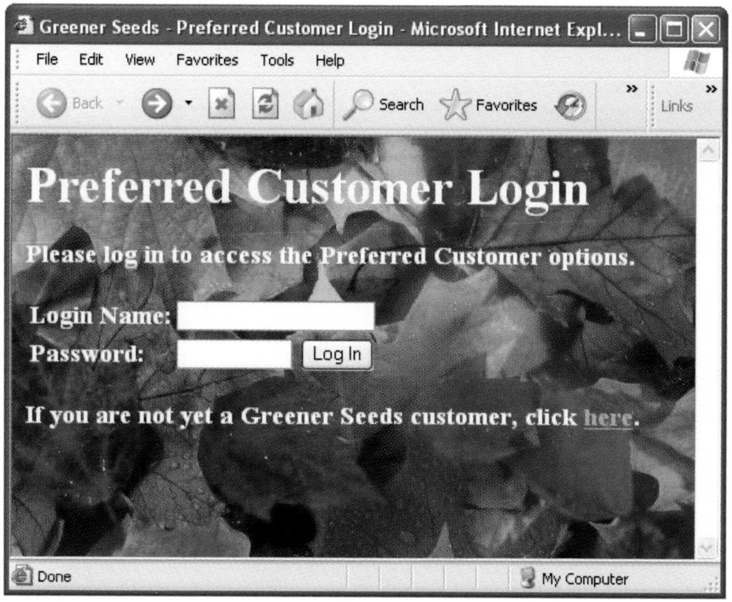

The form contains two text boxes (`input type="text"`), one named `login` and the other named `password`, and a submit button that bears the text "Log In." The `onsubmit` event in the `<form>` tag specifies that when the form is submitted (in other words, when the visitor clicks the Log In button), the script returns the value of the function named `verify` for the current object (`onsubmit="return verify(this);"`).

The code within the `<script>` and `</script>` tags in the document header does the following:

- States that the script language used is JavaScript.

- Declares a function named `verify` and specifies that the object it works on is `loginform`.

- Compares the `value` (the contents) of the text box named `login` on the form named `loginform` (`loginform.login.value`) to an empty string (`' '`). If there is a match, the `alert` statement displays a message box telling the visitor the problem and returns the value `false`, preventing the form from being submitted.

- Similarly, the code compares the `value` (the contents) of the text box named `password` (`loginform.password.value`) to an empty string (`' '`). If there is a match, the `alert` statement displays a message box (shown here) telling the visitor the problem and returns the value `false`, again preventing the form from being submitted.

- If both the `login` text box and the `password` text box contain text, the function returns the value `true`, which allows the form to be submitted.

TIP

The `onsubmit` event is often the most convenient way to validate a form. For complex forms, however, you may find it simpler to use the `onblur` event to validate each text field as the visitor moves the focus away from it.

TABLE 10-3: ATTRIBUTES FOR THE `<eBayUserID>` **TAG**

ATTRIBUTE	DISPLAYS YOUR USER ID
(none)	As a link to your eBay account
bold	In bold font, as a link to your eBay account
e-mail	With your e-mail address
nofeedback	Without your feedback score
nolink	Not as a link to your eBay account
nomask	Omitting shades

Use Special Tags

The HTML tags discussed so far in this book apply to all web pages and all current and recent browsers. Some sites, however, use custom HTML tags for special purposes. This section discusses examples of custom HTML tags for two sites: eBay and Blogger.com.

Develop Your "About Me" Page on eBay

eBay, the widely used online auction site, allows sellers to customize the way their "About Me" pages appear.

CONTROL THE DISPLAY OF YOUR USER ID

eBay enables you to display your user ID in different forms, depending on your requirements, by using the `<eBayUserID>` tag with the appropriate attribute (see Table 10-3).

For example, to display your user ID without your feedback score and not as a link to your eBay account:

```
<eBayUserID nofeedback nolink>
```

CONTROL THE DISPLAY OF YOUR FEEDBACK ITEMS

You can control the display of your feedback item list by using the appropriate attributes (see Table 10-4) with the `<eBayFeedback>` tag.

The following example applies lime and cyan to punch up the feedback table:

```
<eBayFeedback color="cyan" alternatecolor="lime">
```

User: peter_example_44 (35 ☆) **Date**: Oct-29-04 06:54:43 PDT	
Praise: Civil enough, and good, quick service. Correct items.	
User: jane_angry_102 (8 ☆) **Date**: Oct-30-04 18:27:10 PDT	
Complaint: Still waiting for the guitar after 6 weeks. One excuse after another; none believable.	

CONTROL THE DISPLAY OF YOUR ITEMS LIST

You can use the `<eBayItemList>` tag to display a list of some or all of the items you're bidding on or selling. Table 10-5 lists the attributes you can use.

TABLE 10-4: ATTRIBUTES FOR THE `<eBayFeedback>` TAG

ATTRIBUTE	EFFECT ON THE FEEDBACK TABLE
(none)	Displays your feedback with default settings.
`alternatecolor`	Controls the background color of the upper feedback lines—for example, `alternatecolor="cyan"`.
`border`	Sets the border width in pixels—for example, `border="3"`. The default setting is `0`.
`caption`	Adds a caption containing the specified text above the feedback table—for example, `caption="Read What Other Customers Have to Say"`.
`cellpadding`	Specifies the amount of cell padding to use—for example, `cellpadding=5`.
`color`	Controls the background color of the lower feedback lines—for example, `color="lime"`.
`size`	Controls the number of feedback items displayed—for example, `size="5"` displays your first five feedback items.
`tablewidth`	Changes the width of the feedback table from 90 percent of the available space (the default) to the specified percentage—for example, `tablewidth="80%"`.

TABLE 10-5: ATTRIBUTES FOR THE `<eBayItemList>` TAG

ATTRIBUTE	DISPLAYS
(none)	All the items that you are currently selling.
`bids`	All the items on which you're currently bidding.
`border`	Specifies the border width of the table in pixels. The default setting is `0`.
`caption`	Displays the specified text at the top of the items table.
`category`	Restricts the listing to the specified category and its subcategories: `1`: Collectibles `99`: Miscellaneous `160`: Computers `220`: Toys, Bean Bag Plush `237`: Dolls, Figures `266`: Books, Movies, Music `281`: Jewelry, Gemstones `353`: Antiques `866`: Coins & Stamps `870`: Pottery & Glass `888`: Sports Memorabilia `1047`: Photo & Electronics
`cellpadding`	Specifies the amount of cell padding in pixels—for example, `cellpadding=2`.
`since`	`-1` (the default setting) causes only current auctions to appear. A positive setting makes auctions appear for that number of days after they have ended.
`sort`	The specified items sorted by: `2`: date, oldest first `3`: auction end date, newest first `4`: price, ascending `8`: date, newest first
`tablewidth`	Sets the width of the items table to the specified percentage of the available space—for example, `tablewidth="80%"`.

The following example displays the items you're selling in the Computers category listed by auction end date, newest first:

```
<eBayListItem sort="3" category="160">
```

CONTROL THE TIME DISPLAY

You can use the `<eBayTime>` tag by itself to display the current time in the default format (MM/DD/YY, HH:MM:SS and the time zone—for example, 10/21/04, 21:05:22 PDT) or with the `format` attribute and the codes shown in Table 10-6 to create a custom time format. In most cases, the default format is clearest.

To use the `format` attribute, type format, an equal sign, a pair of double quotation marks, the codes for the date and time items you want to display (together with any spaces and punctuation needed), and another pair of double quotation marks. The following example displays the current date in a format such as "Saturday, December 25, 2004":

```
<eBayTime format="%A, %d %B, %Y">
```

TABLE 10-6:
FORMAT CODES FOR THE
`<eBayTime>` **TAG AND THE**
`<eBayMemberSince>` **TAG**

CODE	EXPLANATION	VALUES
%H	24-hour clock	00 to 23
%I	12-hour clock	01 to 12
%M	Minute	00 to 59
%S	Second	00 to 59
%p	AM/PM or local equivalent	AM or PM (or local equivalent)
%A	Full weekday name	Monday to Sunday (or local equivalent)
%a	Abbreviated weekday name	Mon to Sun (or local equivalent)
%B	Full month name	January to December (or local equivalent)
%b	Abbreviated month name	Jan to Dec (or local equivalent)
%d	Day of the month	01 to 28, 29, 30, or 31
%m	Month of the year	01 to 12
%Y	Four-digit year	2004, 2005, 2006, and so on
%y	Two-digit year	04, 05, 06, and so on

Blogger.com uses two main groups of tags:

* *Item-level tags* extract specific pieces of data from Blogger's database so that you can use the data in your pages. Item-level tags start and end with dollar signs inside their angle brackets. For example, `<$BlogTitle$>` is an item-level tag that extracts the blog's title from the database.

* *Page-level tags* are used to enclose item-level tags and place them in the appropriate position in a page. Page-level tags do not include dollar signs, so they are easy to distinguish from item-level tags. Page-level tags have an opening tag (for example, `<BlogSiteFeed>`) and a corresponding closing tag that begins with a forward slash (`</BlogSiteFeed>`):

```
<BlogSiteFeed>
<$BlogSiteFeedUrl$>
</BlogSiteFeed>
```

CAUTION

Blogger's template tags are not actually HTML, but behave similarly to HTML. Unlike in HTML, you must get the case right for Blogger's tags to work correctly.

Use Blogger.com Tags

Blogger.com (http://www.blogger.com) provides special template tags for creating custom templates for your web logs, or blogs.

Some Blogger tags are used only in the header of a page, while others are used only in the body. Table 10-7 lists the Blogger tags, indicating which are used for the header and which are used for the body. The following sections provide examples using some of the most useful Blogger tags.

DISPLAY YOUR BLOG PAGE TITLE IN THE BROWSER TITLE BAR

The following example, which you would place in the header section of your template, displays your blog page title in the browser's title bar:

```
<title><$BlogPageTitle$></title>
```

DISPLAY INFORMATION ABOUT YOURSELF

The following example displays the first name, last name, and URL of the blog owner (for instance, you):

```
<p>This blog belongs to <$BlogOwnerFirstName$> 
    <$BlogOwnerLastName$>.<p>
<p>To read my profile, click <a href="<$BlogOwnerProfileUrl$>
    here</a>.</p>
```

DISPLAY THE NUMBER OF COMMENTS

The following example displays the number of comments for the item and a link to the `#comments` anchor on the page that contains the comments. This example is placed within an opening `<BlogItemCommentsEnabled>` tag and a closing `</BlogItemCommentsEnabled>` tag to restrict it to items on which comments are enabled (so that it doesn't appear on items that don't allow comments):

```
<Blogger>
    <BlogItemCommentsEnabled>
        <a href="<$BlogItemPermalinkURL$>#comments">
        <$BlogItemCommentCount$> Comments So Far</a>
    </BlogItemCommentsEnabled>
</Blogger>
```

INSERT A PERMANENT HYPERLINK TO A BLOG ITEM

The following example inserts a permanent hyperlink to the blog item:

```
<a href="<$BlogItemPermalinkURL$>"
title="Permanent Link to the Post">#</a>
```

TABLE 10-7: BLOGGER.COM TAGS

TAG	TYPE	EXPLANATION
HEADER TAGS		
`<$BlogSiteFeedLink$>`	Item	Returns your site feed's URL.
`<$BlogEncoding$>`	Item	Returns the type of character encoding used for your blog.
`<BlogSiteFeed>`	Page	Contains the `<$BlogSiteFeedUrl$>` tag.
`<$BlogSiteFeedUrl$>`	Item	Returns the URL of the site feed.
`<$BlogMetaData$>`	Item	Returns all the metadata for the blog.
`<$BlogPageTitle$>`	Item	Returns the title of the blog page.
BODY TAGS		
`<Blogger>`	Page	Contains the main body of your blog's content. Most of the other body tags should go between an opening `<Blogger>` tag and a closing `</Blogger>` tag.
`<$BlogTitle$>`	Item	Returns the title of the blog.
`<$BlogMemberProfile$>`	Item	Returns all the shared information in your member profile.
`<$BlogOwnerFirstName$>`	Item	Returns the first name of the blog owner.
`<$BlogOwnerLastName$>`	Item	Returns the last name of the blog owner.
`<$BlogOwnerEmail$>`	Item	Returns the e-mail address of the blog owner.
`<$BlogOwnerFullName$>`	Item	Returns the full name of the blog owner.
`<$BlogOwnerPhotoUrl$>`	Item	Returns the URL of the blog owner's photo.
`<$BlogOwnerNickname$>`	Item	Returns the nickname of the blog owner.
`<$BlogOwnerLocation$>`	Item	Returns the city, state, and country (if applicable) of the blog owner.
`<$BlogOwnerAboutMe$>`	Item	Returns the "About Me" description of the blog owner.
`<$BlogOwnerProfileURL$>`	Item	Returns the URL of the blog owner's profile.
`<BlogDateHeader>`	Page	Contains the `<$BlogDateHeaderDate$>` tag.
`<$BlogDateHeaderDate$>`	Item	Returns the date header for the item.
`<BlogItemTitle>`	Page	Contains the `<$BlogItemTitle$>` tag.
`<$BlogItemTitle$>`	Item	Returns the title of the blog item.
`<BlogItemURL>`	Page	Contains the `<$BlogItemURL$>` tag.
`<$BlogItemURL$>`	Item	Returns the URL for the blog item.
`<$BlogItemBody$>`	Item	Returns the content of a post

BODY TAGS *Continued...*		
`<$BlogItemAuthor$>`	Item	Returns the full name of the item's author.
`<$BlogItemAuthorNickname$>`	Item	Returns the nickname of the item's author.
`<$BlogItemAuthorEmail$>`	Item	Returns the e-mail address of the item's author.
`<$BlogItemAuthorURL$>`	Item	Returns the URL of the item author's home page.
`<$BlogItemDateTime$>`	Item	Returns the date and time the item was posted.
`<$BlogItemNumber$>`	Item	Returns the ID number of the item.
`<$BlogItemArchiveFileName$>`	Item	Returns the archive file name of the item.
`<$BlogItemPermalinkURL$>`	Item	Returns the permanent URL of the item.
`<$BlogItemControl$>`	Item	Returns a Quick Edit link to the item.
`<BlogDateFooter>`	Page	Contains the `<$BlogDateFooter$>` tag.
`<BloggerArchives>`	Page	Contains the `<$BlogArchiveURL$>` tag and `<$BlogArchiveName$>` tag.
`<$BlogArchiveURL$>`	Item	Returns the URL of the blog's archive.
`<$BlogArchiveName$>`	Item	Returns the name of the blog's archive.
`<BloggerPreviousItems>`	Page	Contains the `<$BlogPreviousItemTitle$>` tag and `<$BlogItemPermalinkURL$>` tag.
`<$BlogPreviousItemTitle$>`	Item	Returns the title of the previous item in the blog.
`<$BlogItemPermalinkURL$>`	Item	Returns the permanent URL of the blog item.
`<BlogItemCommentsEnabled>`	Page	Contains the comment tags that you want to display only on items for which comments are enabled.
`<$BlogItemCommentCount$>`	Item	Returns the number of comments for the blog item.
`<BlogItemComment>`	Page	Contains the tags that return the details of the comment.
`<$BlogCommentNumber$>`	Item	Returns the ID number of the comment.
`<$BlogCommentBody$>`	Item	Returns the body text of the comment.
`<$BlogCommentPermalinkURL$>`	Item	Returns the permanent URL of the comment.
`<$BlogCommentAuthor$>`	Item	Returns the author of the comment.
`<$BlogCommentDateTime$>`	Item	Returns the date and time of the comment.
`<$BlogCommentDeleteIcon$>`	Item	Displays a delete button for the comment. (This button can be used only by the blog's administrator or the comment's author.)
`<$BlogItemCreate$>`	Item	Displays a link that lets visitors create new comments.

Numbers

1-7 type sizes, descriptions of, 53–54

256 colors, using, 31

640 x 480 resolution, experimenting with, 31

800 x 600 resolution, experimenting with, 31

1024 x 760 resolution, experimenting with, 31

Symbols

(hash symbol), using with href attribute, *88*

/ (slash)
  Dividing folders with, 22
  Significance of, 3

<!-- --> tag, adding comments with, 8

<> (angle brackets), significance of, 3

" " (double quotation marks), surrounding file names with, 5, 14, 146

; (semicolon), using with style declarations, 144

A

<a> and </a> tags, using with hyperlinks, 11

"About Me" page, developing on eBay, 201–204

above value for frame attribute, effect of, 111

absolute dimension, using with height and width, *129*

absolute links
  definition of, *86*
  guidelines for use of, 87

Access
  choosing General tab options for, 162
  creating web pages from data-access pages in, 180

accesskey attribute, assigning keyboard shortcuts to links with, 90–91

action attribute, using with forms, 183

Add Network Place Wizard, using with Internet Explorer, 34

Adobe GoLive, features of, 12

Adobe Photoshop Elements, resource for, 10

align attribute
  adding to opening <table> tag, 118
  adding to opening <td> tag, 119

adding to opening <tr> tag, 118

applying to elements, 50

using with inline graphics, 75

values for, 75

aligning
inline graphics, 75

text in style sheets, 154–155

all value for rules attribute, effect of, 112

alt attribute
  using with spacer images, 79
  using with inline graphics, 74

ALT+TAB shortcut, switching between web pages and applications with, 7

alternative text
  adding to frameset documents, 134–135
  using with inline graphics, 74

anchor tags
  creating links to, 88, 90
  using with hyperlinks, 11

anchors, connecting hyperlinks to, 169–170

(angle brackets (<>), significance of, 3

Animation Shop tool, features of, 66

asymmetrical broadband, definition of, *25*

Attributes dialog box, displaying in Paint, 64

attributes, relationship to tags, 3

audio files, 25
  creating link for playing of, 100
  creating link for downloading of, 100
  delivery methods for, 99–100
  embedding in web pages, 101–102
  formats for, 99
  playing in background of web pages, 101

AutoRepublish Every Time This Workbook is Saved option, benefit of, *177*

AVI (audio-video interleave) files, features of, 99

B

<b> and </b> (bold) tags, using, 51

backbone, definition of, *24*

background attribute, using with graphics, 80

background audio, playing for web pages, 101

background color. *See also* color attribute

applying to elements, 58

applying to tables, 122

background graphics. *See also* graphics; inline graphics
  adding, 80
  preventing from being tiled or scrolling, 157–158

background pictures. *See also* pictures
  applying to tables, 122
  applying to tables and cells

background-color property, applying, 58

<basefont> tag, changing default text size with, 55

baseline value, effect of, 120

behavior attribute, using with <marquee> tag, 60

below value for frame attribute, effect of, 111

bgcolor attribute, using with <marquee> tag, 60–61

<big> and </big> inline style, effect of, 53

blink value
  advisory about use of, 153
  using with, 57

<blockquote> and </blockquote> tags, indenting margins with, 49

Blogger.com tags, using, 205–206

blue borders, removing from around links, 87

body, purpose in web pages, 4

body sections, creating in tables, 113

body tags, adding to web pages, 4

boldface, applying, 51

borders
  applying, 59
  applying to inline graphics, 77
  controlling display in tables, 111–112
  displaying and hiding in tables, 108, 111
  removing from frames, 136
  specifying widths for tables, 108
  in tables, *105–106*

boxes, creating, 58, 111

.br domain, explanation of, 26

 tag, breaking lines with, 8, 42

browser-generated events, examples of, 194

browsers
  checking web pages in, 17–18
  checking web sites with, 31
  redirecting to other web pages, 16
  redirecting to other pages, 195–196

bulleted lists
  creating, 45
  display of, 44

C

capitalization of text, changing, 5

<caption> and </caption> tags, using with tables, 109

cell height, setting, 117

cell width, specifying, 115

cellpadding attribute, effect of, 116–117

cells
  applying background pictures to, 122–123
  applying horizontal alignment to, 118–119
  applying vertical alignment to, 120
  definition of, *105*
  grouping by rows and columns, 112–114
  position in tables, 106
  spanning, 106
  spanning two columns or rows, 121

¢ special character, code for, 43

center alignment, 9
  applying to row contents within cells, 118
  applying to elements, 50

check boxes, adding to forms, 187–188

class attribute, using as selector, 149–150

client, diagram of, *20*

closing tags, identifying, 3

.cn domain, explanation of, 26

<colgroup> tag, grouping table columns with, 114

color, applying to table borders, 111

color attribute, using with <font> tag, 54

cols value for rules attribute, effect of, 112

colspan attribute, adding to opening <td> tag, 121

columns
  adding to tables, 110
  definition of, *105*
  grouping, 114
  position in tables, 106
  spanning cells over, 121
  using fixed widths and wildcards with, 130
  using fixed widths in pixels with, 130
  using variable widths in percentages with, 130
  using with frames, 132–133

Note: Italicized page numbers denote definitions of new terms.

.com domain, explanation of, 26
command buttons, adding to forms, 189
comments
 adding to web pages, 8
 displaying in blogs, 205
component documents
 adding to framesets, 133
 creating for web pages using frames, 130
compressed audio formats, using, 99
compressing graphics, 73
content
 adding to web pages, 4–9
 planning for web sites, 28–29
 separating by folders, 3
content attribute, using with meta tags, 15, 16
© special character, code for, 43
CSS (Cascading Style Sheets). *See* style sheets
CTRL+S shortcut, saving web pages with, 7
CuteFTP, web address for, 37
CuteHTML editor, web address for, 12

D

↓ special character, code for, 43
data-access pages in Access, creating web pages from, *180*
.de domain, explanation of, 26
default.html file, relationship to URLs, 21
definition lists
 creating, 47
 display of, 44
Deneba Canvas graphics application, web address for, 67
digital cameras
 controlling files sizes with, 71
 downloading pictures from, 71–72
direction attribute, using with <marquee> tag, 60–61
directories
 including index files in, 5
 securing, 5
disc attribute, using with <ul> tag, 45
dithering, definition of, *31*
÷ special character, code for, 43

divisions
 creating for paragraphs, *41*–42
 using as selectors, 151
<dl> and </dl> (definition list) tags, using, 47
DNS (Domain Naming System), overview of, 26
document styles, definition of, *142*
documents, creating hyperlinks to, 170
domain host name, example of, 20
domain names, 24
 registering, 26–28
 selecting, 26
 trademark concerns related to, 28
double quotation marks (" "), surrounding file names with, 5, 14, 146
Dreamweaver, features of, 12
drop-down lists, adding to forms, 186–187

E

eBay, developing "About Me" page on, 201–204
.edu domain, explanation of, 26
<em> and </em> (logical emphasis-text) tags, using, 51
e-mail accounts, considering for web hosts, 23
e-mail addresses
 advisory about using in web pages, 94
 creating hyperlinks to, 171
e-mail buttons, creating, 94–95
e-mail
 creating links for sending of, 92–95
 including form content in, 191–192
e-mail signatures, including graphics in, 82–84
<embed> tag, using with audio and video, 102–103
embedded style sheets, creating, *144*–145
Encoding tab of Web Options, choosing in Office applications, 166–167
.es domain, explanation of, 26
events. *See* user events
Excel, 175–177
 choosing General tab options for, 161
 Files tab of Web Options in, 165–166

external style sheets
 applying to frameset documents, 147
 creating and applying, 146–151
extranets, definition of, 23–24

F

feedback items on eBay, controlling display of, 201–202
fields
 adding to forms, 184–189
 role in forms, *182*
file extensions, using, 14
file properties in Office applications, removing personal information from, 172
file sizes, managing for web pages, 30
files. *See also* HTML files
 creating hyperlinks to, 169
 downloading with links, 91
 transferring to network places, 36–37
 transferring with FTP clients, 38
 using naming conventions, 3
Fireworks graphics application, web address for, 67
first lines of elements, applying different formatting to, 152
first-line indents, creating, 56
:first-line pseudo-element, adding to style sheets, 152
flatbed scanners, benefits of, 72
folders
 creating for web sites, 2
 naming, 2
 navigating, 32
 separating content by, 3
 transferring to network places, 36–37
 using with Office application files, 165
font formatting
 controlling, 53–54, 57
 controlling in style sheets, 153–154
font properties
 for formatting text, 153
 using with style attribute, 57
<font> tag, using, 53
fonts, changing on Internet Explorer, 40
footer sections, creating in tables, 113

form field events, examples of, 194
form structure, defining, 183–184
formatting
 applying to web pages, 9
 considerations for, 40
forms
 adding check boxes to, 187–188
 adding command buttons to, 189
 adding drop-down lists to, 186–187
 adding fields to, 184–189
 adding multiline text boxes to, 185–186
 adding single-line text boxes to, 184–185
 completing, 189–190
 creating reset buttons for, 189
 definition of, *182*
 for e-mailing their contents, 191–192
 including clear buttons on, 190
 starting, 183
 validating with onsubmit event, 200
 verifying filled-in status of, 198–200
&fract*; special characters, codes for, 43
frame attribute, values for, 111
frames. *See also* inline frames
 adding flexibility to, 130
 changing margins for, 136
 considering use of, 129
 controlling scrolling of, 137
 creating component documents for, 130
 creating links to change contents of, 140
 defining height and width of, 129–130
 definition of, *127*
 illustration of, 128
 planning for use of, 128
 preventing resizing of, 137
 removing borders from, 136
 using columns with, 132
 using relative dimensions with, 129
 using rows and columns with, 133
 using rows with, 131–132
frameset documents
 adding alternative text to, 134–135
 applying external style sheets to, 147
 creating, 130–131
 definition of, *128*

framesets
  adding component documents to, 133
  nesting, 138
FrontPage, features of, 12
FTP clients, transferring web sites with, 32, 37–38
FTP sites
  accessing instantly, 36
  accessing with Internet Explorer, 33–35
  moving objects from, 37

G

get, specifying for method attribute, 184
GIF (Graphics Interchange Format), creating
  with Paint Shop Pro, 68–69
.gov domain, explanation of, 26
graphic links
  creating, 86–87
  using with e-mail, 92–93
graphics. See also background graphics; inline
  graphics
  compressing, 73
  controlling size of, 73
  converting to different formats with Paint, 66
  copyright concerns related to, 65
  creating two or more links in, 95–97
  creating with Paint application, 64–66
  removing white space around, 135
  resizing with Paint, 66
  scanning from documents or pictures, 72–73
  using effectively on web sites, 30
graphics applications, choosing, 66–67
groups value for rules attribute, effect of, 112
> special character, code for, 43

H

<h1> and </h1> tags, example of, 6
hash symbol (#), using with href attribute, 88
header sections, creating in tables, 112
header tags, adding to web pages, 4
headers
  placing meta tags in, 15
  purpose in web pages, 4

headings
  adding to web pages, 6
  creating, 43–44
  including descriptions for, 6
height attribute
  adding to opening <table> tag, 117
  adding to opening <td> tag, 117
  creating boxes with, 58
  using with inline graphics, 76
  using with pop-up windows, 198
horizontal alignment, applying to cells, 118–119
horizontal rules, adding to web pages, 80
HostSearch, web address for, 22
<hr> (horizontal rule) tag, using, 80–81
href attribute, using with hyperlinks, 11, 88, 91
href='#' statement, effect of, 197
hsides value for frame attribute, effect of, 111
.htm and .html file extensions, using, 14
HTML editors, benefits of, 11–12
HTML elements, creating with Word, 176
HTML files. See also files
  copying structures of, 14
  creating form existing documents, 11
  saving in Notepad, 5
  selecting contents of, 14
  transferring via FTP, 32
HTML (Hypertext Markup Language)
  definition of, 3
  example of, 14
HTML signature files
  creating, 82–83
  using in Outlook Express, 83–84
HTML tags. See tags
<HTML> tags, adding to text documents, 3
http://
  versus https://, 22
  significance of, 21–22
http-equiv meta tag, redirecting browsers with, 16
hyperlinks. See also graphic links; links; text links
  adding ScreenTips to, 169
  adding to web pages, 11–12
  connecting to anchors, 169
  creating files associated with, 13
  creating in Office applications, 168–171

creating to e-mail addresses, 171
creating to new documents, 170
creating to place in current document, 170
definition of, 85
inserting into blog items, 206
turning off autoformatting in Office
  applications, 172
using with inline frames, 140
hyphenation, controlling, 42

I

<i> and </i> (italic) tags, using, 51
id attribute, using as selector, 149
¡ special character, code for, 43
<iframe> (inline frame) tag, using, 139
Image Mapper dialog box, displaying in Paint
  Shop Pro, 98
imagemaps, creating, 95–97
<img src=> tag, adding pictures with, 10
<img> tag, using with inline graphics, 74
.in domain, explanation of, 26
indents
  applying, 49
  applying to first line of paragraphs, 56
  setting in style sheets, 155
  using with spacer images, 79
index files, including in directories, 5
index.html page, including hyperlink back to,
  14, 21
inline frames, creating, 138–140.
  See also frames
inline graphics. See also background graphics;
  graphics
  aligning, 75
  applying borders to, 77
  including alternative text for, 74
  inserting, 74
  positioning with spacer images, 78–79
  resizing, 75–77
  specifying both dimensions for, 76
inline styles, applying, 51–52
interlaced GIFs, creating with Paint Shop Pro,
  68–69
interlaced PNGs, creating with Paint Shop Pro, 70
internal style sheets, creating, 144–145

Internet connection speed and uptime,
  considering for web hosts, 24
Internet, definition of, 19
Internet Explorer
  applying style sheets in, 157
  benefits of, 17–18
  changing fonts on, 40
  checking web sites with, 31
  transferring web sites with, 33–37
intranets, definition of, 23
IP addresses
  definition of, 20
  relationship to DNS, 26
¿ special character, code for, 43
ISPs (Internet Service Providers)
  choosing, 22–25
  evaluating, 25
.it domain, explanation of, 26
italics
  applying, 51
  simulation of, 51

J

JavaScript, performing malicious actions with, 195
.jp domain, explanation of, 26
JPEG (Joint Photographic Experts Group)
  format, using with Paint Shop Pro, 68–69
justify alignment, applying to row contents
  within cells, 118

K

<kbd> and </kbd> (keyboard) inline style,
  effect of, 53
keyboard events, examples of, 194
keyboard shortcuts
  assigning to links, 90
  for saving web pages, 7
Konqueror browser, web address for, 17

L

← special character, code for, 43
left alignment
  applying to row contents within cells, 118
  applying to elements, 50
left margins, indenting, 49
left property, using with pop-up windows, 198
letter spacing, changing, 55–56
lhs value for frame attribute, effect of, 111
<li> tag
  using with bulleted lists, 45
  using with numbered lists, 46
line breaks
  adding to web pages, 8
  controlling, 42
line height, setting for style sheets, 156
line spacing, changing, 56
line-height property, using, 56
linked files, creating, 13–14
links. *See also* graphic links hyperlinks; text links
  assigning keyboard shortcuts to, 90
  changing tab order of, 90–91
  components of, 85
  creating for anchors on other web pages, 90
  creating in graphics, 95–97
  creating to change frame contents, 140
  creating to download audio and video files, 100
  creating to download files, 91
  creating to play audio and video files, 100
  creating to send e-mail, 92–95
  creating within web pages, 88–89
  displaying ScreenTips for, 92
  opening in new windows, 90
lists
  bulleted lists, 45
  definition lists, 47
  nested lists, 48
  numbered lists, 46–47
Log On As dialog box, displaying in Add
  Network Place Wizard, 35
logical emphasis-text tags, using, 51
lossy and lossless compression, explanation of, *68*
< special character, code for, 43
Lynx browser, web address for, 17

M

MacLynx browser, web address for, 17
Macromedia Dreamweaver, features of, 12
mailto hyperlinks
  creating, 171
  using graphics as, 93
margins
  changing for frames, 136
  indenting, 49
  resizing for inline frames, 139
  setting in style sheets, 156
markup tags. *See* tags
<marquee> tag
  advisory about, 60
  creating moving text with, 60–61
meta tags
  describing web pages with, 15
  http-equiv, 16
method attribute, using with forms, 183
Microsoft FrontPage, features of, 12
Microsoft Office applications, creating HTML
  documents with, 11
.mil domain, explanation of, 26
monspaced fonts, using, 40–41
mouse events, examples of, 194
moving text, adding with <marquee> tag, 60–61
Mozilla browsers, web addresses for, 17
Mozilla Firefox, using default fonts and colors
  in, 158
MP3 files, creating link for downloading of, 100
multiline text boxes, adding to forms, 185–186
My Documents window, opening, 2
My Webs folder, using, 2

N

name attribute
  using with frames, 133
  using with meta tags, 15
named anchor, definition of, *88*
naming conventions, using with files, 3

navigating web sites, 90
 special character, code for, 43
 (nonbreaking spaces), keeping text
  together with, 42
nesting
  framesets, 138
  lists, 48
  tables, 123–124
.net domain, explanation of, 26
Netscape browser, web address for, 17
network places
  accessing, 36
  creating for web servers, 33–35
  transferring files to, 36–37
Network Solutions, web address for, 27
<nobr> and </nobr> (no-break) tags, using, 42
<noframes> text, including in frameset pages, 134
none value for rules attribute, effect of, 112
noresize attribute, using with frames, 137
Notepad
  adding .txt extension by default in, 5
  opening, 3
  pinning to Start menu, 2
  preventing addition of .txt extension in, 146
nowrap attribute, using with <td> tag, 115
ñ special character, code for, 43
numbered lists
  creating, 46–47
  display of, 44

O

objects, moving from FTP sites, 37
OC (optical carrier) channels, considering for
  web hosts, 24
Office applications
  checking appearance of documents in, 171
  choosing Browser tab options for, 163–164
  choosing Files tab options for, 164
  configuring web options in, 160–167
  creating HTML documents with, 11
  creating hyperlinks in, 168–171
  removing personal information from file
  properties in, 172
Office Web Components, using interactive
  spreadsheets in, 166

<ol> and </ol> tags, creating numbered lists
  with, 46–47
onclick event, 92–94
  definition of, *193*
  displaying pop-up windows with, 196
onload event, advisory about, 193
onmouseover and onmouseout events,
  definitions of, *193*
onselect event, definition of, *193*
onsubmit event
  definition of, *193*
  validating forms with, 200
onunload event, advisory about, 193
Opera browser, web address for, 17
option buttons, adding to forms, 188
optional hyphens, placing, 42
ordered lists, display of. *See* numbered lists
Outlook Express, using HTML signature files
  in, 83–84
outside borders, displaying in tables, 112
overlining, applying to paragraphs, 57

P

<p> and </p> tags, using, 7, 41
pages. *See* web pages
Paint application, creating graphics with, 64–66
Paint Shop Pro graphics application
  creating imagemaps with, 98–99
  creating interlaced GIFs with, 68–69
  creating interlaced PNGs with, 70
  creating progressive JPEGs with, 67–68
  web address for, 66
paragraphs
  applying first-line indents to, 56
  applying underlining, overlining, and
  strikethrough to, 57
  centering, 9
  creating, 41
  grouping into divisions, 41–42
  indicating, 7
personal information, removing from File
  properties in Office applications, 172
Photoshop Elements graphics application,
  features of, 66
pictures. *See also* background pictures

adding to web pages, 10
downloading from digital cameras, 71–72
PivotTable, definition of, *177*
pixels, specifying in Paint, 65
± special character, code for, 43
PNG (Portable Network Graphics) format, description of, *68*
pop-up windows
displaying, 195–197
propeties for, 198
post, specifying for method attribute, 184
PowerPoint, 178–179
choosing General tab options for, 162
Files tab of Web Options in, 165
<pre> and </pre> tags, preformatting text with, 50–51
preformatted text, using, 50–51
progressive JPEGs, creating with Paint Shop Pro, 67–68
properties, setting for styles, 145
proportional fonts, using, 40–41
protocol, definition of, *32*

Q

QuickFacts
Choosing Graphics Applications, 66
Choosing Suitable Web File Formats, 174–175
Dealing with Script Threats, 195
Deciding Whether to Use Frames in Your Web Pages, 129
Keeping Down Graphic Size to Make Pages Load Faster, 73
Laying Out Your Web Pages, 82
Making Useful Imagemaps, 95
Organizing Your Site, 3
Running Your Own Web Server, 25
Understand CSS Versions, 146
Understanding Absolute and Relative Links, 86–87
Understanding Domains, 26
Understanding GIF, JPEG, and PNG, 68–69
Understanding How Search Engines Work, 16
Understanding How the Office Applications Use HTML, 160–161
Understanding Intranets and Extranets, 23

Understanding Item-level Tags and Page-level Tags, 205
Understanding Other Inline Styles, 53
Understanding Other Ways of Creating Style Rules, 145
Understanding the Header and the Body, 4
Understanding the Method Attribute, 184
Understanding the Style Cascade, 143
Understanding Tools for Creating HTML, 11–12
Understanding URLs, 22
Using Proportional and Monospaced Fonts, 40
Working with Fonts, 54
QuickSteps
Creating an Imagemap with Paint Shop Pro, 98–99
Inserting Special Characters, 43
Letting Visitors Upload Files, 191
Making Your Site Navigable, 90–91
Overriding Style Sheets in Your Browser, 157
Setting Table and Cell Height, 117
Using Graphics to Control How Text Appears, 78
Using Word to Create HTML Elements, 176

R

radio buttons, adding to forms, 188
→ special character, code for, 43
red text, significance of, 3
redirection, using in web pages, 16
refresh intervals, setting, 16
refreshing web pages, 6
® special character, code for, 43
Register.com, web address for, 27
registration sites for domain names, 27
relative dimension, using with height and width, *129*
relative links
definition of, *86*
guidelines for use of, 87
reset buttons, creating for forms, 189–190
resizable property, using with pop-up windows, 198
resolutions, experimenting with, 31
rhs value for frame attribute, effect of, 111

right alignment
applying to row contents within cells, 118
applying to elements, 50
right margins, indenting, 49
robots meta tag, description of, 15
rows
adding to tables, 110
aligning contents of, 118, 120
definition of, *105*
grouping, 112–113
position in tables, 106
spanning cells, 121
using with frames, 131–133

S

<s> and </s> (strikethrough) tags, using, 52
<samp> and </samp> (sample) inline style, effect of, 53
scanners, using, 72–73
screen resolutions, experimenting with, 31
ScreenTips
adding to hyperlinks, 169
displaying for links, 92
scripts
definition of, *192*
user events for, 194
using in web pages, 192–199
scroll bars, displaying on inline frames, 140
scrollbars property, using with pop-up windows, 198
scrolling, controlling for frames, 137
search engines
functionality of, 16
preventing web pages from appearing in, 15
secure servers, considering for web hosts, *25*
selectors. *See also* special selectors
class attributes as, 149–150
definition of, *144*
divisions as, 151
id attributes as, 149
setting properties for, 145
spans as, 150–151
semicolon (;), using with style declarations, 144
servers. *See* web servers
shape attribute, using with imagemaps, 96

shopping carts, considering for web hosts, *25*
&shy code, creating soft hyphens with, 42
signature, definition of, *82*
single-line text boxes, adding to forms, 184–185
size attribute, using with fonts, 53–54
slash (/)
dividing folders with, 22
significance of, 3
<small> and </small> inline style, effect of, 53
soft hyphens, placing, 42
source code, viewing for web pages, 9
space, considering for web hosts, 23
spacer images, positioning graphics with, 78–79
spanning cells
definition of, *106*
over two columns or rows, 121
spans, using as selectors, 150–151
special characters, inserting in web pages, 43
special selectors, using, 148–152. *See also* selectors
special tags, using, 201–206. *See also* tags
start attribute, using with <ol> tag, 47
Start menu, pinning Notepad to, 2
streaming, definition of, *25*
strikethrough, applying, 52, 57
style attribute
versus <style> element, 55
border properties for, 59
changing style of elements with, 55–60
font properties for, 57
style rules, creating, 144–145
style sheets. *See* CSS (Cascading Style Sheets)
adding :first-line pseudo element to, 152
aligning, centering, and justifying text in, 154–155
definition of, *141*
controlling font formatting in, 153–154
linking to on other servers, 148
linking to web pages, 148
overriding, 153
overriding in browsers, 157–158
overview of, 142–143, 146
setting indents in, 155
setting margins in, 156
_{and} (subscript) tags, using, 52
subscript, applying, 52

T

tab order, changing for links, 90–91

tabindex attribute, using, 91

table borders

adding, 111–112

setting different colors for, 111

table height, setting, 117

<table summary> tag, expanding caption information with, 109

table width, specifying, 115–116

<table> and <> tags, using, 107–108

tables

adding captions to, 109

adding rows and columns to, 110

aligning horizontally, 118

applying background colors to, 122

applying background pictures to, 122

changing layout of, 106

components of, *105*

creating, 107–109

nesting, 123–124

planning, 106

specifying widths of borders for, 108

tags. *See also* special tags

<!-- -->, 8

<caption> and </caption>, 109

<a> and </a> (anchor), 11

<b> and </b> (bold), 51

<basefont> (default text size), 55

<big> and </big> inline style, 53

<blockquote> and </blockquote> (indentation), 49

 (break line), 8

 (line break), 42

case of, 4

<colgroup>, 114

definition of, *1*

<dl> and </dl> (definition list), 47

<em> and </em> (logical emphasis-text), 51

<font>, 53

<h1> and </h1> (heading), 6

<hr> (horizontal rule), 80–81

<i> and </i> (italic), 51

<iframe> (inline frame), 139

<img src=> (picture), 10

<img> (image), 74

<kbd> and </kbd> (keyboard) inline style, 53

<li> (list), 45–46

<marquee>, 60–61

meta tags, 15

<nobr> and </nobr> (no-break), 42

<noframes>, 134

<ol> and </ol> (ordered list), 46–47

<p> and </p> (paragraph), 7, 41

<pre> and </pre> (preformat), 50–51

<s> and </s> (strikethrough), 52

<samp> and </samp> (sample) inline style, 53

<small> and </small> inline style, 53

<strike> and </strike> (strikethrough), 52

_{and} (subscript), 52

<table summary>, 109

<table> and <>, 107–108

<tbody> and </tbody> (table body), 113

<td> and </td> (table data), 107–108

<tfoot> and </tfoot> (table footer), 113

<thead> and </thead> (table header), 112

<tr> and </tr> (table row), 107–108

<u> and </u> (underline), 52

<ul> and </ul> (unordered list), 45

<var> and </var> (variable text) inline style, 53

target attribute, using with links, 90

<tbody> and </tbody> tags, creating table body sections with, 113

<td> and </td> (table data) tags, using, 107–108

templates, creating, 41

text

changing capitalization of, 56

keeping together with nonbreaking spaces, 42

using effectively on web sites, 30

using with inline graphics, 74

text appearance, controlling with graphics, 78

text files, creating, 13

text, indenting, 41

text links. *See also* graphic links; hyperlinks; links

creating, 86

using with e-mail, 92–93

text paragraphs, adding to web pages, 7

text size, changing default for, 55

text-align property

using with style sheets, 154–155

values for, 154

text-decoration property, using, 57

text-indent property, using, 56

text-transform property, using, 56

<tfoot> and </tfoot> tags, creating footer sections in tables with, 113

<thead> and </thead> tags, creating table header sections with, 112

tiling, preventing, 158

time display on eBay, controlling, 204

× special character, code for, 43

titles

adding for web pages, 4–5

including descriptions for, 6

toolbar property, using with pop-up windows, 198

top borders, displaying in tables, 112

top property, using with pop-up windows, 198

TopHosts.com, web address for, 22

top-level headings, adding to web pages, 6

<tr> and </tr> (table row) tags, using, 107–108

™ special character, code for, 43

trademarks, considering when selecting domain names, 28

traffic, considering for web hosts, 23

.txt extension

adding by default in Notepad, 5

preventing as default in Notepad, 146

type attribute, using with <ul> tag, 45

type color, controlling, 54

type size, controlling, 53–54

typeface, controlling, 53

U

<u> and </u> (underline) tags, using, 52

↑ special character, code for, 43

.uk domain, explanation of, 26

<ul> and </ul> tags, creating bulleted lists with, 45

underline, applying, 52, 57

Unicode, definition of, *166*

unordered lists, display of. *See* bulleted lists

uptime, definition of, *24*

URLs (Uniform Resource Locators)

definition of, *20*

format of, 22

.us domain, explanation of, 26

usemap attribute, using with imagemaps, 95

user events, types of, 193–194

user ID on eBay, controlling display of, 201

V

valign attribute, adding to opening <tr> tag, 120

<var> and </var> (variable text) inline style, effect of, 53

vertical alignment, applying to cells, 120

vertical lines, creating, 125

VGA resolution, explanation of, 99

video

delivery methods for, 99–100

formats for, 99

video files

creating link for playing of, 100

creating link for downloading of, 100

embedding in web pages, 103

video streaming, considering for web hosts, 25

View Source Code command, using, 9

Virtual PC emulator, downloading trial copy of, 17

visibility property, hiding elements with, 60

void value for frame attribute, effect of, 111

vsides value for frame attribute, effect of, 111

W

web client, diagram of, *20*

Web, definition of, *19*

web file formats, choosing for Office applications, 174–175

web hosts, choosing, 22–25

web options, configuring in Office applications, 160–167

Web Options dialog box

displaying for Access, 162

displaying for Excel, 161

displaying for PowerPoint, 162

Web Page Preview option, using with Office applications, 171
web pages
  accessing, 20–21
  accessing in browsers, 17
  adding audio and video to, 98–100
  adding comments to, 8
  adding content to, 4–9
  adding headings to, 6
  adding horizontal rules to, 80
  adding hyperlinks to, 11–12
  adding line breaks to, 8
  adding pictures to, 10
  adding text paragraphs to, 7
  adding titles for, 4–5
  applying formatting to, 9
  applying formatting to elements in, 40
  assessing requirements for, 22
  basic structure of, 41
  checking appearance of, 171
  checking on PCs and Macs, 17
  checking with other browsers, 17–18
  creating from data-access pages in Access, 180
  creating from Excel workbooks, 175–177
  creating from PowerPoint presentations, 178–179
  creating hyperlinks to, 169
  CuteFTP, 37
  describing with meta tags, 15
  embedding audio in, 101–102
  embedding video in, 103
  headers and bodies in, 4
  indenting text on, 41
  inserting special characters in, 43
  inserting vertical lines in, 125
  laying out, 82
  linking to external style sheets, 146–147
  linking two or more style sheets to, 148
  linking within, 88–89
  managing files sizes of, 30
  placing e-mail links in, 92
  playing background audio for, 101
  redirecting browsers to, 16
  refreshing, 6
  reloading automatically, 15–16
  requirements for, 40
  saving, 5, 6
  saving with keyboard shortcuts, 7
  saving Word documents as, 173
  setting refresh intervals for, 16
  showing last-update status of, 195
  speeding up loading of, 73
  starting in Word, 167
  switching to applications from, 7
  using scripts in, 192–199
  viewing, 5
web servers
  creating network places for, 33–35
  definition of, 20
  running, 25
  transferring web sites to, 32–38
web sites
  Blogger.com, 205
  checking, 31
  for color-codes reference, 54
  creating folders for, 2
  for CuteHTML, 12
  definition of, 20, 23
  Deneba Canvas graphics application, 67
  documenting, 3
  Fireworks graphics application, 67
  for HostSearch, 22
  Joker.com, 27
  for Konqueror browser, 17
  for Lynx browser, 17
  for MacLynx browser, 17
  for Mozilla browsers, 17
  navigating, 90
  for Netscape browser, 17
  for Network Solutions, 27
  for Opera browser, 17
  optimizing effectiveness of, 29–30
  organizing, 3, 30
  Paint Shop Pro, 66
  Photoshop Elements graphics applications, 66
  planning contents of, 28–29
  for Register.com, 27
  storing in My Webs folder, 2
  for TopHosts.com, 22
  transferring to web servers, 32–38
  transferring with FTP clients, 37–38
  transferring with Internet Explorer, 33–37
  updating and maintaining, 31–32
  for Virtual PC emulator, 17
web tools, considering for web hosts, 24
web-authoring applications, examples of, 12
web-hosting features, deciding on, 23–25
web-hosting services, evaluating, 26
web-site visitors, getting feedback from, 92–95
width attribute
  adding to opening <td> tag, 115
  adding to opening <table> tag, 115
  creating boxes with, 58
  using with inline graphics, 76
  using with pop-up windows, 198
Windows Explorer, copying objects from, 37
WMV (Windows Media Video) files, features of, 99
Word
  creating HTML elements with, 176
  Files tab of Web Options in, 165
  starting new web pages in, 167
Word documents
  removing Office-specific tags from, 174
  saving as web pages, 173
word spacing, changing, 55–56
WS_FTP Connection Wizard, starting, 38
www designation
  advisory about omission of, 21
  purpose in URLs, 22

International Contact Information

AUSTRALIA
McGraw-Hill Book Company Australia Pty. Ltd.
  TEL +61-2-9900-1800
  FAX +61-2-9878-8881
  http://www.mcgraw-hill.com.au
  books-it_sydney@mcgraw-hill.com

CANADA
McGraw-Hill Ryerson Ltd.
  TEL +905-430-5000
  FAX +905-430-5020
  http://www.mcgraw-hill.ca

GREECE, MIDDLE EAST, & AFRICA
  (Excluding South Africa)
McGraw-Hill Hellas
  TEL +30-210-6560-990
  TEL +30-210-6560-993
  TEL +30-210-6560-994
  FAX +30-210-6545-525

MEXICO (Also serving Latin America)
McGraw-Hill Interamericana Editores S.A. de C.V.
  TEL +525-1500-5108
  FAX +525-117-1589
  http://www.mcgraw-hill.com.mx
  carlos_ruiz@mcgraw-hill.com

SINGAPORE (Serving Asia)
McGraw-Hill Book Company
  TEL +65-6863-1580
  FAX +65-6862-3354
  http://www.mcgraw-hill.com.sg
  mghasia@mcgraw-hill.com

SOUTH AFRICA
McGraw-Hill South Africa
  TEL +27-11-622-7512
  FAX +27-11-622-9045
  robyn_swanepoel@mcgraw-hill.com

SPAIN
McGraw-Hill/Interamericana de España, S.A.U.
  TEL +34-91-180-3000
  FAX +34-91-372-8513
  http://www.mcgraw-hill.es
  professional@mcgraw-hill.es

UNITED KINGDOM, NORTHERN,
EASTERN, & CENTRAL EUROPE
McGraw-Hill Education Europe
  TEL +44-1-628-502500
  FAX +44-1-628-770224
  http://www.mcgraw-hill.co.uk
  emea_queries@mcgraw-hill.com

ALL OTHER INQUIRIES Contact:
McGraw-Hill/Osborne
  TEL +1-510-420-7700
  FAX +1-510-420-7703
  http://www.osborne.com
  omg_international@mcgraw-hill.com